T0329992

The Changing Face of US Patent Law and its Impact on Business Strategy

NEW HORIZONS IN INTERNATIONAL BUSINESS

Series Editor: Peter J. Buckley
Centre for International Business,
University of Leeds (CIBUL), UK

The New Horizons in International Business series has established itself as the world's leading forum for the presentation of new ideas in international business research. It offers pre-eminent contributions in the areas of multinational enterprise—including foreign direct investment, business strategy and corporate alliances, global competitive strategies, and entrepreneurship. In short, this series constitutes essential reading for academics, business strategists and policy makers alike.

Titles in the series include:

The Changing Face of US Patent Law and its Impact on Business Strategy

Edited by

Daniel R. Cahoy

Pennsylvania State University, USA

Lynda J. Oswald

University of Michigan, USA

NEW HORIZONS IN INTERNATIONAL BUSINESS

Edward Elgar

Cheltenham, UK • Northampton, MA, USA

Published by
Edward Elgar Publishing Limited
The Lypiatts
15 Lansdown Road
Cheltenham
Glos GL50 2JA
UK

Edward Elgar Publishing, Inc.
William Pratt House
9 Dewey Court
Northampton
Massachusetts 01060
USA

A catalogue record for this book
is available from the British Library

Library of Congress Control Number: 2012952877

This book is available electronically in the ElgarOnline.com Economics Subject Collection, E-ISBN 978 1 78100 785 3

MIX
Paper from
responsible sources
FSC® C018575

ISBN 978 1 78100 784 6

Typeset by Servis Filmsetting Ltd, Stockport, Cheshire
Printed by MPG PRINTGROUP, UK

Contents

v

Contributors

Cassandra Aceves is a doctoral student studying management and organizations at the Stephen M. Ross School of Business, University of Michigan. Her current research focuses on innovation, technology and how firms influence their environments through corporate political action. Before entering her doctoral program, Cassandra received her bachelor of arts degree in political science from the University of California, Los Angeles, and a master of business administration from the Warrington College of Business, University of Florida.

T. Leigh Anenson is an Associate Professor of Business Law at the Robert H. Smith School of Business, University of Maryland. Her research involves rethinking the role of medieval equity in modern business litigation in the United States. Anenson's research has earned the two most prestigious awards given by the Academy of Legal Studies in Business. Her papers have been widely cited in academic articles, leading law textbooks and court opinions. She has won numerous teaching awards and has held visiting appointments at the University of Sydney and the University of Cambridge. She served on the editorial board of *American Business Law Journal* and is the past president of the International Section of the Academy of Legal Studies in Business and its Pacific Southwest region. Before embarking on an academic career, Anenson practiced business law and regularly litigated cases involving equitable principles and defenses.

David L. Baumer, PhD, JD, Attorney at Law, is a Professor of Business Management in the Poole College of Management at North Carolina State University in Raleigh, North Carolina. He earned his undergraduate economics degree from Ohio University and his PhD in economics from the University of Virginia. He earned his JD from the University of Miami in Florida. Baumer is also a licensed attorney in the state of North Carolina. Baumer has taught undergraduate and graduate courses in law, economics, and law and technology. Between 2006 and 2012, he was Head of the Business Management Department within the Poole College of Management. Baumer's work has been published 37 times in peer-reviewed journals in law, economics, technology and accounting. In addition to 50 or so presentations at academic conferences, Baumer's research has been funded several times by the National Science Foundation. He has also been an expert witness in a number of patent and antitrust cases. His articles have been published in a variety of journals including *American Business Law Journal, IEEE Privacy and Security, Computers and Security, ACM*, and the *Journal of Internet Law* among others.

Robert C. Bird is an Associate Professor of Business Law and the Northeast Utilities Chair in Business Ethics at the University of Connecticut School of Business. Bird received his JD and MBA from Boston University. Robert's research interests focus on employment law, intellectual property law, and the study of law as a source of competitive advantage. He has also received many teaching awards, as well as best paper awards for his scholarly research. Bird has authored over 40 articles, including publications in *American Business Law Journal, Harvard Journal of Law & Public Policy, Cincinnati Law Review, Journal of Law and Economics, Stanford Journal of Law, Business and Finance*, and the *Kentucky Law Journal*.

Daniel R. Cahoy is an Associate Professor and Dean's Faculty Fellow in Business Law at Penn State University's Smeal College of Business. He is a registered US patent attorney and has a research expertise in intellectual property and regulatory law related to biotechnology and pharmaceuticals. Cahoy has written extensively on the topic of patent rights and innovation incentives, and his works include papers that address reforming the US patent system, FDA regulatory policy and the characterization of patent landscapes in fields related to energy policy and sustainability. He is a past editor in chief of *American Business Law Journal* and serves on the Executive Committee of the *Academy of Legal Studies in Business*. Cahoy researched international IP issues as a Fulbright Scholar and has a great interest in the global environment for IP incentives and ownership.

Wade M. Chumney, JD, MSc, Attorney at Law, is the Cecil B. Day Assistant Professor of Business Ethics and Law in the Scheller College of Business at the Georgia Institute of Technology in Atlanta, Georgia. He earned his undergraduate degree in political science from Davidson College, his master's degree in information systems from Dakota State University, and his juris doctor from the University of Virginia School of Law. Chumney is also a licensed attorney in the state of South Carolina. He has taught undergraduate and graduate courses in a variety of subjects, including law, business ethics, and the law and ethics of technology. He has been invited to present his research at numerous institutions, including the University of California, Berkeley, the University of Idaho, ICN Business School in France, and the University of Applied Sciences in Austria. Chumney has received numerous honors and awards for his research, including the Holmes-Cardozo Best Paper Award, the Academy of Legal Studies in Business (ALSB) Distinguished Proceeding Award, the United States Association for Small Business and Entrepreneurship (USASBE) Best Case Award, the Belmont University Outstanding Scholarly Activity Award, and the Southeastern Academy of Legal Studies in Business (SEALSB) Junior Scholar Award of Excellence. He has published nearly a dozen peer-reviewed articles in numerous journals, including *American Business Law Journal, Journal of Business Ethics, Entrepreneurship Theory and Practice, Boston University Journal of Science and Technology Law*, and *American Taxation Association Journal of Legal Tax Research*.

Joel Gehman is an Assistant Professor of Strategic Management and Organization at the Alberta School of Business, University of Alberta. His research examines the impact of cultural concerns regarding sustainability and values on organizational practices, technology innovation and institutional arrangements. Gehman's research has been published or is forthcoming in the *Academy of Management Journal, Organization Studies, Research Policy, Social Studies of Science*, the *Michigan Telecommunications and Technology Law Review*, and *Research in the Sociology of Organizations*.

Donna M. Gitter is a Professor of Law at Baruch College, City University of New York with scholarly expertise in the fields of international patent and biotechnology law. Gitter has published numerous articles in academic journals, such as the *Berkeley Journal of International Law*, the *Columbia Science and Technology Law Review*, the *Duke Journal for Comparative and International Law*, and the *New York University Law Review*. In recent years, she has been invited to contribute and present articles as a sponsored guest of the Australian National University College of Law, the University of Edinburgh Law School in Scotland, the University of Trento in Italy, the University of Michigan Stephen M. Ross School of Business, Drake University Law School, Seton Hall Law School, and The John Marshall Law School. She has also presented at Cornell University Law School and Oxford University in England. Moreover, she has received several awards in recognition of her excellence in research and teaching and competed successfully for numerous fellowships and research grants. Gitter graduated Phi Beta Kappa and *cum laude* from Cornell University's College of Arts and Sciences, where she earned a BA in government. She earned her JD from the University of Pennsylvania Law School, where she served as senior editor of the *Comparative Labor Law Journal*.

Zhen Lei is currently an Assistant Professor of Energy and Environmental Economics in the Department of Energy and Mineral Engineering at Penn

State University. His research interests include economics of innovation and intellectual property, science and technology policy, energy and environmental economics, and applied econometrics.

Gideon Mark is an Assistant Professor of Business Law at the Robert H. Smith School of Business, University of Maryland. He holds degrees from Brandeis University, Columbia University, Harvard University, New York University, and the University of California. His research has focused on securities regulation, corruption, corporate governance, and intellectual property. Professor Mark was in private practice for many years before beginning his academic career.

Susan J. Marsnik is an Associate Professor in the Department of Ethics and Business Law, Opus College of Business, University of St. Thomas. She has taught comparative intellectual property law in specialized graduate programs at European universities and as a Fulbright Senior Specialist at Beni Suef University in Egypt. Prior to her academic career, Marsnik practiced law with a boutique firm in Minneapolis. She also has over a decade of other business experience including in the book publishing industry, marketing of legal services and consulting on management and comparative law issues. Marsnik's primary area of substantive research focuses on public and private international law by analyzing US intellectual property law in the context of international and foreign laws. She regularly presents her research at academic conferences in the US and Europe and has spoken on cultural factors impacting copyright law in Jordan. Her research has been published in law and business journals, encyclopedias, and as part of legal practitioner and legal education programs.

David Orozco is an Assistant Professor of Legal Studies in the College of Business at Florida State University. Professor Orozco's research focuses on intellectual property management topics and the regulation of knowledge-based assets. His articles have appeared in top academic journals such as *American Business Law Journal*, *Indiana Law Journal*, *Penn State Law Review*, *Catholic University Law Review* and *Journal of Marketing*. His research has also been featured in *The Wall Street Journal*.

Lynda J. Oswald is a Professor of Business Law at the Stephen M. Ross School of Business at the University of Michigan, where she teaches and researches in the field of intellectual property law, with a particular emphasis on patent law and infringement liability. She has published in numerous journals, including *American Business Law Journal*, *Vanderbilt Law Review*, *Northwestern University Law Review*, *Washington and Lee Law Review*, and *Washington University Law Quarterly*. Oswald has received numerous awards for her research, including the Hoeber Memorial

Award and the Holmes-Cardozo Award for Research Excellence from the *American Business Law Journal*. Her work has been cited by numerous courts, including the US Supreme Court in *United States v. Bestfoods*. Oswald is a past president of the Academy of Legal Studies in Business, and served on its Executive Committee from 2003–08. She has held visiting appointments at the University of Florida Law School, the University of Michigan Law School, China University of Political Science and Law in Beijing, L'viv State University in Ukraine, the Hopkins-Nanjing Center in Nanjing, China, and the University of Sydney in Australia.

Roby B. Sawyers, PhD, CPA, CMA is a Professor in the Poole College of Management at North Carolina State University in Raleigh, North Carolina. He earned his undergraduate accounting degree from the University of North Carolina at Chapel Hill, his master's from the University of South Florida and his PhD from Arizona State University. He teaches a variety of undergraduate and graduate courses in taxation and has been a visiting professor in the International Management Program at the Catholic University in Lille, France and the Vienna School of Economics and Business (Wirtschaftsuniversitat Wien). He is an author of *Managerial Accounting—A Focus on Ethical Decision Making, Managerial ACCT and Federal Tax Research*. He has published articles in a variety of journals including *American Business Law Journal, Journal of the American Taxation Association, ATA Journal of Legal Tax Research, National Tax Journal, Advances in Taxation, Journal of Business Ethics, Journal of Accountancy, CPA Journal, Tax Adviser, Tax Notes*, and *State Tax Notes*.

Robert E. Thomas is Associate Professor and Huber Hurst Professor of Legal Studies and Technology and Chair of the Department of Management in the Warrington College of Business at the University of Florida. In addition, he is the director of the prestigious Huber Hurst Legal Research Seminar and president-elect of the Academy of Legal Studies in Business. He is an expert in the areas of intellectual property, technology law and negotiation and has published multiple articles and lectured throughout the United States and Europe in these areas. His current research examines current patent law reform efforts. His analysis is multi-disciplinary, employing tools from law, economics and institutional political theory. Prior to his University of Florida appointment, Professor Thomas held dual faculty appointments at the University of Michigan Business School and Department of Economics. He has also taught at the Wharton School of Business at the University of Pennsylvania and the Institut D'Administration Des Entreprises in Aix-en-Provence, France. Professor Thomas is a Princeton University graduate and received his JD and PhD in business economics from Stanford Law and Business Schools, respectively.

Introduction

As one of the world's most important markets, the United States is a critical space for developing new products and services. Firms that innovate require legal protection to ensure that they capture a return on their investment. In the context of new and useful articles and methods, that protection is largely provided by the US patent system. Intuitively, one may conclude that having a well-functioning patent system in America is essential for a prosperous business environment in the US. In fact, the system has been cited as an important tool for economic growth and jobs creation (Rai, Graham & Doms, 2010). The substantial patenting activity by non-US companies means that the US patent system benefits the global economy as well.

Any modern firm seeking a competitive advantage must therefore understand the nature and functioning of the patent system. First and foremost, patents provide a period of exclusivity for maximizing profits. Additionally, patents can confer a myriad of ancillary advantages for a firm, such as acting as a signaling device or providing a vehicle for accessing competitor technology through licensing. For competitors and society, patents serve as a key conduit of information that fuels broader innovation by disclosing a fully enabled invention even before it is in the public domain. When firms fall on hard times, investors often rest their hopes on patents—often as an important source of remaining value (Mattioli, Spector & Jones, 2012).

Evidence of just how much patents can shape an industry is readily available in the news. For example, on any given day in 2011 or 2012, one was likely to encounter a story about litigation in the mobile communications sector. Nearly all of the major players—including Apple, Google, Microsoft, Samsung and HTC—have been involved in one case or another in a variety of venues across the US. They have played the role of both plaintiff and defendant in cases involving a dizzying array of technologies from touchscreen inputs to software for enhancing messaging. The litigations are high stakes to say the least. In the battle between Apple and Samsung involving cell phones and tablet computing devices, Apple scored a decisive victory in August 2012 when it received a jury verdict of infringement in the amount of nearly $1.5 billion (*Apple Inc. v. Samsung*

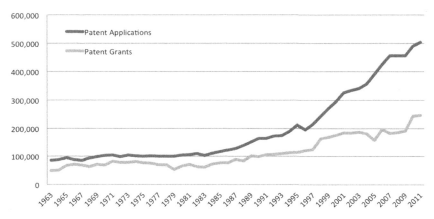

Source: US Patent & Trademark Office, 2012.

Figure 0.1 US Patent Applications and Grants, 1963–2011

Electronic Co., 2012; Wingfield, 2012). The consequences may be a "tax" added onto the price of mobile computing devices that compete with Apple's (Ante, 2012). One might be tempted to view the mobile communications sector as an outlier; however, just weeks earlier Monsanto won a $1 billion verdict over Du Pont in the completely unrelated field of genetically modified seed patents (*Monsanto Co. v. E.I. Dupont De Nemours & Co.*, 2012). Clearly, patent rights have a great impact on business.

There is reason to believe that the US patent system will play an even greater role for businesses in the future. After leveling off slightly in the first part of the 21st century, the number of issued patents has exploded, rising to 247,713 in 2011.

As more and more patents issue, firms are increasingly compelled to integrate patent strategy into their business plans. Moreover, patents have extended into industries that are not necessarily perceived as high technology, such as food production and clothing manufacture. It is no longer optional for the business community to care about the patent environment; understanding patents is a baseline requirement.

However, as important as the US patent system is to the global business community, it is not without problems. Concerns have arisen over the years that there is a substantial misalignment between the interests of society and the actual impact of the system. Some believe that patents are too easy to obtain or that the quality of issued patents is poor, clogging the marketplace with blocking property rights and stunting competition (Jaffe & Lerner, 2004; Heller, 2008). Others have argued that patents can limit follow-on innovation by preventing the sharing of technology necessary to serve as a foundation for others (Murray & Stern, 2007). The rules are often archaic and poorly suited for emerging industries, particularly those related to the Internet. Even when there is a theoretical advantage to the system, the costs of ownership and enforcement may prevent many patent owners from seeing a benefit to pursuing rights. In fact, it has been suggested that patents may not be cost-effective for any industry outside of pharmaceuticals and biotechnology (Bessen & Meurer, 2008).

To address the problems in the patent system, there have been many proposals for change from academics, business leaders and policymakers. While it is not always easy to agree on the specific reforms necessary—divisions exist between industry sectors like pharmaceuticals and electronic communications that experience the system differently—most agree that the system should be improved.

And indeed, much change has come to patent law over the years. The courts in particular have been very active in reinterpreting of the Patent Act of 1952 and articulating common law rules that fill in the spaces. Some of most important changes have come from the US Supreme Court, which until recently appeared to cede most patent issues to the specialized US Court of Appeals for the Federal Circuit. For example, in *eBay Inc. v. MercExchange, LLC* (2006), the Supreme Court curtailed the use of injunctions in patent cases, which weakened the negotiating power of patentees. In *KSR International Co. v. Teleflex Inc.* (2007), the Supreme Court broadened the test of obviousness, retroactively calling into question the enforceability of many issued patents. More recently, in *Mayo Collaborative Services v. Prometheus Laboratories Inc.* (2012), the Supreme Court addressed the scope of patentable subject matter by further defining what activity transformed a method from a law of nature to a protectable invention.

In addition, Congress has been active in patent reform. Typically, the legislative branch is the slowest to change due to the consequences of altering such an important system, not to mention the complexity of the rules and differing interests. However, in 2011 Congress pushed through some of the most significant reforms in decades when it enacted legislation known as the America Invents Act (AIA). The most prominent and controversial of the AIA's changes is shifting the US from a first-to-invent to a first-to-file system, meaning that rights will normally be determined by the first inventor to file an application at the US Patent and Trademark Office (PTO). Other changes include expanding prior user rights, eliminating the best mode requirement and making it nearly impossible to claim a patent on a tax strategy. For businesses, an important but less discussed revision was the elimination of private *qui tam* actions for false patent marking, which had previously led to significant liability for manufacturers that neglected to remove expired patent numbers.

The PTO has also been very busy in changing the way it operates in response to demands from the business community. The office has dramatically increased the number of examiners to deal with the deluge of patents, created accelerated exam procedures to account for important technology, drafted guidelines for examination of inventions in areas of tenuous patentability, and increased its outreach to the business community. When the PTO's efforts are combined with its collaboration with other patent offices across the globe, it is fair to say that the amount of information available to the business community has never been greater.

Still, many believe that much more is required for the system to function properly so that it optimally encourages innovation while preserving competition. One of the United States' most widely respected scholars and jurists, Judge Richard Posner, issued a strong critique of the patent system after sitting as a trial judge in a case between Apple and Motorola (Posner, 2012). According to Judge Posner, most industries do not benefit from patent rights.

> In most [industries], the cost of invention is low; or just being first confers a durable competitive advantage because consumers associate the inventing company's brand name with the product itself; or just being first gives the first company in the market a head start in reducing its costs as it becomes more experienced at producing and marketing the product; or the product will be superseded soon anyway, so there's no point to a patent monopoly that will last 20 years; or some or all of these factors are present. Most industries could get along fine without patent protection.

The problems caused by factors such as patent trolls, defensive patenting and search costs can render the system a burden on industry rather than a catalyst for innovation. Judge Posner suggests that a variety of reforms, such as reduced patent terms and widespread compulsory licenses, are necessary.

The business community is therefore faced with an extremely important patent rights system that can also create barriers and is in a constant state of flux. This book is intended to highlight some of the most important changes in US patent law in recent years and describe their impact on domestic and global businesses. The changing face of US patent law can be broadly categorized in terms of: (1) the forces that impact patent policy; (2) modifications to the patent application process; (3) issues and reform related to patent oppositions and litigation; and (4) rights regimes that supplement protection in industries where patents are less effective.

Individual chapters within this book provide detailed consideration of various issues within these categories.

FORCES THAT INFLUENCE PATENT POLICY

Because the overall functioning of the US system is complex, lawmakers and the courts must keep in mind policies to guide decision-making and provide a measuring stick for success. General principles of course include the creation of incentives for increased invention as well as follow-on innovation. But many other policies could be integrated into the patent system, such as support for green technology, assistance for independent inventors, preference for domestic patent applicants or high standards for the examination of gene sequences. Unfortunately, a well-functioning patent system cannot be all things to all interest groups, so choices must be made. How is this done in the context of a system that has the potential to so dramatically influence the business community? The answer can be found in an understanding of the forces that influence patent policy.

In Chapter 1, Robert Thomas and Cassandra Aceves confront this topic head-on by considering the formation of interest coalitions to effectuate intellectual policy revision. The chapter contrasts the experiences of copyright interest groups with those of patent interest groups in recent years, and assesses how each has fostered change. It considers why some groups appear to be more successful than others in influencing the debate, building on interest-group politics theory and other descriptions in the literature (e.g., Thomas, 2006). The chapter provides a model that identifies variables motivating intellectual property political action and the coalitions that are likely to form based on these factors. It then applies the model to explain the influences on international treaties such as the Trade-Related Aspects of Intellectual Property Agreement (TRIPS, 1994) as well as domestic legislation such as the AIA. The chapter concludes that successful influence occurs when efforts are drawn narrowly and suggests that future coalitions are likely to follow a conservative model. It argues that such a model facilitated passage of the AIA and the lack of such an approach in controversial efforts to expand copyright met with predictable failure.

In Chapter 2, David Orozco considers a narrower venue for influence: the PTO. The chapter explains the underappreciated significance of the PTO in making patent policy in industries such as software, biotechnology and clean technology. It focuses on the PTO's rulemaking authority and argues that, despite court-imposed limitations, the agency engages in substantive policymaking. The chapter refers to such power as an "administrative policy lever" and states that it can be explained by positive political theory, a construct that examines legal actors' decisions and motivations in response to larger political forces and frameworks (McCubbins, Noll & Weingast, 1989). It then discusses the trajectory of future administrative patent levers in light of the passage of the AIA. The chapter predicts that the PTO will increase in policy-oriented activities and notes that an attendant risk is a balkanized patent policy.

THE IMPACT OF REVISIONS TO THE PATENT APPLICATION PROCESS

Within the scope of agreed-upon patent policies, change occurs most immediately and directly in the context of the patent application process. To be sure, actions regarding core patentability issues such as allowable subject matter and the means for determining the winner of a contest between inventors with similar claims are extremely important. The failure to design workable rules can disenfranchise a large segment of future patent owners, suppressing innovation. However, even minor modifications to the process can have an impact. Setting workable fee structures, rational examiner workload or incentives, and clear guidelines may determine who is willing to play the patent game. Any revisions to the patent application process must be understood by the business community and integrated into management practices.

In Chapter 3, Robert Bird provides a broad overview of changes imposed by the AIA and then drills down for an in-depth discussion of the new rules relating to inventor determination and erasing the stain of inequitable conduct. The chapter contextualizes the narrower discussion by noting the significance inventor contests and inequitable conduct accusations have had on patentees throughout history. Regarding inventor determination, the chapter explains the rationale for shifting the US from a first-to-invent system to a first-to-file system. It reviews the available evidence on the likely impact of the law such as Abrams and Wagner's (2012) widely discussed empirical study of Canada's earlier shift, and finds clear conclusions to be lacking. However, the chapter notes that there may be important advantages to first-to-file in a global system, particularly for domestic filers. Conversely, the chapter argues for caution in the application of the new supplemental exam procedure. Without a careful restraint of this "amnesty," low-quality patents may proliferate.

In Chapter 4, T. Leigh Anenson and Gideon Mark examine the recent changes to the inequitable conduct doctrine and the possibility that they may ultimately harm the patent system. Inequitable conduct is a defense that exists when a patentee has violated his or her obligations to be fully forthcoming in the course of an ex parte examination. Withholding evidence of prior art may compromise an examiner's ability to determine patentability. This chapter reviews the availability of the inequitable conduct defense as a remedy to this breach of good faith. It considers new rules under both the AIA and the recent decision in *Therasense, Inc. v. Becton, Dickinson & Co.* (2011) that effectively restrict the application of the doctrine. The chapter concludes that these changes go too far in reducing the incentive for patent applicants to make a full disclosure, permitting abuse of the system and endangering its integrity.

The discussion by Wade Chumney, David Baumer and Roby Sawyers in Chapter 5 assesses the impact of the expansive boundaries of patentable subject matter on professions. The chapter considers the possibility that, absent an effective defense, patent owners may end up severely hampering the practice of professions such as accounting. It reviews the history of business method patents and describes the emergence of flexible rules. The chapter then demonstrates how these flexible rules can essentially allow one to patent key aspects of the accounting profession. It provides several examples of patents that appear to offer such a level of control. The chapter then details the policy arguments against the issuance of accounting-related patents, noting that great costs are necessarily imposed. It proposes a "learned profession defense" as a solution, explaining that a similar infringement exemption has been successful in the context of medical methods. The chapter concludes that limits are necessary, or professions will suffer and society will bear much of the burden.

THE CHALLENGES OF A SHIFTING ENFORCEMENT ENVIRONMENT

Obtaining a patent is only part of the equation for a business interested in exploiting its innovative advantage. Similarly, the fact that many patents exist in a technology space does not mean that competitors have no room to maneuver. Businesses must appreciate the critical second step of patent enforcement as an element of the intellectual property environment. Unfortunately, the rules are often in a state of transition due to the delicate balance of preserving the advantages of strong property rights in inventions while maintaining competition whenever possible. For example, invalid patents may be identified as a problem and eliminated after enforcement is threatened, but the procedures must not unduly weaken a patentee's investment expectations. Additionally, what actions constitute enforcement plays an important role in clarifying infringement risk. Shifting them after the fact undermines confidence in the marketplace. The unanticipated spillover effects of strong patent enforcement that impact the dissemination of health or safety information are a primary concern to businesses and the public. There have been many changes in these patent enforcement principles over the years, and the business community must keep abreast in order to stay competitive.

In Chapter 6, Lynda Oswald addresses the ever more common issue of infringement through the action of multiple parties, or "joint infringement." With the emergence of patented business methods and software systems with several components, courts are seeing more cases in which no single party infringes all elements of a claim. Courts must fashion a rule that eliminates infringement loopholes while not inappropriately drawing innocent parties into a case. The chapter reviews the Federal Circuit's recent en banc decision in *Akamai Technologies, Inc. v. Limelight Networks, Inc.* (2012) that significantly changed the joint infringement landscape. Assessing its lack of adherence to conventional tort theory as well as departure from existing precedent, the chapter argues that the Federal Circuit has strayed into patent policymaking. It suggests that the specialized nature of the court has led to overly isolated jurisprudence as predicted by commentators (Nard & Duffy, 2007). The chapter concludes that returning to more traditional legal doctrine would better serve patent law and the business community.

Daniel Cahoy, Joel Gehman and Zhen Lei in Chapter 7 consider the possibility that patents can serve an ancillary purpose as an information containment tool. By design, patents are information disclosure devices, and providing a full and complete understanding of the invention is part of the patent owner's bargain with society. However, when follow-on use of an invention is necessary to generate information on safety or effectiveness, patents may actually serve as a barrier. This chapter considers the issue as a matter of theory and how the Federal Circuit's decision in *Madey v. Duke* (2002) eliminated an essential exemption for such use. It then explores its real-life application in the context of natural gas extraction (fracking). It suggests that the application is broader and notes that there are both attendant business strategies and societal concerns that may influence the future development of doctrine. For now, the chapter concludes, there are limited means that society can exploit to avoid the issue of patents as information containment tools.

In Chapter 8, Susan Marsnik considers the issue of post-grant, administrative review of patents. Such review has existed for some time in US law in the form of reexamination, which was considered to be substantially more restrictive than the European Patent Office's (EPO) opposition system (EPC, 2010, Art. 99). As a result of amendments in the AIA, the

PTO will be the venue for three new or revised post-grant review procedures. This chapter discusses the rationale behind strong post-grant review and why the pre-AIA system was lacking in the US. It details the European system and then explores how the new procedures in the US adopt many of the EPO provisions. The chapter analyzes whether the new US procedures will fulfill the goal of reducing the number of bad patents while preserving innovation incentives. It concludes that limitations related to cost and litigation estoppel will make the US procedures less effective, and render them an unlikely tool for improving patent quality or stemming the tide of litigation.

THE EMERGENCE OF EXCLUSION SYSTEMS BEYOND PATENTS

As important as patents can be in research-intensive industries, they can in some cases actually be too weak to provide a return on investment. This is particularly the case in industries with long product development times and extensive regulatory procedures. In such cases, innovators may need a supplemental protection system that provides many of the same advantages as patents. Congress has responded to this need from time to time by creating specialized information exclusion systems that provide additional value to businesses.

In Chapter 9, Donna Gitter reviews the implications of a supplemental rights regime in the context of the new Food and Drug Administration (FDA) approval pathway for follow-on protein products or biosimilars. In 2010, Congress enacted the Biologics Price Competition and Innovation Act (BPCIA), which allows for generic biologic treatments. Modeled on an existing procedure for generic pharmaceutical drug products, the law is intended to facilitate competition once innovator exclusivity has expired. However, to preserve innovator incentives, the BPCIA includes long data and market exclusivity periods that operate apart from the patent system. The chapter addresses the controversy in the interpretation of the data and market exclusivity provisions, and provides an optimal interpretation of the statute. It examines the academic literature and considers the impact of the new regime on international trade agreements. The chapter concludes that some amendment of the new law may be necessary to increase its clarity and improve its function as a supplemental innovation protection system.

By considering the many changes US patent law has undergone over the years, one can appreciate the dynamic nature of the system and take full advantage of it. This book provides an overview of many of the most important changes that impact businesses. Its comprehensive treatment can serve as a tool for firms and aid policymakers in generating ideas for future revision.

REFERENCES

Abrams, D. & Wagner, R.P. (2012). Poisoning the Next Apple: How the America Invents Act Harms Inventors. *Stanford Law Review*, **65**. Retrieved from http://ssrn.com/abstract=1883821.

Akamai Technologies, Inc. v. Limelight Networks, Inc., 2012 U.S. App. LEXIS 7531 (Fed. Cir. Aug. 31, 2012).

America Invents Act, Pub. L. No. 112-29, 125 Stat. 284 (2011).

Ante, S.E. (2012, Sept. 28). The Apple Tax. *Wall Street Journal Online*. Retrieved from http://online.wsj.com/article/SB10000872396390444270404577610013613 551038.html.

Apple Inc. v. Samsung Electronic Co., No. 11-CV-01846 (N.D. Cal., Aug. 24, 2012) (jury verdict). Retrieved from http://www.patentlyo.com/files/juryverdict applesamsung.pdf.

Bessen, J. & Meurer, M. (2008). *Patent Failure: How Judges, Bureaucrats, and Laywers Put Innovators at Risk*. Princeton, NJ: Princeton University Press.

Biologics Price Competition and Innovation Act of 2009 (BPCIA), 42 U.S.C. § 262 (2010).

Convention on the Grant of European Patents (EPC), Oct. 5, 1973, as revised Nov. 29, 2000. (2010). *The European Patent Convention* (14th ed.), Munich, Germany: European Patent Office.

eBay Inc. v. MercExchange, L.L.C., 547 U.S. 388 (2006).

Heller, M. (2008). *Patent Gridlock*. New York: Perseus Books.

Jaffe, A.B. & Lerner, J. (2004). *Innovation and its Discontents*. Princeton, NJ: Princeton University Press.

KSR International Co. v. Teleflex Inc., 550 U.S. 398 (2007).

Madey v. Duke, 307 F.3d 1351 (Fed. Cir. 2002).

Mattioli, D., Spector, M. & Jones, A. (2012, Aug. 10). Kodak Patent Bidding is Tame. *Wall Street Journal*, B1.

Mayo Collaborative Services v. Prometheus Laboratories Inc., __ U.S. __, 132 S. Ct. 1298 (2012).

McCubbins, M.D., Noll, R.G. & Weingast, B.R. (1989). Structure and Process, Politics and Policy: Administrative Arrangements and the Political Control of Agencies. *Virginia Law Review*, **75**(2), 431–82.

McCubbins, M.D. & Schwartz, T. (1984). Congressional Oversight Overlooked: Police Patrols versus Fire Alarms. *American Journal of Political Science*, **28**(1), 165–79.

Monsanto Co. v. E.I. Dupont De Nemours & Co., No. 09-CV-00686 (E.D. Mo., Aug. 2, 2012) (jury verdict).

Murray, F. & Stern, S. (2007). Do Formal Intellectual Property Rights Hinder the Free Flow of Scientific Knowledge? An Empirical Test of the Anti-Commons Hypothesis. *Journal of Economic Behavior & Organization*, **63**(4), 648–87.

Nard, C. & Duffy, J. (2007). Rethinking Patent Law's Uniformity Principle. *Northwestern University Law Review*, **101**(4), 1619–76.

Posner, R.A. (2012, July 12). Why There are Too Many Patents in America. *The Atlantic*.

Rai, A., Graham, S. & Doms, M. (2010). *Patent Reform: Unleashing Innovation, Promoting Economic Growth & Producing High Paying Jobs*. Washington, D.C.: US Department of Commerce. Retrieved from www.commerce.gov/sites/default/files/.../Patent_Reform-paper.pdf

Therasense, Inc. v. Becton, Dickinson & Co., 649 F.3d 1276 (Fed. Cir. 2011) (en banc).

Thomas, R.E. (2006). Vanquishing Copyright Pirates and Patent Trolls: The Divergent Evolution of Copyright and Patent Laws. *American Business Law Journal*, **43**(4), 689–739.

Trade-Related Aspects of Intellectual Property Rights Agreement, Apr. 15, 1994, Marrakesh Agreement Establishing the World Trade Organization, Annex 1C, 1869 U.N.T.S. 299 (1994).

United States Patent & Trademark Office (2012, May 22). *U.S. Patent Statistics Report*. Retrieved from http://www.uspto.gov/web/offices/ac/ido/oeip/taf/us_stat.htm.

Wingfield, N. (2012, Aug. 24). Jury Awards $1 Billion to Apple in Samsung Patent Case. *New York Times*, A1.

PART I

Influences on patent policy

1. Coalition formation and battles to effect intellectual property policy change in the age of ACTA, AIA and the SHIELD Act

Robert E. Thomas and Cassandra Aceves*

Until 2011, copyright interest holders (Creative Content) had been remarkably successful in enhancing copyright legal protection both internationally, through the negotiation of two treaties, the World Intellectual Property Organization Copyright Treaty (WCT) and the WIPO Performances and Phonograms Treaty (WPPT), and domestically, through the Digital Millennium Copyright Act (DMCA). Creative Content's success is in marked contrast to the lack of success that patent interest holders have enjoyed during this period in effectuating favorable legislative change post-negotiation of the Trade-Related Aspects of Intellectual Property Agreement (TRIPS) in 1994.

However, in 2011–12, these roles have reversed with patent interest holders enjoying the enactment of the Leahy-Smith America Invents Act (AIA) and Creative Content being stymied in its effort to get the pro-Creative Content Anti-Counterfeiting Trade Agreement (ACTA) adopted by an international alliance of nations. As of summer 2012, the moribund ACTA is on life support at best, whereas patent interests are looking to follow the successful enactment of the AIA with the unapologetically pro-technology-sector (High Tech) Saving High-Tech Innovators from Egregious Legal Disputes Act (SHIELD Act). Indeed, it seems as if fortunes have changed.

This chapter develops a theory that explains why different intellectual property (IP) interest groups enjoy different degrees of success in influencing multi-lateral and legislative policymaking. The chapter builds on interest-group politics theory and the authors' prior work (Thomas, 2006). Key factors in determining the success of such initiatives include the nature and strength of the coalition formed, the expansiveness of the policy change sought, the strength of opposing forces, and the type of harm that the policy attempts to address. Specifically, IP interest groups attempt to minimize losses due to unauthorized, non-paying users of their intellectual property.

This chapter employs the comparatively neutral term "misappropriation," rather than "theft," to refer to all types of unauthorized uses of intellectual property. This chapter identifies two types of IP misappropriation: misappropriation due to (1) end-users (users of intellectual property for personal consumption) and (2) industrial users (users of intellectual property as inputs to production). Pre-TRIPS, end-user misappropriations were smaller sources of losses than were losses due to industrial-user misappropriations because end-users misappropriated very small quantities of IP goods. By contrast, industrial users (unauthorized users of intellectual property who intend to sell goods produced with misappropriated intellectual property in volume and for profit) constituted a greater threat of loss due to the substantial impact on IP product markets.

Thus, formation of a "grand coalition" that included members from all IP industry sectors was possible to address the shared interest of developing a global system to address industrial misappropriation. The results of this grand coalition's efforts became TRIPS.

The IP landscape became more complex post-TRIPS, with the Internet and digitalization elevating end-user misappropriation above the threat from industrial misappropriation, thereby uniting Creative Content. Meanwhile, patent interest groups splintered around the relative importance of reducing lawsuits brought by non-practicing entities (NPEs). Although the united-versus-splintered interest-groups hypothesis explains the divergence in success enjoyed by Creative Content relative to patent interest groups in getting favorable policy initiatives enacted prior to the 112th Congress, at first blush it fails to explain influence efforts since 2011.

This chapter argues that recent events do indeed fit within the interest-group influence framework. Creative Content's failure to enact policy to dramatically expand copyright protection was due to overly ambitious initiatives that engendered opposition from major interest groups that previously were unaffected by Creative Content's effort to expand tools available to address its problems with end-user misappropriation. Thus, with large Internet players such as Google opposed, Creative Content suffered its first defeat.

Patent interest groups took the opposite approach by scaling back the scope of policy initiatives in order to reduce opposition to reform efforts. Thus, the AIA succeeded by eliminating provisions that were strongly opposed by strong patent interest groups. High Tech hopes to continue this recent legislative success with the SHIELD Act, a bill drawn very narrowly to address the concerns of High Tech without impacting the interests of other major patent interest groups. Thus, Creative Content and patent interest groups are most likely to experience future success in influencing policymakers by narrowly drawing proposals to avoid heated and frequently doomed interest group battles.

Part I of this chapter provides a model that identifies the variables that motivate IP political action and the coalitions that are likely to form based on these factors. The section also describes the tools available to influence policy change and the likelihood of success of influence efforts based on coalitions formed. Part II then discusses how the model of influence applies to IP influence efforts from TRIPS to ACTA. Successful influence efforts invariably were drawn narrowly to avoid debilitating interest-group politic battles. TRIPS had no organized opposition outside the developing world and the WIPO treaties and the DMCA also enjoyed smooth, relatively opposition-less, paths to enactment. By contrast, pre-AIA patent reform efforts were ambitious, with provisions that adversely affected major patent industry sectors. Part III provides concluding observations. The conclusion hypothesizes that future influence efforts will follow the conservative approach of the AIA rather than the ambitious expansive approach of ACTA. Thus, rather than seeing the end of IP-policy influence efforts, future influence efforts will be crafted more precisely with an awareness of all interest groups that may be impacted.

I. A MODEL OF INTELLECTUAL PROPERTY POLICY INFLUENCE

In previous work, we analyzed the divergent successes copyright and patent interest groups enjoyed in influencing IP public policy by combining to influence the enactment of TRIPS. Creative Content enjoyed the ratification of the WCT and WPPT and adoption of the DMCA. By contrast, since TRIPS ratification, US patent right holders surrendered some gains achieved under TRIPS due to resistance from developing nations (Sell, 2003) and until the enactment of the AIA in 2011 had not obtained any substantive patent reform legislation despite trying for over a decade (Thomas, 2006).

This chapter extends that previous analysis by explaining the dynamic process of coalition formation and breakup that has characterized the development of intellectual property law. This chapter augments that analysis by developing a theory that explains why diverse copyright and patent interest groups united to collectively push through the ratification of TRIPS, but no longer cooperate in pursuing IP law changes. The theory developed here also provides an explanation for the critical role that digitalization played in changing the legislative strategy of copyright interest holders while having very little impact on the strategic behavior of most patent interest groups. Our analysis suggests that factors that enabled diverse intellectual property interest groups to coalesce and engineer the enactment of TRIPS no longer exist and that it is unlikely that such unified collective action organized to change IP law will ever reoccur.

A. The Dynamics of Intellectual Property Economics

Our theory is interdisciplinary in employing legal analysis, microeconomic theory and interest-group political theory to analyze the political economy of the development of IP law. The analysis uses standard microeconomic assumptions. It assumes that: (1) there are markets for intellectual property; (2) IP creators and owners are profit-maximizers; and (3) consumers demand products produced using intellectual property (Landes & Posner, 2003). Thus, IP value is a function of what business and consumers are willing to demand and pay for intellectual property. In this simple model, if there is no demand or no ability to charge for intellectual property, the value of the intellectual property is zero. Consumers of intellectual property maximize their objective functions by acquiring intellectual property for the lowest offered price. Therefore, consumers acquire goods they demand for as little as zero. In this model, there are no ethical constraints, so consumers take goods and services without permission ("misappropriate") when the cost of such behavior is low.

At this point, a comment on terminology is required. This chapter uses the term "misappropriate" and "misappropriation" instead of "theft" and "piracy" because the former terms are less biased and relatively neutral. Labeling IP consumers as thieves, pirates, trolls and, now, counterfeiters is used to demonize unauthorized users of intellectual property politically and in the media (Patry, 2009). We believe strongly that using such highly charged terms—regardless of how popular they have become—to describe uses and users of intellectual property is inappropriate in an analytical study.

Moreover, misappropriation is actually a more accurate description of unauthorized or unlawful use of intellectual property. Black's Law Dictionary defines theft as "the felonious taking and removing of another's personal property with the intent of depriving the true owner of it" (Garner, 2009). By contrast, Black's Dictionary defines misappropriation as "the application of another's property or money dishonestly to one's own use." The dictionary describes the elements of misappropriation as: (1) an investment to acquire (or in our case, create) the information; (2) a taking of the information without a similar investment; and (3) a competitive injury to the plaintiff as the result of the taking.

This definition describes what happens when someone takes intellectual property without permission. The plaintiff does not lose its intellectual property; however, it suffers a competitive loss: either lost profits or a reduction in the value of its monopoly position with respect to its intellectual property. Thus, such popular terms as theft and piracy are not only biased, but they are less accurate than available alternatives.

Before discussing the misappropriation threats that IP holders face, it is helpful to describe consumption patterns in IP markets. Some types of misappropriation are more costly than others. To advance this discussion, this chapter asserts that there is a distinction between consuming a product produced with legally protected intellectual property—an indirect form of IP consumption—and consuming the intellectual property directly. IP products are frequently tangible (with the notable exception of processes), whereas the underlying intellectual property is intangible (Landes & Posner, 2003). When a consumer takes a drug, uses a patented chemical product, reads a book or watches a movie, she is an indirect consumer of intellectual property. However, when a consumer manufactures a drug, uses a process to produce electronics or distributes music over the Internet, she is directly using or distributing intellectual property. As the subsequent analysis argues, the type of consumption—direct or indirect as well as other characteristics—strongly influences the policies IP right holders prefer.

This analysis identifies three types of non-creative uses of intellectual property: industrial, trading, and consumption. Industrial users are businesses that use intellectual property either in the manufacture, sale, or provision of goods and services. Industrial users may use intellectual property directly or indirectly. An industrialist's use of intellectual property may be part of a patent-protected process, a patented component or chemical entity, or may be subsumed in the manufacture of an intermediate product used in the production of another product. In some cases industrialists may produce products that consist of a myriad of components, many of which may contain intellectual property (Burk & Lemley, 2003). In other cases, the product may be synonymous with its encapsulated intellectual property. For example, pharmaceuticals may consist of a single patented chemical entity. Or, in the realm of copyright, a movie, photograph, book, or song each is a creative work entitled to intellectual property protection.

Traders, the second type of user, differ from industrial users in that they do not use intellectual property for the production or provision of goods and services. Instead, traders profit or gain value from intellectual property primarily through the sale, licensing and distribution of intellectual property. Traders include NPEs—also known pejoratively as patent trolls—who acquire patent rights through trade or purchase (Thomas, 2006). Do note that NPEs also include creators who choose not to directly exploit their creations. The NPE trader is generally a company that profits by seeking license fees from industrial users or court awards when negotiations fail. However, NPEs may also enhance efficiency by playing the role of broker between firms with a competitive edge in creating innovations and firms that are better at exploiting and marketing innovations. Hence, NPEs are not invariably negative rent seekers and may at times increase societal welfare.

The third type of user is the IP consumer. Consumers, or end-users, use intellectual property for personal enjoyment. They obtain utility through personal use, and use by friends and family, of IP products. They do not use intellectual property to add value to products or services that are subsequently sold or distributed. Thus, consumers and industrial users are mutually exclusive. Consumers are end-users of industrial products containing intellectual property, such as pharmaceuticals and electronics. Consumers are also end-users of creative works such as music, film, art and literature. Note that when consumers share or distribute intellectual property to users outside their sphere of friends and family, this analysis treats them as traders rather than as end-using consumers.

We assume that relative to total production of a good, a single end-user consumes only a small quantity of that good. An end-user can enjoy a relatively small number of televisions, automobiles and other consumer goods at a time. A business end-user may enjoy a larger volume of a good, but the volume is most likely to be small relative to the total output of the good. An end-user would have little personal use for multiple copies of a book or movie. Moreover, in using a pharmaceutical product, the consumer would need and therefore consume amounts too small to affect overall market demand for the product. Thus, consumer end-user consumption is finite and discrete. When individual end-users significantly impact markets, as in the case of file sharing, this chapter classifies that individual as a trader.

One of the most difficult problems facing IP rights holders is preventing IP misappropriation. Compounding this problem are the tremendous losses that IP misappropriation can cause. A single act of IP misappropriation can reduce the value of intellectual property to zero. By contrast, losses resulting from tangible property theft are almost never that substantial (Landes & Posner, 2003). Theft of tangible property typically requires some unauthorized party to take physical control of the property. Moreover, theft of a tangible service such as a haircut, a meal at a restaurant or car repairs requires some sort of contact between the service provider and the consumer or the consumer's physical property. Thus, theft of tangible property and services is extremely limited. Basic security such as locks and police action can be employed to minimize or eliminate such theft. Clearly, the logistics of stealing tangible property limits losses from this unlawful activity. Theft of products from a warehouse may be significant but is unlikely to drive the value of the company's products to zero. As long as the product is consumable or rival in consumption, the theft will not reduce demand from consumers who do not receive any of the stolen good (Nicholson, 2004). Therefore, the firm is able to produce more products to meet future demand. Even when the loss is calamitous— for example, the theft of a rare diamond or an artistic masterpiece—there is a possibility that the owner can recover the stolen property, thereby minimizing the loss.

By contrast, the taking of intangible intellectual property can result in the market value of the intellectual property falling to zero. As discussed above, end-users usually interact with IP goods rather than directly with intellectual property. Even when intellectual property such as music and information is delivered in a less tangible form, consumers require an electronic device such as a radio, television or computer to consume or retain the intellectual property. We categorize intellectual property contained in a product by the extent to which the intellectual property is "secured" by that tangible product from end-user consumption. A product containing intellectual property is highly secured if the cost of unauthorized access or distribution of the encapsulated intellectual property to an end-user exceeds the total benefit that the end-user obtains from obtaining direct access to the targeted intellectual property. Examples of secured IP products include legal drugs, electronics and industrial processes. The intellectual property in a drug may be intrinsic to the drug, but it would be difficult and expensive for an end-user to extract, directly use or distribute the encapsulated intellectual property. End-users have similar difficulty directly accessing and consuming the intellectual property contained in electronics and industrial processes. End-users may enjoy industrial processes that produce cars that are more fuel efficient and safer, but they would have little use for the underlying intellectual property that enables such enhancements. The costs necessary to exploit the value of such intellectual property far exceed any gain that an end-user could obtain from such activities.

Other IP products—including many products based on creative content—are less secure. Books, journals and recorded media are such examples. Although IP law protects the containers, the intrinsic value in such IP products is the published and recorded content—words, images and sounds. End-users—even pre-digital era—can access such intellectual property at a cost. Books and journal articles can be transcribed and photocopied, and recorded media can be copied either in analog or digital form. Pre-digital era, the costs of copying creative content still exceeded benefits that an end-user could obtain from such unauthorized use. An end-user might incur such costs in order to make copies of literary materials or recorded media for friends and family. However, an end-user—facing a positive marginal cost for each unit produced—would have little incentive to produce large amounts of creative content since each photocopied book would require significant time and effort. Therefore, IP interest holders faced greater losses from misappropriation of less-secure intellectual property, but such losses were nevertheless limited.

However, losses from IP misappropriation due to industrial users and IP traders were potentially far greater than end-user misappropriation. The fixed and marginal costs that deterred consumers from misappropriating secured intellectual property did not have similar deterrence effects for misappropriating industrial users. IP industrial misappropriators generally face lower total costs of production than do authorized producers. Unlike IP creators and licensees, industrial users face zero development and licensing costs. Thus, assuming production costs are similar across industry players, IP misappropriators have a cost advantage in production provided their IP acquisition costs are lower than the costs of licensing the intellectual property. For inventions these costs are very low because patent law requires patent applicants to describe their inventions in detail in publicly available patent filings (Patent Act, 1952). Similarly, the costs of misappropriating creative works are also low. The cost of acquiring and reproducing a book, a music CD or movie DVD is minimal, and access control technologies provide little deterrence (Thomas, 2006).

Accordingly, it follows that unauthorized industrial users can drive IP holders' and licensees' profits to zero by selling goods produced with the misappropriated intellectual property at a price below that of authorized industrial users. Thus, whereas encapsulating intellectual property within secured products could—pre-digital era—limit losses due to end-user misappropriation, IP rights holders had few effective self-help defenses against industrial misappropriation. Thus, most legislative and geo-political efforts to control IP misappropriation focused on containing industrial IP misappropriation (Sell, 2003).

B. Strategic Implications of the Misappropriation Problem

The above discussion has implications for IP rights holders' strategic choices for misappropriation control. These implications differ based on the time period. Prior to the digital era, consumer misappropriation was likely to have limited impact on the value of intellectual property because this misappropriation was discrete and limited in nature. Consumer misappropriation was likely to come from physical theft of goods containing intellectual property. Reproducing intellectual property without a profit motive was prohibitively expensive relative to the low opportunity costs of purchasing goods. Before the invention of photocopiers and audio recording devices, a consumer unwilling to pay or physically steal IP goods could copy a book by hand or re-record a musical composition. Such activities were costly in terms of time and resources (Thomas, 2006).

The invention of photocopying technology reduced this cost significantly. Photocopying a book was far less expensive than copying the book by hand. In addition, analog-recording devices, such as cassette tapes or videocassette recorders, dramatically lowered the costs of copying these creative works. However, even with these reductions in the costs of misappropriation, lost profits attributable to such uses did not render creative enterprises unprofitable (Patry, 2009). Both types of replication were highly labor intensive and both types still required a positive expenditure of resources. Finally, neither form of replication was "lossless." Both types produced duplicates that were clearly inferior to the original. Photocopied books did not include bindings and were visually inferior to the original copy. Similarly, analog recordings of audio and video performances were audibly and visually inferior to the original products (Thomas, 2006).

In the digital age the problem of consumer misappropriation became significant for creative works but not for inventions (Marsnik & Thomas, 2011). Potential losses from industrial misappropriation did not change. However, the reduced costs of replicating creative works removed a major deterrent to consumer misappropriation. Essentially all creative works can be digitized and transmitted electronically at near-zero marginal cost (Ginsburg, 2011). Moreover, unlike copies in the pre-digital era, digital copies were either perfect or near-perfect copies of the original creative work. Once digitized, the cost of replication and distribution of a creative work goes to zero. With zero costs of replication and distribution, consumers face no barrier to posting creative works on the Internet or exchanging creative works. Although the motivation for unauthorized distribution of creative works is unclear, many consumers engaged in this activity. The zero cost of distribution and consumers' willingness to acquire goods for the lowest available cost meant that one sale could theoretically reduce the value of creative intellectual property to zero. Thus, acquisition of a single unit of a creative product can result in unlimited distribution of products containing the creative work at a price—often zero—below the level that the legal owner or licensee of the intellectual property must charge to obtain a profit. Moreover, once unauthorized distribution begins, it may be essentially impossible to stop continued distribution of the creative work. Once placed on the Internet, the sources for misappropriated work multiply, and some sources may be in locations that present jurisdictional difficulties (Thomas, 2006).

Hence, whereas misappropriation by industrial users remained a concern for creative rights holders in the digital era, these concerns became subordinated to the bigger threat of end-user misappropriation. The magnitude of industrial user misappropriation did not decline; rather, the harm from consumer misappropriation grew from an insignificant to an industry-threatening level in a very short period. Creative Content responded to this changing landscape by shifting its focus from industrial misappropriation to end-user misappropriation. This new focus provided Creative Content with even less reason to participate in a coalition with patent interest holders. Although the copyright coalition was smaller, as will be discussed below, the lack of concerted opposition allowed this smaller coalition to nonetheless achieve significant success in influencing policy.

C. The Political Economy of IP Protection

This section posits that law facilitates efforts to advance strategic interests discussed in previous sections. Law enables economic actors to enlist the policing powers of the state to exclude, confiscate or destroy infringing products, and to penalize and punish economic actors involved in such unauthorized activities. Even more critical, law can scale IP enforcement effort, allowing rights holders to exclude unauthorized use at the national or global level (Thomas, 2006).

The value of legal enforcement of IP rights provides incentives for actors to influence the legislative process. Convincing or inducing legislative bodies to enact laws that enhance legal rights or the effectiveness of enforcement mechanisms is a common strategy (Shell, 2004). Considerable attention has been paid to the political influence process (Wilson, 1980). Lobbying is the term used to describe the process that interest groups employ to influence the legislative process. Lobbying exploits the self-interest of political actors by providing them with resources required to achieve their objectives. The self-interest model posits that elected officials are motivated by the desire to get elected and, once elected, remain in office (Stigler, 1973).

Competing in elections is a very expensive process that requires political candidates to raise large sums of money. The model assumes that voters vote for candidates who they believe are most likely to benefit their constituencies. Political candidates through campaigning attempt to show voters that they are more likely to effectively address voter interests than their opponents. However, convincing voters is difficult because the opposition has the same objective. Therefore, voters must evaluate the often-voluminous amounts of information they receive from each candidate to decide who is presenting the most convincing case. While imperfect, outspending the other candidate increases the probability of success, and being substantially outspent by the other side dramatically increases the probability of losing. Therefore, as candidates battle to outspend or at least keep pace with their opponents, the cost of campaigning can increase dramatically. Many Senate and House of Representatives campaigns spend in the millions of dollars. Thus, it is critical that political actors raise large amounts of money (Shell, 2004). Interest groups attempting to influence the legislative process willingly contribute to the campaigns of political actors who they believe are likely to advance their interests. Although elected officials may not explicitly trade votes for donations, there are correlations between contributions and responsiveness of legislators.

The simple model of legislative influence increases in complexity quickly when competing interest groups are added to the model. In our previous work, we considered these effects in detail (Thomas, 2006). In summary, the described model posits that legislators enact laws that interest groups favor when the law is uncontroversial and unopposed. When opposition exists and one side is significantly more powerful than the other side, the stronger side has a greater probability of prevailing. This outcome is much more likely when the benefits of the proposed law are concentrated in the strong party and the costs to the opposing party are defused. Thus, a powerful interest group that benefits greatly from enacting the new law is likely to get their way when the other side faces defused benefits from opposing the powerful interest group.

For example, interest groups in finance industries may block or blunt regulatory reform affecting their industries. Successfully blocking such reform is likely to be worth many millions or billions of dollars for a few large players. In contrast, the benefit to individual consumers may be insignificant or may only provide a future or indirect benefit. Most consumers and small businesses have limited interactions with banking and finance players, and only a fraction of those who do interact with the banking industry receive a measurable benefit. Thus, the cost of organizing consumer interests to counter the blocking effort is likely to exceed the benefits consumers receive from regulatory reform (Wilson, 1980).

The outcome of such influence efforts is not deterministic. When opposing interest groups face high benefits and costs, the results are less predictable. Whereas legislative actors wish to please their constituencies, they abhor conflict and generally choose not to act when powerful interest groups oppose each other. In addition, legislative bodies abhor controversy and negative publicity. Therefore, a weaker group can block or blunt the efforts of more powerful interest groups to influence legislative behavior by raising the profile of the subject matter of the influence effort (Shell, 2004). Thus, for example, in early 2012 the Stop Online Piracy Act (SOPA) and the Protect IP Act (PIPA) appeared to be on the fast track for legislative passage. However, Google, Wikipedia, and other Internet players protested by shutting down for a 24-hour period in January 2012. What had previously been considered an uncontroversial, esoteric legislative act that was designed to benefit a prominent legislative constituency suddenly became a high-profile controversial action with civil liberties ramifications that quickly became too hot to handle. This chapter discusses the events surrounding this incident in a later section.

In the face of controversial legislative topics, copyright IP interest groups often turn to the process Peter Yu calls "legislative laundering" to get desired initiatives onto the legislative fast track (Yu, 2008). Powerful interest groups have used the treaty-making process and multilateral negotiations for some time to create what they hope to be insurmountable momentum and instantaneous legitimacy to get legislative initiatives enacted. By getting a number of power nations to adopt a treaty—which process is frequently dominated or spearheaded by a set of US interest groups—the desired policy gains an air of inevitability. Whether or not this inevitability is a psychological fabrication, it gives elected officials political cover for enacting legislation that may subsequently turn out to be controversial. Proposed law based on treaty deliberations is framed as an obligation rather than a proposal subject to congressional debate. Therefore, rejections of or attempts to amend such proposed legislation are viewed as violation of US treaty obligations entered into by authorized representatives of the United States.

Thus, as long as the treaty-initiated proposals are not overly controversial or opposed by powerful interest groups, policy laundering provides an efficient and effective means of getting desired policy enacted into law while avoiding compromises and amendments associated with the legislative process. It also provides a means of getting ambitious policy enacted without alerting the press or interest groups that might oppose or wish to amend the proposed legislation. When employed effectively, new law may be implemented before opposition has time to mobilize to either block or amend the new law. Creative Content interest groups were extremely effective in using policy laundering to get the DMCA enacted in the 1990s (Sharp, 2002; Yu, 2008).

II.   HOW WE GOT HERE: IP PROTECTION FROM TRIPS TO ACTA AND AIA

Since the 1990s, IP interest groups have acted collectively to influence the passage of IP-related legislation. In this section, we discuss these actions within the framework of the theory developed in the previous section. The first major action, enactment of the TRIPS treaty, stands in stark contrast to subsequent influence efforts in that the coalition that backed it uniquely included all patent, copyright (and trademark) interest groups. None of the subsequent influence efforts included both copyright and patent interest groups, and some of these efforts—especially on the patent side—have been even more splintered. This section examines these influence efforts with the assumption that each involved party sought to address its particular interests as described in the previous section. The chapter notes that—as Axlerod et al. hypothesize—interest groups form coalitions when the coalition's objectives address shared interests (Axlerod, Mitchell, Thomas, Bennett & Bruderer, 1995). The probability that the coalition bond between members is strong is greater when the coalition objectives do not provide a subset of the coalition with significant competitive advantages against other coalition members.

A.   The TRIPS Coalition: The All-inclusive IP Coalition

The coalition formed to advance IP interests that resulted in TRIPS was unique in that it included all the major copyright and patent interest groups. The Intellectual Property Committee (IPC) (which included, among others, Bristol-Myers, CBS, DuPont, GE, GM, HP, IBM, Johnson & Johnson, Merck, Monsanto, and Pfizer) was the major force behind US TRIPS efforts. While this group included both copyright and patent interests, it was clear that patent interests predominated in the IPC's mission (Sell, 2003). TRIPS ambitiously set out to create a uniform set of rules for enforcing IP rights at the national level. This included greater levels of transparency in the decision-making process, appeal procedures, timely, fair and non-costly enforcement, decisions in writing and a judicial review, injunctions if necessary, awards for damages and disposal of infringing material (TRIPS, Art. 41–49). TRIPS also established the TRIPS Council; made up of member nations, its sole responsibility was to evaluate members' adherence to TRIPS provisions (TRIPS, Art. 63). Additional enforcement mechanisms included dispute resolution between TRIPS members handled under the WTO's dispute settlement procedures.

The TRIPS bias in favor of patent interests was apparent. Sell observed that patent interests were "particularly pleased" with the TRIPS agreement because of its new enforcement provisions (Sell, 2003). Pharma (which was the strongest sub-interest group within the IP coalition) achieved its long-sought-after objective of worldwide protection for drug patents even in nations without established patent systems. By contrast, Creative Content received few benefits and was dissatisfied with the TRIPS agreement. From its perspective, the TRIPS focus on national-level enforcement did little to address the budding problem of end-user misappropriation. Evidencing Creative Content's dissatisfaction, the main copyright advocacy group—the International Intellectual Property Alliance (IIPA)—lobbied aggressively for reform in WIPO even before the culmination of TRIPS (Sharp, 2002). TRIPS—where the digital rights debate began without any immediate results—marked the birth of an aggressive copyright campaign to tighten protection over digital content, and the culmination of protection for products vulnerable to industrial misappropriation.

Patent interest groups during this period clearly feared industrial misappropriation. It was apparent that they were concerned about governments implicitly allowing or even authorizing large-scale industrial misappropriation. This concern was a particular priority for Pharma, which believed that without the stick that TRIPS offered, developing countries would allow or even encourage their domestic industrial interests to exploit pharmaceutical patents from Western countries with impunity. Creative Content, by contrast, was skeptical from the beginning about whether the TRIPS deliberations would advance its interests in any significant way (Sell, 2003). Creative Content preferred to employ Section 301 and other bilateral agreements to address its industrial misappropriation concerns. Creative Content's skepticism was validated when proposals to address end-user misappropriation were dropped during treaty negotiations. Nonetheless, Creative Content continued to support the TRIPS IP coalition through its conclusion even though copyright interest groups such as the movie industry received limited gains during the GATT rounds leading to TRIPS (Jakubowicz & Jeanray, 1994).

B. Creative Content: Exerting Influence outside the Grand Coalition

Creative Content legislative influence efforts have been successful post-TRIPS. Due to the onset of the digital era, advances in computer technology blurred the boundaries between end-user goods and intellectual property. The method of delivering creative content ceased to be a barrier to misappropriation because digitalization allowed content to be transformed and transferred regardless of the original transmission format. This phenomenon facilitated the growth of end-user misappropriation and therefore lowered the priority of industrial copyright misappropriation

(Thomas, 2006). To combat the new threat posed by computer-enabled end-user misappropriation, copyright sought additional provisions within TRIPS that would address this growing concern. However, awareness of the digital threat emerged late in the TRIPS negotiations and therefore was not resolved in time to meet the TRIPS Dunkel draft of 1991 (J.M., 1992). Therefore, Creative Content, while encouraged by the new enforcement standards in TRIPS, did not receive the level of gains that it had sought in the GATT negotiations as a whole. As Jack Valenti, the former president of the MPAA and the principal IIPA spokesperson, remarked, "The GATT as currently proposed is an arrow aimed straight at the heart of the US motion picture industry. We cannot support—and—we will actively oppose the agreement if placed before the Congress in its present form" (TV Trade Media, 1992). In contrast to patent interest groups, which strongly supported TRIPS, the film industry—one of the leading lobbying sources for increased copyright protection—saw itself losing out in GATT as a result of inclusion of the cultural exemption in the final TRIPS agreement. This exemption allowed countries to restrict the flow of foreign creative content in order to protect domestic creative content industries (Broder, 1993).

As a result of its disappointment with the TRIPS negotiation under GATT, Creative Content negotiated the WCT and WPPT (the Internet Treaties) towards the end of the TRIPS deliberations. The Internet Treaties focused directly on end-user misappropriation concerns by ensuring that rights holders could effectively use technology to protect their rights and to license their works online (Pike & Fischer, 2003). Unlike many patent rights holders, Creative Content could create technological devices or anti-circumvention provisions to protect copyright-protected materials by reestablishing a physical barrier to the underlying intellectual property in end-user products. The Internet Treaties—in contrast to TRIPS—bolstered technological efforts to address end-user misappropriation by requiring member nations to provide adequate legal protection for Creative Content and outlaw the circumvention of technological protection measures such as encryption. Simultaneously, the Internet Treaties formalized protection of creative rights for the online/digital marketplace by compelling member states to prosecute the intentional alteration or deletion of electronic rights management information (Pike & Fischer, 2003).

Creative Content pushed to include a plethora of provisions designed to enhance the protection of the interests of Creative Content in the Internet Treaties. For example, the Internet Treaties included provisions addressing major concerns of the creative-content-delivery industries: film, television and music. These provisions increased restrictions on the broadcast and rental of copyright-protected materials. Notably, these provisions were some of the same hotly contested cultural initiatives that were discarded during the TRIPS discussion in an effort to garner sufficient support for the final draft. The end result of these multilateral deliberations was to "shift the debate concerning technological circumvention measures and online service provider liability back to the national level for further consideration" (Pike & Fischer, 2003).

One of the principal goals of Creative Content was the creation of the most expansive systems of protection possible in order to establish a baseline to use as leverage in subsequent domestic and international IP policy negotiations (Yu, 2011). Through the multilateral treaty process that produced the Internet Treaties, Creative Content employed a recursive strategy of policy laundering in which inclusion of policy reforms in international treaties was used to push for domestic legislation to implement the multilateral treaty obligations. Once such provisions were implemented domestically, Creative Content could employ these domestic successes to pressure foreign governments to implement similar policies into their domestic laws. This recursive process could continue indefinitely with successes at the multilateral level used to pressure domestic legislative bodies into elevating creative content protections, which in turn could be used to pressure foreign governments into reciprocating.

Putting this strategy into effect after adoption of the Internet Treaties, Creative Content began lobbying for implementation of the pro-copyright provisions outlined in the Internet Treaties. The DMCA was crafted not only to protect Creative Content's domestic interests but also to promote these interests internationally. Supporters argued that the DMCA had to be as expansive as possible in order to maximize the impact on international agreements (Note, 2008). The DMCA was extremely one-sided in advancing the interests of Creative Content. Backers sought to include provisions that would help copyright holders maximize the size of the economic rents they could extract from marketing their products in the digital realm (Okediji, 2009). Conspicuously absent from these discussions were any concessions to end-users, including fair-use exceptions or allowances for unauthorized use of content that could help increase creative outputs and further enhance user participation in the creative process. Initial propositions were aggressively overreaching. They awarded control over all digital reproductions of works "transmitted over the Internet, even those reproduced in temporary form," and also provided for "elimination of the first-sale doctrine; elimination of fair use when licensing of the work is possible; and giving control to owners over every digital transmission" (Okediji, 2009). Thus, US legal code adopted policy provisions that had proven to be too controversial for the international community.

The DMCA instituted five main provisions: refinement of performance rights in sound recordings; guidelines for Internet service providers (ISPs) regarding infringement; conforming recording provisions to the realities of the Internet; updating the library and archival procedures for the digital environment; and categorizing the development of devices that circumvent protection technology as a criminal activity (Pike & Fischer, 2003). In an effort to stave off misappropriation of digital works, the DMCA included anti-circumvention provisions, which prohibited breaking encryptions on copyright works as well as the creation of devices that "circumvent technical protections of copyrighted works" (Wang, 2003).

The anti-circumvention clause of the DMCA proved to be its most controversial provision. The district court determined, based on its interpretation of the DMCA, that the widely disseminated DeContent Scramble System (DeCSS)—a code written to break the Content Scramble System (CSS) created to prevent the copying of movies recorded on DVDs—was illegal (*Universal v. Reimerdes*, 2000). Ruling in favor of the MPAA, the court implied that IP protection was more important than the harm to free speech associated with restricting fair use access to materials subject to access control and copy prevention systems. This shift in favor of Creative Content, due in large part to DMCA requirements, provides strong evidence of the shift in the judicial interpretation of the balance between copyright enforcement and personal civil liberties that passage of the DMCA engendered.

The DeCSS ruling is in sharp contrast to pre-DMCA rulings on recording devices. For instance, a casebook argues that if the DMCA had been in force, the "Sony Betamax case" (*Sony Corp. v. Universal Studios*, 1984) would have most likely have been decided differently (Pike & Fischer, 2003). In *Sony*, the court determined that the manufacturers of video cassette recorders (VCRs) could not be held liable for infringement because consumers used VCRs for "time shifting purposes" and that this act enlarged the viewing audience, thereby augmenting, rather than reducing, the economic value of creative content. Therefore, rather than harming content holders, VCRs used for time-shifting purposes did not infringe copyrights. Thus, whereas VCRs could be used to infringe copyrights, there were also "substantial noninfringing uses" which were privileged. However, with the advent of the DMCA courts concluded that the substantial noninfringing use defense did not apply if the defendant had to circumvent an anti-circumvention technology to employ the use (Pike & Fischer, 2003). The shift in favor of Creative Content at the expense of end-user rights and access is indicative of the substantial realignment of rights with respect to creative content effectuated by passage of the DMCA.

C.   ACTA and Post-DMCA Pro-creative Content Laws

Post-DMCA, Creative Content continued its efforts to expand its ability to counter end-user misappropriation through the creation of increasingly more powerful enforcement tools. In the mid-2000s, Creative Content attempted to develop momentum by getting relatively uncontroversial domestic policy enacted before targeting the international forum. The first step in this policy-laundering effort was the 2008 passage of the Prioritizing Resources and Organization for Intellectual Property Act (PRO-IP). As an apparent precursor to ACTA, PRO-IP created aggressive search and seizure measures that enable border patrol officials to seize and destroy any property "used or intended to be used to commit or assist in the violation of trademark and copyright law" (Prioritizing Resources and Organization for Intellectual Property Act, 2008).

Due to the similarities between PRO-IP and ACTA, it is likely that Creative Content used PRO-IP to develop momentum for ACTA. Much of the PRO-IP Act was recycled into ACTA. But far from just an international extension of PRO-IP, ACTA provisions would greatly expand copyright protection by means that are sweeping and politically charged. ACTA achieved this wish list of copyright enforcement by piecing together the strictest elements from its member states' national copyright laws to form the most stringent international copyright law on record (Kaminski, 2009). For instance, ACTA obligates all member nations to classify the aiding and abetting of copyright infringement as a criminal act. For the first time, criminal prosecutors would not have to allege the existence of a monetary gain motive in order to get a conviction in such infringement action.

ACTA further introduced a number of more controversial provisions. These provisions included a new emphasis on border enforcement measures, the formation of an international cooperative information-sharing and enforcement task force, enhanced criminal sanctions and statutory damages, and further cooperation measures between ISPs and member states (Ayoob, 2010). Groups opposed to ACTA alleged that the act might limit free speech as well as increase the authority of border agents to confiscate personal property such as laptops, iPods and other electronics and allow at-will searches of music libraries. These new powers would allow flagrant violations of civil liberties (Goff, 2010).

This approach of seeking extremely expansive new methods of content protection in treaty negotiations is consistent with the policy-laundering approach that Creative Content has employed successfully during earlier multilateral negotiations. There are clear discrepancies between US and European legal codes, which would require modification of US copyright law to enforce ACTA—the goal of policy laundering (Yu, 2008). ACTA outlined a global standard on copyright infringement and it did so without being vetted through an open multilateral process (Kaminski, 2009). As it was in early TRIPS negotiations, many developing nations were excluded from deliberations over a legal framework with which they would eventually have to comply. Although no written record has surfaced, it is likely that developing nations would be coerced into endorsing ACTA, through mechanisms similar to those used to gain broad acceptance of TRIPS.

D.   ACTA Adoption Process and Subsequent Missteps

The ACTA implementation process followed the Creative Content playbook with some significant adjustments. Building on the momentum gained from the 2008 passage of the PRO-IP Act, the United States—along with Australia, Canada, the European Union (EU), Japan, Korea, Mexico, Morocco, New Zealand, Singapore and Switzerland—finalized the text of ACTA in November 2010. Perhaps recognizing the controversial nature of proposed provisions, these nations drafted this multilateral agreement outside of the usual WTO and WIPO trade forums in secrecy (Kaminski, 2009). The secrecy allowed member nations to present ACTA to the public as a *fait accompli* after adoption.

However, news of the negotiations broke prematurely during the Wikileaks scandal. In May 2008, two public interest groups, the Electronic Frontier Foundation and Public Knowledge, filed suit under the Freedom of Information Act to receive access to information related to ACTA negotiations. Specifically, these groups requested access to ACTA documents, including participant lists, records of meetings between the USTR staff and representatives from the entertainment, luxury goods and services, and pharmaceutical industries. The US executive branch blocked these requests, asserting that ACTA negotiations required confidentiality due to national security (Ayoob, 2010). European countries also denied access to information requests (Anderson, 2008).

Although the leaks did not slow down the negotiation process, policy-laundering efforts in the United States may have doomed ACTA passage. Negotiating nations proceeded with agreement ratification despite the unwelcomed publicity. In October 2011, Japan, the United States, Australia, Canada, Morocco, New Zealand, Singapore and South Korea ratified ACTA and the European Union and Mexico promised to follow. Before ratification, Creative Content began pushing Congress to pass legislation to incorporate ACTA into US law. In May 2011, the Senate introduced the Protect Intellectual Property Act of 2011 (PIPA) and the Commercial Felony Streaming Act (CFSA). These bills would dramatically enhance the enforcement actions available to law enforcement agents for the protection of creative content on the Internet.

These bills (especially PIPA and its companion bill in the House, the Stop Online Piracy Act (SOPA)) had acquired an air of inevitability. Backers of these bills pitched them as targeting infringing Internet sites that are based in foreign countries. These backers assured the public that average citizens with personal websites had little to worry about from bill enforcement provisions. Thus, passage of PIPA and SOPA would be a simple case of client politics: benefits would be concentrated among creative content providers—a very powerful influence group—and the public would shoulder highly dispersed costs (Wilson, 1980). PIPA had 40 co-sponsors and passed the Senate Judiciary Committee by unanimous voice vote. Similarly, SOPA enjoyed broad bipartisan support in the House of Representatives at its introduction. There seemed to be little that could slow down, much less stop, the momentum pushing this pro-copyright legislation towards enactment.

However, the smooth sailing of the pro-Creative Content legislative flurry did not last. Despite assurances that average citizens would not be penalized under these bills, the actual text suggested otherwise. For example, the CFSA provided for enhanced criminal penalties for copyright violations in the United States. Particularly alarming to opponents was the severe penalty this bill exacted for what Internet experts identified as commonplace usage: posting a file subject to copyright protection without permission that receives as few as ten views. This offense could result in a sentence of up to five years in prison. Given the accessibility of online creative content and the fact that many videos become "viral"— extremely popular and widely disseminated—in a short period of time, the assurance that average Internet users would not be subject to these harsh penalties was not credible.

The anti-streaming provisions of CFSA, which were subsequently incorporated into SOPA, became a rallying point to generate organized opposition to PIPA and SOPA. Recording artist Justin Bieber, who gained fame in part from posting clips of himself performing commercial music without authorization on YouTube, became the poster child for PIPA and SOPA opponents. They claimed that Bieber could be jailed under SOPA if he posted such videos after the enactment of these bills. Bieber rallied PIPA and SOPA opposition by demanding that Senator Amy Klobuchar of Minnesota be jailed for co-sponsoring PIPA. A variety of grassroots organizations developed opposition to these bills and organized using Internet-based tools such as YouTube and Twitter. Congressional support for PIPA and SOPA began peeling away in late 2011. By mid-January an Internet strike or blackout was announced for January 18. Thousands of websites including such prominent Internet actors as Google, Wikipedia, Craigslist, and Mozilla participated in the blackout (SOPA Strike, 2012). By the end of January 2012, it was very clear that PIPA and SOPA, while not abandoned, would not be passed without major substantive revisions.

The concerted grassroots opposition to PIPA and SOPA not only stalled the momentum to get these bills enacted, but may have also been responsible for halting ACTA globally. The activism of Internet action groups is what Wilson identifies as "entrepreneurial politics" (Wilson, 1980). As Shell describes it, "Entrepreneurial Politics entails a head-on challenge by an underdog against an entrenched interest" (Shell, 2004). In entrepreneurial politics, the political benefits are spread thin and the associated cost of political action is relatively high. In the case of PIPA and SOPA, the Internet provided a means of lowering the cost of organizing against powerful copyright interest groups. Often an external event occurs that allows these entrepreneurial groups to exploit favorable publicity. Here, the image of a jailed Justin Bieber may have been the catalyst that propelled the growth of anti-PIPA and SOPA collective action. The 18 January 2012 Internet "blackout" protest catapulted this esoteric IP issue to the front pages of newspapers, making support for what was believed to be a simple matter of client politics untenable for elected officers. Although PIPA, SOPA and ACTA are not officially dead, with the European Union's July 2012 rejection of ACTA, these initiatives will require substantial revision before they resurface in Congress.

E. Post-TRIPS Patent Reform and the 2011 AIA

Post-TRIPS, patent interest groups have achieved much less success in influencing legislation than have their copyright counterparts. Unlike the client politics and policy laundering initially enjoyed by the cohesive copyright coalition, the patent coalition has been handicapped in pursuit of legislative change by far more diverse and fractured interests. Therefore, prior to 2011, instead of exploiting client politics to enact ambitious enforcement laws, patent interest groups engaged in contentious interest-group battles each time Congress considered patent reform. These battles stand in stark contrast to the highly cohesive TRIPS IP coalition and post-TRIPS copyright coalitions.

The grand TRIPS coalition did not extend past the TRIPS-enactment period. TRIPS provided patent interest groups with the tools they needed to address industrial misappropriation on the global stage. Post-TRIPS, the patent coalition fractured based on industry type with the Old Tech (pharmaceutical, chemical, traditional industrial, and semiconductors) and High Tech (computer, electronics, software, and Internet companies) coalitions being the main opposing factions. In general, the interests of these two factions diverge on whether they benefit from enhanced or weakened patent protection. For Old Tech, patents often are the primary source of revenue. Often, a patent serves as the most important input in the production of Old Tech products and may have required large R&D expenditures to create. As a result Old Tech companies may depend on strong patents to produce significant revenue for extended periods (Thomas, 2006).

By contrast, High Tech's patents tend not to be as critical to the profitability of High Tech products. A High Tech product can contain thousands of technologies, many of which may be subject to patents (Burk & Lemley, 2003). Patents used in such products are generally not as expensive to develop and their useful life cycle before replacement is likely to be much shorter than the 20-year patent term. Due to rapid technological change, time is of the essence. Therefore, delays in getting products to market or failure to keep them in the market during their peak life cycle is often fatal to product success. Therefore, the IP policy that Old Tech prefers diverges substantially from policies that High Tech wants enacted into law. Old Tech prefers policies that maximize the value, strength and longevity of its successful patents, whereas High Tech prefers policies that make it difficult for NPE to successfully bring infringement actions targeted at its products (Thomas, 2006).

Since 2005, Congress has considered a patent reform bill each session and, prior to 2011, each bill has been unambiguously pro-High Tech. These bills, named the Patent Reform Act of 2005, 2007 and 2009, respectively, contained provisions that favored raised barriers to NPE patent infringement lawsuits. The Patent Reform Act of 2005—containing multiple ways for third parties to challenge patent claims both pre- and post-issuance—made it more difficult to bring willful infringement and inequitable conduct claims, and placed limits on the ability of patent holders to obtain injunctions in infringement actions. This bill never became law. However, in 2006, in *eBay v. MercExchange*, the Supreme Court provided much of the relief from the threat of injunctions that the 2005 Patent Reform Act would have provided by raising the bar to obtaining a preliminary injunction. Prior to *eBay v. MercExchange*, successful patent infringement plaintiffs almost always received injunctions without proving, for example, irreparable injury, or that monetary damages were inadequate. This case held patent plaintiffs to the same elevated standard of proof required of plaintiffs in other lawsuits seeking injunctive relief.

The 2007 Patent Reform Act discarded the injunction-relief provision and instead focused on other ways to limit the effects of NPE lawsuits. This bill required damages to be related to the patent value added to the infringing product, removed limitations on the post-grant opposition process that made the process risky, and restricted the venue of patent infringement actions. In addition, the bill banned tax-planning patents, and exempted financial institution from patent infringement for using a check-cashing system. These latter two provisions garnered support from the accounting and financial industries, with the provision on check cashing being targeted at a single patent owned by Data Treasury. However, the provisions most favored by High Tech proved to be the most controversial. In particular, a broad range of interest groups opposed the damages limitations. As a result, bill supporters were unable to garner sufficient support for passage. With the Patent Act of 2009, High Tech appeared to concede defeat or lose its remaining influence with respect to patent reform. Bill sponsors removed the venue restriction and damages limitation provisions, the provisions likely to provide the biggest relief from NPEs. Even with these modifications, this bill never reached the Senate floor.

The 2011 America Invents Act (AIA) provided a plethora of changes but few directed towards addressing High Tech's NPE problem. Significant new provisions included a switch from a first-to-invent system to a first-to-file system, an effective prohibition against tax-strategy patents (by classifying them as being known in the prior art), the previously discussed prohibition against check-processing patents, and inclusion of provisions allowing unlimited post-grant review of financial business method patents. This last provision, contained in Section 18 of the AIA, is the only provision with a direct impact on NPEs. However, that impact is confined to the financial services sector. Parties can challenge "covered" (finance-related) business method patents under a new streamlined review process that circumvents costly civil court proceedings. However, High Tech does not benefit from this provision. Technology-related patents are specifically excluded from Section 18 review.

In light of these failed efforts, High Tech has decoupled its efforts to obtain legislative relief from patent reform efforts. In August 2012, two representatives introduced the SHIELD Act. The SHIELD Act is completely transparent in targeting NPEs that bring lawsuits against High Tech companies. Moreover, the provisions of the SHIELD Act are designed to apply solely to computer hardware and software patents. The SHIELD Act would add Section 285A to the Patent Act, which would allow a defendant in a "computer hardware or software infringement" claim to recover full costs of defending the lawsuit if the court determines that the plaintiff did not have a reasonable likelihood of prevailing on its infringement claims.

The SHIELD Act takes a substantially different approach to obtaining legislative relief. Rather than encapsulating desired policy change inside a comprehensive reform effort with provisions that apply to all patent holders, the SHIELD Act proposes provisions that precisely and specifically address High Tech's interests. With this precisely worded bill, High Tech is trying to escape the scrutiny of other major patent interest groups who should not be impacted by its enactment. High Tech may have adopted this approach after observing the success of the accounting/ tax preparation and financial industry interest groups in getting highly specific provisions successfully included in the AIA without significant opposition. If High Tech is successful in this approach, it may enjoy the smooth-sailing benefits of client-politics treatment in Congress.

III. CONCLUSION

This chapter has shown that the post-TRIPS differential success of copyright and patent interest groups in achieving favorable legislative policies enacted into law is due primarily to the difference in the nature of the threat they face in protecting their intellectual property. Creative Content is most concerned with the threat of end-user misappropriation. This focus has allowed these interest groups to act as a powerful influence group employing policy laundering and exploiting client politics to get ambitious policy enacted to address the threat of end-user misappropriation.

Patent interest groups, by contrast, continue to deal with the threat that industrial misappropriation poses. However, industrial misappropriation is more complex than end-user misappropriation in that it splits patent groups based on industry sector. Some industry sectors are solely owners of patents; others are both owners and users of patents; some industry groups are primarily users. Patent owners diligently fight for and support laws that target industrial misappropriation, whereas patent owners push to enact laws that make it difficult for NPEs to target them for patent infringement. This dichotomy has resulted in High Tech companies pushing for protection from NPEs and Old Tech companies, including Pharma, blocking the implementation of such policies because the policies could weaken their valuable patents.

However, the playing field is changing dramatically. The most recently proposed copyright acts—ACTA, SOPA and PIPA—have expanded to include industrial users of copyright in their coverage. Such large ISPs as Google, Wikipedia, Craigslist and Mozilla have found their potential liability and obligations under these acts unacceptable and as a result are opposing these bills. Thus, grassroots efforts fortified by these large ISPs have turned what had been previously client-politics passage of laws favoring Creative Content into entrepreneurial and interest-group-politics battles. Thus, future expansion of copyright interests are likely to occur at a much slower rate and will require narrowing the impact of such proposals to avoid antagonizing large Internet and technology players.

The outlook for legislative change on the patent side has changed as well. The AIA passed by carving out the most controversial provisions from earlier reform efforts, thereby leaving provisions that did not antagonize powerful patent interest groups. More telling, the AIA included provisions that through precision drafting advance the interests of narrowly defined interest groups without impacting major players. We expect that this approach will be adopted in the future by other IP interest groups. Rather than push for comprehensive reform with little possibility of garnering support from all major interest groups, future legislative initiatives will be small, compact bills that are carefully and narrowly targeted to meet the needs of specific interest groups without provoking opposition from major players. This is clearly the strategy that High Tech is employing in pushing Congress to consider the SHIELD Act. Using this approach, such interest groups are much more likely to enjoy success in their efforts to influence the legislative process and avoid likely doomed-from-the-start interest-group battles.

Our analysis suggests that this approach will be essential for all IP interest groups, whether copyright or patent, to employ in order to achieve success influencing change in IP law. The ability to influence broad policy change through the smooth client-politics process has likely passed. Both copyright and patent interest groups have discovered that there is too much scrutiny and too many interest groups involved to wield a blunt instrument. Rather, future legislative initiatives, if they are to succeed, must be crafted using the precision of a surgeon's scalpel.

NOTE

REFERENCES

Anderson, N. (2008, Nov. 11). EU Denies ACTA Document Request; Democracy Undermined? *arstechnica*. Retrieved from http://arstechnica.com/uncategorized/2008/11/eu-denies-acta-document-request-democracy-undermined/.

Anti-Counterfeiting Trade Agreement. Retrieved from http://www.ustr.gov/acta.

Axelrod, R., Mitchell, W., Thomas, R.E., Bennett, D.S. & Bruderer, E. (1995). Coalition Formation in Standard-Setting Alliances, *Management Science*, **41**(9), 1493–1508.

Ayoob, E. (2010). The Anti-Counterfeiting Trade Agreement. *Cardozo Arts & Entertainment Law Journal*, **28**(1), 175–93.

Broder, J.M. (1993, Jan.11). Hollywood Opposes Trade Pact: Entertainment: The industry is hoping its interests under GATT accord will be better served later, under Clinton. *Los Angeles Times*. Retrieved from http://articles.latimes.com/1993-01-11/business/fi-1110_1_entertainment-industry.

Burk, D.L. & Lemley, M.A. (2003). Policy Levers in Patent Law. *Virginia Law Review*, **89**(7), 1575–1696.

Commercial Felony Streaming Act, S. 978, 112th Cong., 1st Sess. (2011).

Digital Millennium Copyright Act, Pub. L. No. 105-304, 112 Stat. 2860 (Oct. 28, 1998).

eBay Inc. v. MercExchange, L.L.C., 547 U.S. 388 (2006).

Gale Group (2012, Jul. 31). Jack Valenti Opposes GATT. Retrieved from http://www.thefreelibrary.com/Valenti+opposes+GAAT+text.-a012041511.

Garner, B.A. (ed.) (2009). *Black's Law Dictionary* (9th ed.). Eagan, MN: West/Westlaw.

Ginsburg, J.C. (2011). Copyright in the Digital Environment: Restoring the Balance: 24th Annual Horace S. Manges Lecture, April 6, 2011. *Columbia Journal of Law and the Arts*, **35**(1), 1–15.

Goff, J.T. (2010). Regulation of Digital Copyrights and Trademarks at the U.S. Border: How the Proposed Anti-Counterfeiting Trade Agreement and the Enacted Pro-IP Act Will Destabilize the Current System. *Southwestern Journal of International Law*, **16**, 207–28.

Jakubowicz, K. & Jeanray, P. (1994). *Central and Eastern Europe: Audiovisual Landscape and Copyright Legislation*. Belgium: Maklu.

J.M. (1992, Jan. 25). GATT, the Dunkel Draft and India. *Economic and Political Weekly*, **27**(4), 140–42.

Kaminski, M. (2009). The Origins and Potential Impact of the Anti-Counterfeiting Trade Agreement (ACTA). *The Yale Journal of International Law*, **34**(1), 247–56.

Landes, W.M. & Posner, R.A. (2003). *The Economic Structure of Intellectual Property Law*. Cambridge, MA: Belknap Press of Harvard University Press.

Leahy-Smith America Invents Act, Pub. L. No. 112-29, 125 Stat. 284 (2011).

Marsnik, S.J. & Thomas, R.E. (2011). Drawing a Line in the Patent Subject-Matter Sands: Does Europe Provide a Solution to the Software and Business Method Patent Problem? *Boston College International and Comparative Law Review*, **34**(2), 227–327.

Nicholson, W. (2004). *Intermediate Microeconomics and Its Application* (9th ed.). Mason, OH: South-Western.

Note (2008). Harmonizing Copyrights Internationalization with Domestic Constitutional Constraints. *Harvard Law Review*, **121**(7), 1798–1819.

Okediji, R. (2009). The Regulation of Creativity under the WIPO Internet Treaties. *Minnesota Legal Studies Research Paper No. 09-30*. Retrieved from http://ssrn.com/abstract=1433848.

Patent Act of 1952, 35 U.S.C. §§ 1-376 (1952) (as amended).

Patent Reform Act of 2005, H.R. 2795, 109th Cong., 1st Sess. (2005).

Patent Reform Act of 2007, H.R. 1908, S. 1145, 110th Cong., 1st Sess. (2007).

Patent Reform Act of 2009, H.R. 1260, S. 515, 111th Cong., 1st Sess. (2009).

Patry, W. (2009). *Moral Panics and the Copyright Wars*. Oxford: Oxford University Press.

Pike & Fischer, Inc. (2003). *The Digital Millennium Copyright Act: Text, History, and Caselaw*. Silver Springs, MD: Pike & Fischer, Inc.

Prioritizing Resources and Organization for Intellectual Property Act, Pub. L. No. 110-403, 122 Stat. 4256 (October 13, 2008).

Protect IP Act of 2011, S. 968, 112th Cong., 1st Sess. (2011).

Saving High-Tech Innovators from Egregious Legal Disputes Act of 2012, H.R. 6245, 112th Cong., 2nd Sess. (2012).

Sell, S.K. (2003). *Private Power, Public Law: The Globalization of Intellectual Property Rights*. Cambridge: Cambridge University Press.

Sharp, J. (2002). Coming Soon to Pay-Per-View: How the Digital Millennium Copyright Act Enables Digital Content Owners to Circumvent Educational Fair Use. *American Business Law Journal*, **40**(1), 1–81.

Shell, G.R. (2004). *Make the Rules or Your Rivals Will*. New York: Crown Business.

Sony Corporation of America v. Universal City Studios, Inc., 464 US 417 (1984).

SOPA Strike (2012, Jan. 18). *Victory! Fight for the Future*. Retrieved from http://sopastrike.com.

Stigler, G.J. (1973). The Theory of Economic Regulation. *The Bell Journal of Economic and Management Science*, **2**(1), 3–21.

Stop Online Piracy Act, H.R. 3261, 112th Cong., 1st Sess. (2011).

Thomas, R.E. (2006). Vanquishing Copyright Pirates and Patent Trolls: The Divergent Evolution of Copyright and Patent Laws. *American Business Law Journal*, **43**(4), 689–739.

Trade-Related Aspects of Intellectual Property Rights Agreement, Apr. 15, 1994, Marrakesh Agreement Establishing the World Trade Organization, Annex 1C, 1869 U.N.T.S. 299 (1994).

TV Trade Media (1992). Valenti Opposes GATT Text. *The Free Library by Farlex*. Retrieved from http://www.thefreelibrary.com/Valenti+opposes+GAAT+text.-a012041511.

Universal City Studios, Inc. v. Reimerdes, 111 F.Supp.2d 346 (S.D.N.Y. 2000).

Wang, S. (2003). Recontextualizing Copyright: Piracy, Hollywood, the State and Globalization. *Cinema Journal*, **43**(1), 25–43.

Wilson, J.Q. (1980). *The Politics of Regulation*. New York: Basic Books.

World Intellectual Property Organization Performances and Phonograms Treaty, December 20, 1996, Geneva, S. Treaty Doc. No. 105-17 (1997).

World Intellectual Property Organization Copyright Treaty, Dec. 20, 1996, Geneva, S. Treaty Doc. No. 105-17 (1997).

Yu, P.K. (2008). The Political Economy of Data Protection. *Chicago-Kent Law Review*, **84**(3), 777–801.

Yu, P.K. (2011). Six Secret (and Now Open) Fears of ACTA. *Southern Methodist University Law Review*, **64**(3), 975–1094.

2. Administrative patent levers in the software, biotechnology and clean technology industries

David Orozco*

With the recent passage of the America Invents Act (AIA), the US patent system has undergone a transformative realignment. Numerous significant changes have been made as a result of this legislation; among the most significant are the implementation of a first-to-file system, fee-setting authority at the United States Patent and Trademark Office (PTO) and several changes involving post-grant review proceedings (Leahy-Smith America Invents Act, 2011). Many questions remain, however, regarding how these statutory changes will impact patentees, innovators and society. Scholars have been called upon to address these significant, largely open questions.

One particular question relates to the rulemaking authority that has been statutorily delegated to the PTO. As recognized by scholars, a power struggle has been waged between the PTO and the Court of Appeals for the Federal Circuit (CAFC), a specialized appellate court with exclusive jurisdiction over patent cases decided by the federal district courts. This struggle relates to the CAFC granting the PTO limited or no deference and limiting the PTO's ability to engage in substantive and policy-oriented rulemaking. The CAFC has on various occasions held that the PTO is limited solely to procedural rulemaking and that any rulemaking that extends beyond this function is beyond the PTO's delegated administrative authority (Orozco, 2012; Tran, 2012b).

This chapter will examine this struggle in light of the AIA's passage and will build from the author's previous research to examine how the PTO has engaged in policymaking in response to industry-specific challenges, despite the significant limitations imposed by the CAFC (Orozco, 2012). In particular, the PTO's rulemaking and policymaking will be analyzed in relation to three controversial and challenging industries: software, biotechnology and clean technology.

The author's prior work examined the PTO's engagement in policymaking through what were labeled *administrative patent levers* (Orozco, 2012).

As defined in that prior work, administrative patent levers are PTO rules that: (1) address particular technological challenges or controversies; (2) are technology-specific; and (3) are guided by policy motivations and institutional signals initiated by actors among all three branches of government. These policymaking levers are explained by positive political theory, which examines legal actors' decisions and motivations in response to larger political forces and frameworks (McCubbins, Noll & Weingast, 1989). The three industries examined in this chapter will be analyzed from this positive political theory perspective.

As discussed in the author's prior work, PTO rules that fall under the category of administrative patent levers are substantive in nature. The rules emerge in response to actions or signals initiated among all three branches of government and obtain legal legitimacy from this broad base of support in light of the PTO's limited, procedural rulemaking authority. The author's prior work specifically examined administrative patent levers related to business method patents (Orozco, 2012). It was demonstrated that the legislature had reviewed business methods in a significant number of hearings and had implemented or proposed legislation that would curtail the harmful effects of business methods. The judiciary had also responded negatively to business methods and limited their negative impacts on industry. The executive branch engaged in various policy studies that were critical of business methods in general. The result of this broad institutional attention was the emergence of various administrative patent levers germane to business methods (Orozco, 2012).

This work builds from the prior study on business method patents. The contribution of this chapter is twofold. First, the chapter provides additional evidence that the PTO engages in policymaking and relies on administrative patent levers to achieve its policy-oriented goals. This is despite the CAFC's narrow view of the PTO as an agency entrusted solely with procedural rulemaking authority. As discussed in prior work, these administrative patent levers are explained as a response to the pressure and signals sent among all three branches of government, some of which are referred to as "fire alarms" in the positive political theory literature (McCubbins & Schwartz, 1984). Second, this chapter discusses the potential trajectory of future administrative patent levers in light of changes brought about by the AIA. More specifically, the AIA introduces new language that on its face grants the PTO the authority to engage in substantive policymaking by allowing it to prioritize patent applications with respect to technologies that the PTO deems are important to American competitiveness. As will be argued, this authority grants the PTO greater leeway in its future implementation of administrative patent levers.

This chapter will proceed to discuss the three technological domains of software, biotechnology and clean technology. All of these industries raise special concerns that in turn trigger a high level of institutional attention. This institutional attention is expressed within the legislature, the judiciary and the executive branch. The PTO responds to these signals by developing administrative patent levers unique to each technology sector. Each section is concluded with a discussion of the AIA's impact on the development of the PTO's administrative patent levers.

I. SOFTWARE

A. Industry-specific Patent Concerns

Software patents have been extremely controversial from the outset because they test the limits of what is patentable and raise significant interoperability concerns in the technology community, and increasingly so in light of the open source movement. Software is often characterized as a complex or cumulative technology, and patents in this field have been criticized as reducing the freedom to operate among software engineers (Thomas, 2008). Another aspect of software patents that scholars perceive as reducing the need for the patent monopoly grant in this area is the low research and development expenditures necessary to undertake software innovations (Federal Trade Commission, 2003).

Software patents were not legally recognized until the United States Supreme Court allowed them in *Diamond v. Diehr* in 1981. Prior to *Diehr*, software alone was considered too abstract to qualify as patentable subject matter, and thus in violation of the principle that laws of nature or abstract ideas are beyond patentability. Ever since *Diehr*, however, software patents have been upheld by the courts as patentable subject matter, even though they have been severely criticized as unduly broad and undeserving of patent protection (Marsnik & Thomas, 2011).

B. Institutional Pressure

1. The legislature
Unlike with business methods or gene patents, the legislature has never devoted a hearing to specifically address software as a unique category of patents. The legislature has, however, on a few occasions indirectly heard testimony related to software patents. A proponent of the open source community testified against the dangers of software patents. The general counsel of Red Hat, Inc., a leading open source software company, testified in a hearing that:

The open source community largely disdains patent protection of software. The community does so in part because of a strong perception that by extending patent protection to software, software developers are provided two bites at the intellectual property apple: one under copyright, and a second under patent. The open source community also believes that patents on software have actually stifled innovation, rather than promoted it, because software development occurs at a much more rapid pace than one finds in the other patent arts (Webbink, 2002).

In a separate Senate hearing, Marshall Phelps, the deputy general counsel for intellectual property at Microsoft, testified that:

> [T]he IT industry, like so many others, is encountering the enormous cost of dealing with patents of questionable quality. Today hundreds of patent infringement cases are pending against computer software and hardware companies, costing the industry hundreds of millions of dollars each year. Too many of these cases are brought by speculators who do not develop, make or distribute anything. Our industry is particularly vulnerable to such claims because our complex products often have hundreds of patent or patentable features contained in them (Phelps, 2005).

On another occasion, the legislature considered a modification to the Patent Act[1] that would negatively impact software patent holders by providing an exemption for software companies to practice software patents without incurring liability (Patent Act of 1952, § 271(f)(1)). One industry representative critical of this measure testified that:

> [T]he language in Section 10 of the Committee Print is much broader than necessary for that purpose and will create a loophole that will allow software and firmware houses to avoid liability for patent infringement of U.S. patents by exporting their wares as "intangible" e-mail signals and files on master disks with full knowledge that they will be converted to tangible, physical form when received by their overseas customers (Haken, 2005).

This statutory amendment was never enacted. As will be discussed below, however, the Supreme Court in *ATT v. Microsoft* essentially endorsed creating this loophole for software patents in its holding (*ATT v. Microsoft*, 2007).

2. The judiciary

Recently, in *Microsoft v. i4i*, the Supreme Court upheld a lower court's decision to apply a clear and convincing standard of proof for patent validity challenges (*Microsoft v. i4i*, 2011). That case dealt with the nonpracticing entity i4i asserting a software patent against Microsoft related to a document editing process. Although the case dealt with the broader issue of the standard of proof in patent challenges, it was also an indirect attack on software patents. Several *amici* supporting the defendant critiqued software patents as a unique category of low-quality patents (Business Software Alliance, 2011). In this case, the Supreme Court refrained from targeting software patents in a *sui generis* manner.

In the prior *Microsoft v. AT&T* case, however, the Supreme Court took the opportunity to weaken the reach of software patents. In that case, the CAFC had agreed with AT&T that liability under Section 271(f) applied to software. The Supreme Court reversed the CAFC. In its opinion, the Supreme Court considered the loophole that would be created in reference to software patents as a separate patent category under its holding. The Court was ultimately not persuaded by the loophole argument, although the Court recognized its potential in the software industry when it stated that: "[t]he 'loophole,' in our judgment, is properly left for Congress to consider, and to close if it finds such action warranted" (*Microsoft v. AT&T*, 2007).

The most significant and recent cases involving software patents include the CAFC's *In re Bilski* decision and the Supreme Court's review of this decision. In *Bilski*, the CAFC revisited the holding of *State Street Bank v. Signature Financial Group*, which allowed patenting business methods. The CAFC held that business methods, including those expressed as software, had to meet the machine-or-transformation test (*In re Bilski*, 2008). On appeal, the Supreme Court held that the machine-or-transformation test was not the sole test, but could be used to determine the patentability of method claims. Notably, the Supreme Court stated that exclusively applying the machine-or-transformation test might actually hinder software patents (*Bilski v. Doll*, 2009).

3. The executive branch

In what might be the first instance of fire alarms related to software patents, industry lobbied the executive branch in a 1966 presidential commission report to prevent patents from applying to software (Samuelson, 1990). More recently, the Federal Trade Commission (FTC) has taken the lead for raising the alarms related to software patents within the executive branch. The FTC is a prominent administrative agency that has been critical of certain patenting activities. In October 2003, the FTC published a report, *To Promote Innovation: The Proper Balance of Competition and Patent Law and Policy*, which has been cited by the Supreme Court and in legislative hearings. This FTC report criticizes business methods and software patents. That report states that "a questionable patent that claims a single routine in a software program may be asserted to hold up production of the entire software program. This process can deter follow-on innovation and unjustifiably raise costs to businesses and, ultimately, to consumers." The Commission praised the second-pair-of-eyes review that the PTO implemented for business methods, and went on to advocate its implementation in the field of software patents (Federal Trade Commission, 2003).

C.   The PTO's Software-related Administrative Patent Levers

Given the significant criticisms of software patents among influential stakeholders, the prediction could be made that software patents would be candidates for additional regulation across institutional settings. According to some commentators, the CAFC was in the best position to narrow the scope of software patents, yet it failed to do so (Burk & Lemley, 2003). The Supreme Court likewise had the opportunity to address the patentability of software and other abstract method claims, but it largely shied away from doing so in *Bilski*. From various accounts, the courts have largely failed to constrain the harms posed by software patents. This area is, therefore, particularly well suited for regulation by the PTO's administrative patent levers. What follows is an account of several administrative patent levers that in practice have heightened the requirements for obtaining software patents.

Recent PTO examination guidelines have targeted software claims and held them unpatentable in light of *Bilksi*. For example, the PTO's Board of Patent Appeals and Interferences (BPAI) issued precedential opinions in cases involving software patents. In the case of *Ex parte Gutta*, the BPAI set out a new set of rules for assessing the patentability of software algorithms (*Ex parte Gutta*, 2009). In this precedential case dealing with a software algorithm patent, the BPAI defined a two-pronged test to determine the algorithm's patentability in light of *Bilski*. The first prong asks whether the claim was limited to a tangible practical application that results in a real-world use. The second prong asks whether the claim encompasses substantially all practical applications of the mathematical algorithm. In that case, the BPAI rejected the patent application by applying this novel test (*Ex parte Gutta*, 2009).

In addition to these more restrictive patent examination guidelines, the PTO reached out to industry when it established its peer-to-patent pilot program, which allows third parties to submit prior art to a patent examiner. The peer-to-patent project was an effort undertaken by the PTO in June 2007 to open up the application review process to external reviewers who may submit relevant prior art and statements to a patent examiner. Originally, this limited pilot project was undertaken to examine software patents, but shortly after its announcement business methods were added to its scope (Orozco, 2012). As stated by the PTO:

Recently a group of academic and business professionals have proposed a collaborative, online process in which members of the public pool together their knowledge and locate potential prior art. This pilot will test whether such collaboration can effectively locate prior art that might not otherwise be located by the Office during the typical examination process (USPTO, 2008).

The project has been conducted on a purely voluntary basis, with patent applicants choosing to opt into the peer-to-patent review process. In exchange for volunteering, the applicant receives an expedited review process and in theory a more robust examination that yields a higher-quality issued patent. Although the PTO participated in the project, it was conducted in collaboration with the Community Patent Review Project of the Institute for Information Law and Policy at New York Law School.

The second anniversary report of the peer-to-patent project stated that a total of 187 patent applications had been reviewed as of May 2009. The PTO has deemed the initial two-year pilot program a success and agreed to continue the project. The extended period for receiving peer-to-patent submissions into accepted applications would end on 3 February 2012, or eighteen (18) weeks after the latest date on which an application is accepted into the program, whichever occurred last (USPTO, 2008).

Last, the PTO has collaborated with industry to expand the level of prior art databases available to its corps of examiners. One frequently asserted criticism of software patents is the PTO's inability to secure comprehensive and up-to-date prior art databases to assess software patent applications with the prior art in this field. Software is a rapidly evolving field, and it is extremely difficult for the PTO to maintain its databases current in light of this challenge. To overcome this problem, the PTO has partnered with the software industry to help update its technical literature databases in the software-related arts. In one interesting development, the PTO partnered with the open source community to develop a partnership to provide the PTO with more current and broad software-related prior art (USPTO, 2006).

D. The AIA's Impact on Software Patents

The AIA does not include any provisions that deal with software patents in a *sui generis* manner. Section 18 of the Act, however, will have significant impact on some software patent owners. This section allows those who have been sued for infringing a financial method patent to challenge the patent's validity at the PTO. A substantial number of financial method patents are implemented with the use of software. The Financial Services Roundtable lobbied for this section as a limitation on check-processing patents that rely on a scanning method (Thomas & Aceves, 2013).

II. BIOTECHNOLOGY

A. Industry-specific Patent Concerns

Biotechnology is another technological field where the utility or desirability of patents has been questioned. A frequent concern in this area relates to the desirability of subjecting fundamental and broad aspects of human biological science to the property system (Heller & Eisenberg, 1998). Patents related to genetic sequences, for example, have generated a significant amount of criticism. Naturally occurring genes by themselves, however, are not patentable and claims related to genes vary widely in terms of their scope.

The popular media and policy debates often overlook the critical distinction between a patent claiming ownership of a product or process involving a genetic sequence versus ownership of the underlying gene itself. As a matter of law genes occurring in nature are classified as unpatentable natural phenomena. Difficulties arise when genes are manipulated, recombined or isolated in ways that do not occur in nature or when patent claims are attached to these gene-related discoveries. Another problem involves the use of research tools involving genetic sequences. The use of these tools, which are often used to screen the potential utility of pharmaceutical compounds or to detect genetic mutations that predispose individuals to diseases, has generated controversy in several high-profile cases, as illustrated in the *Association of Molecular Pathology v. Myriad Genetics* case discussed below.

Another controversy surrounding biotechnology patents is their association with the rising costs of drug treatments. Biotechnology patents are increasingly obtained to develop novel drug compounds and therapeutic techniques that reach consumers after regulatory approval is secured. Biologic pharmaceuticals, which are derived from living organisms, represent the fastest growing segment of pharmaceuticals, and 25 percent of drugs in the development pipeline are biopharmaceuticals. Biologic pharmaceuticals accounts for a 17.4 percent increase in prescription spending, the fastest level of growth of any drug category (Gitter, 2013).

B. Institutional Pressure

1. The legislature

Since 1995, in three separate circumstances the legislature held hearings on biotechnology patents. For example, during hearings related to the Biotechnology Process and Patent Protection Act,[2] the legislature heard testimony from biotechnology constituents advocating in favor of an amendment to the patent statute that would make it easier for biotechnology companies to obtain process patents for genes, in light of a CAFC decision and PTO practice that had narrowed biotechnology process patents (*In re Durden*, 1985). That legislation was ultimately enacted and biotechnology patents were thus afforded greater protection.

On 13 July 2000 the House of Representatives held a hearing to specifically address issues related to gene patents. As with business methods, this was a rare instance when the legislature devoted an entire hearing to a particular patent category. This hearing specifically addressed the difficulties that the PTO faces when issuing gene patents and the risks of issuing gene patents that are overly broad. In 2007, Congressman Xavier Becerra introduced a bill that would have amended the Patent Act to make gene patents altogether unlawful. One can therefore glean from the congressional record that, like business method patents, biotechnology patents are one of the few technological areas that Congress is willing to oversee.

In 2009, Congress enacted the Biologics Price Competition and Innovation Act (BPCI). The BPCI Act allows manufacturers of follow-on proteins (biosimilars) to file abbreviated applications for Food and Drug Administration (FDA) approval. This would allow the follow-on biosimilar manufacturers to avoid some of the costly pre-clinical and clinical testing requirements and access to data generated by the branded manufacturers (Gitter, 2013).

2. The judiciary

Gene patents have been attacked as unethical, as claiming fundamental aspects of nature given the advent of the Genome Project, and as impediments to innovation under an anti-commons theory (Heller & Eisenberg, 1998). The courts, however, have held a somewhat mixed view on this issue. The Supreme Court, for example, allowed a bio-engineered bacterium to be patented in *Diamond v. Chakrabarty*, famously saying that Congress intended patentable subject matter to include "anything under the sun that is made by man" (*Diamond v. Chakrabarty*, 1979). Ever since that decision, the courts have held that many sorts of organisms, even mammals, are patentable within the goals and meaning of the Patent Act.

Recently, a New York district court held that a patent issued on a genetic sequence used to detect breast cancer was not patentable subject matter, reversing the settled expectations of several years of precedent related to genetic sequence patents (*Association of Molecular Pathology v. Myriad Genetics*, 2010). On appeal, the CAFC reversed the district court's holding that the genetic sequences in question were unpatentable *per se*. The US Supreme Court granted certiori in the Myriad case in December 2012 to determine whether human genes are patent-eligible.

3. The executive branch

Unlike with business methods, the FTC did not criticize gene patents in its influential report.[3] The National Institute of Health (NIH), however, has voiced concerns over gene patents and has exerted considerable influence over government and PTO policy with respect to gene patents. As stated by one top PTO official, the agency views the NIH as one of the most important stakeholders in the field of gene patents (Dickinson, 2000). The NIH is one of the primary funding agencies that sponsors genetic research that may eventually become the subject of a patent application. The NIH does not advocate for the categorical elimination of gene patents. It does, however, advocate in favor of information-sharing and restraint in enforcing these rights. As that agency stated:

> The NIH expects that NIH-supported genotype-phenotype data made available through the NIH GWAS data repository and all conclusions derived directly from them will remain freely available, without any licensing requirements, for uses such as, but not necessarily limited to, markers for developing assays and guides for identifying new potential targets for drugs, therapeutics, and diagnostics. The intent is to discourage the use of patents to prevent the use of or block access to any genotype-phenotype data developed with NIH support. The NIH encourages broad use of NIH-supported genotype-phenotype data that is consistent with a responsible approach to management of intellectual property derived from downstream discoveries, as outlined in the NIH's Best Practices for the Licensing of Genomic Inventions and its Research Tools Policy (National Institute for Health, 2007).

Another criticism of gene patents arose from a report issued in April 2010 by the Department of Health and Human Services Secretary's Advisory Committee on Genetics, Health and Society—*Gene Patents and Licensing Practices and Their Impact on Patient Access to Genetic Tests*. This report advocates a statutory change that provides immunity from gene patent liability to "anyone who infringes a patent on a gene while making, using, ordering, offering for sale, or selling a genetic test for patient care purposes," or for "those who use patent-protected genes in the pursuit of research."

In 2006, the National Research Council (NRC) published *Reaping the Benefits of Genomic and Proteomic Research: Intellectual Property Rights, Innovation, and Public Health*. In this comprehensive report, the NRC provided recommendations that support the NIH's policy of information-sharing and for universities to retain the right to retain "in their license agreements the authority to disseminate their research materials to other research institutions and to permit those institutions to use patented technology in their nonprofit activities."

Also, in response to rising healthcare costs, President Obama has called for the biologic pharmaceutical exclusivity term under the BPCI to be shortened from twelve years to seven years to promote economic growth and to reduce the deficit (Gitter, 2013). In 2011, the FDA decided whether the FDA could, under the BPCI, begin to review biosimilar applications during the 12-year exclusivity period mentioned in the statute. Responding to calls from the executive branch and several senators advocating for increased public access to biosimilars, the FDA resolved the issue in favor of allowing biosimilar manufacturers to submit their applications within the 12-year exclusivity period (Gitter, 2013).

C. The PTO's Biotechnology-related Administrative Patent Levers

The PTO was caught in a difficult scenario after the implementation of the Biotechnology Process and Patent Protection Act as that legislation was aimed at facilitating the patenting of biotechnology-related innovations in light of the PTO and the CAFC narrowing the scope of biotechnology patents. The PTO still had to balance the competing concerns related to the potentially chilling effect that gene patents have on innovation. To deal with this scenario, the PTO published the "Revised Interim Utility Examination Guidelines" in the *Federal Register* on 21 December 1999. The rules were adopted to deal with the fears that upstream genes would be patented and hinder research and innovation due to patent thickets. The PTO was required to clarify the level of utility that genetic sequence patents would have to satisfy as neither the courts nor the legislature had spoken on this matter. As mentioned by scholars, the patent utility requirement is a policy lever that the courts have used to narrow or expand patent scope in cases where technological challenges exist (Burk & Lemley, 2003). In this case, the PTO used this well-known policy lever to suit its own purposes. Speaking on this topic at a Congressional hearing, the PTO Director stated:

> In order to assure the highest standards of utility, the PTO recently published revised utility examination guidelines in the Federal Register. These new utility guidelines, which we expect to finalize this fall, require patent applicants to explicitly identify, unless it's already well established, a specific, substantial, and credible utility for all inventions. In other words, one simply can't patent a gene itself without also clearly disclosing a real world use. . . . One simply cannot patent a gene itself without also clearly disclosing a use to which that gene can be put. As a result, we believe that hundreds of genomic patent applications may be rejected by the PTO, particularly those that only disclose theoretical utilities (Dickinson, 2000).

A white paper issued by the PTO in 2000 called *PTO, Patent Pools: A Solution to the Problem of Access in Biotechnology Patents?* also targeted gene patents and discussed using patent pools as a method for reducing their harmful impact on information-sharing and innovation. This report stated:

> The use of patent pools in the biotechnology field could serve the interests of the public and private industry, a win-win situation. The public would be served by having ready access with streamlined licensing conditions to a greater amount of proprietary subject matter. Patent holders would be served by greater access to licenses of proprietary subject matter of other patent holders, the generation of affordable pre-packaged patent "stacks" that could be easily licensed, and an additional revenue source for inventions that might not otherwise be developed. The end result is that patent pools, especially in the biotechnology area, can provide for greater innovation, parallel research and development, removal of patent bottlenecks, and faster product development.

In 2010, the PTO expanded its pilot peer-to-patent process to encompass biotechnology patents. The peer-to-patent project was an effort undertaken by the PTO in June 2007 to open up the application review process to external reviewers who may submit relevant prior art and statements to a patent examiner. Originally, this limited pilot project was undertaken to examine software patents, but shortly after its announcement business methods were added to its scope.

D.   The AIA's Impact on Biotechnology

Section 27 of the AIA directs the PTO to engage in a study on "effective ways to provide independent, confirming genetic diagnostic test activity where gene patents and exclusive licensing for primary genetic diagnostic tests exist" (Leahy-Smith America Invents Act, 2011). The goal of this study is to shed light on patents that involve genetic diagnostic tests and to determine whether patients suffer detriment because of the exclusivity granted to these testing procedures. The study will be prepared by the PTO's chief economist and will be submitted to Congress, with recommendations for potentially excluding genetic testing procedures from patentability or allowing compulsory licenses that would allow third parties to provide second opinion genetic diagnostic tests. Representative Debbie Wasserman, a cancer survivor, sponsored the AIA amendment requiring this study.

III. CLEAN TECHNOLOGY

A. Industry-specific Patent Concerns

The perspective on clean technology patents is not that they are controversial and that PTO administrative patent levers are necessary to constrain them, as in the cases of software or gene-related patents. Rather, the argument is that clean technology patents need to be promoted via patent levers as a matter of national security and competitiveness. Interestingly, this category of innovation triggers institutional concerns that, from a policy perspective, veer towards aggressive encouragement rather than mitigation. According to one scholar, the clean technology industry needs governmental support for three reasons: (1) America's over-dependence on foreign energy; (2) global climate change concerns; and (3) an international race to dominate the renewable energy industry (Tran, 2012b).

Regulating clean patents, however, poses several challenges. One major challenge involves classifying the technologies that need support. Defining clean technology is not a straightforward matter. For example, some clean coal technologies might reduce greenhouse gas emission, yet still emit pollutants. It is unclear whether to label such a technology a clean technology since its environmental impact is mixed. Clean technologies are defined by the United Nations as energy-generating technologies that have the potential for reducing greenhouse gases (United Nations, 2010).

B. Institutional Pressure

1. The legislature

The clearest signal sent by the legislature regarding the importance of clean technology patents was expressed by Senator Robert Menendez. The senator played a key role in introducing a section in the AIA that allows the PTO to prioritize applications based on nationally important technologies. Senator Menendez specifically made the case for clean technologies when he introduced the amendment:

> The amendment I am offering here today would do just that. It would incentivize innovation and investment by prioritizing patents that are vital to the American economy and American competitiveness. It will enable us, in essence, to incentivize that innovation by creating that prioritizing. My amendment would allow the Patent Office to prioritize patent applications that are vital to our national interests. Specifically, the amendment says the Patent Office Director may prioritize the examination of applications for technologies that are important to the national economy or national competitiveness, such as green technologies designed to foster renewable energy, clean energy, biofuels,

agricultural sustainability, environmental quality, conservation, or energy efficiency. Currently, the Patent Office runs a green technology pilot program. An application for green technologies may be fast-tracked, leading to an expedited decision. This fast-track process is reserved for a small number of applications that are vitally important, so it has little to no adverse impact on other patent applications (Menendez, 2011).

2. The judiciary

The courts have had the chance to rule on clean technology patents. In some instances, the courts endorse the proposition that green technologies are socially useful activities that should be widely diffused under particular circumstances (*Paice v. Toyota*, 2007). There is, for example, the growing concern that the courts need to restrict clean technology patents held by non-practicing entities. The courts are well equipped to do so by applying the policy lever related to denying a permanent injunction and awarding a reasonable royalty instead, shifting the patent system from a property rule to a liability rule regime in these cases (*eBay v. MercExchange*, 2006).

In *Paice v. Toyota*, a trial court refused to grant the patent owner Paice a permanent injunction after a jury had returned a verdict of infringement against Toyota. Applying the *eBay v. MercExchange* factors for determining equitable relief, the trial court judge found that the balance of hardships would fall on Toyota and an injunction would likely stifle "the burgeoning hybrid market." According to one commentator, the impact of *eBay v. MercExchange* has been to encourage settlements in cases that involve other green technologies, such as LED lights and smart grids (Lane, 2010).

3. The executive branch

The issue of energy security has risen to the forefront of policy discussions within the executive branch of government. The President has prioritized energy security as a top-level concern within his administration. In 2011, the White House published its *Blueprint for a Secure Energy Future*. This report reiterates the President's goal of generating 80 percent of domestic electricity from a variety of clean sources. The impetus for clean technology has international dimensions.[4] The issue involves one of national security and competitiveness, in light of the fact that many clean technologies are being developed and owned by other nations, such as China (Obama, 2011; Cahoy, 2012).

C. The PTO's Clean Technology-related Administrative Patent Levers

The most significant administrative patent lever implemented by the PTO to deal with clean technology is the Green Technology Pilot Program. This program accelerates the processing of applications on environmentally beneficial inventions. The program was criticized as being overly narrow in its admissions criteria, and in 2010 the PTO announced a revision to the pilot program that eliminated the narrow eligibility criteria for expedited processing under the original program (Ackerman, 2011). The green technology pilot program is not the only prioritization program.[5] In general the PTO has the administrative authority to prioritize applications based on its statutory authority to "facilitate and expedite the processing of patent applications" (Patent Act of 1952, § 2(b)2). Commentators point out that the significant backlog at the PTO justifies prioritizing certain patents over others (Tran, 2012a).

D.   The AIA's Impact on Clean Technology

Section 25 of the AIA allows the PTO to prioritize patent applications that are important for national competiveness. Section 25 of the Act states that the PTO:

> may, subject to any conditions prescribed by the Director [of the PTO] and at the request of the patent applicant, provide for prioritization of examination of applications for products, processes, or technologies that are important to the national economy or national competitiveness without recovering the aggregate extra cost of providing such prioritization, notwithstanding section 41 or any other provision of law (Leahy-Smith America Invents Act, 2011).

Given the legislative history behind this unique provision, with the support Senator Menendez exhibited for this provision in relation to environmentally beneficial inventions, it seems natural that the PTO will use this provision to expand its administrative patent lever involving the prioritization of clean technology patents.

IV.   CONCLUSION

This chapter highlights additional technological areas where the PTO seeks to expand its substantive policymaking role. The PTO engages in various types of administrative patent levers to implement policy-oriented goals. Administrative patent levers are defined as substantive PTO rules that are technology-specific and guided primarily by policy motivations and institutional signals initiated by actors among all three branches of government (Orozco, 2012).

With the AIA's enactment, the PTO is likely to increase its activities that cross into the boundary of substantive and policy-oriented rulemaking.

This decision-making behavior has the potential to address technology-specific challenges facing the PTO and our nation. The implementation of technology-specific rules within the PTO requires oversight, however, as a risk attendant with overreliance on administrative patent levers is a balkanized patent policy, with different patentability standards based on different technology classifications. This would be a substantial departure from the prior norm and aim to implement the Patent Act in a technology-neutral manner. Also, the CAFC will likely seek to limit the PTO's authority as evidenced by its prior decisions. The boundaries or contours of the PTO's substantive rulemaking authority via administrative patent levers, in light of the greater authority granted to it by the AIA, is an important legal issue that may have to be resolved with greater clarity in the near future.

NOTES

*   I'd like to extend my gratitude to Professors Lynda Oswald and Dan Cahoy for organizing "The Changing Face of American Patent Law and its Impact on Business Strategy" Colloquium, sponsored by the Stephen M. Ross School of Business at the University of Michigan and the Smeal College of Business at Penn State University, where this chapter was first presented. I'd also like to thank the attending legal studies professors and contributors to this volume, who provided many insightful comments. Any errors remain exclusively mine. Copyright 2013, David Orozco.

1.   The section of the Patent Act that would have been modified is 35 USC § 271. This section permits the owners of a US patent to restrict the export from the US of any components that can be assembled abroad to produce a device that infringes the patent even though the patent is not enforceable in the place where the assembly takes place.

2.   This legislation amended § 103 of the Patent Act. The amendment permits claims for biotechnological processes where at least one of the starting materials or end products are novel and non-obvious.

3.   The FTC Report stated that: "Although panelists agreed that poor patent quality can adversely affect innovation, disagreement existed whether patent quality in the biotechnology area was any different from that in other industries" (Federal Trade Commission, 2003).

4.   For example, the United Nations Framework Convention on Climate Change (UNFCCC) article 4.5 requires developed countries to "take all practicable steps to promote, facilitate and finance, as appropriate, the transfer of, or access to environmentally sound technologies and know-how to other Parties, particularly developing country parties to enable them to implement the provisions of the Convention."

5.   For example the Accelerated Examination Program allows patent applicants across any technology field to obtain a prioritized examination as long as they comply with some rather onerous requirements such as submitting an Information and Disclosure Statement to the PTO.

REFERENCES

Ackerman, L.J. (2011). Prioritization: Addressing the Patent Application Backlog at the United States Patent and Trademark Office. *Berkeley Technology Law Journal*, **26**(1), 67–92.

Association of Molecular Pathology v. Myriad Genetics, 94 USPQ2d 1683 (S.D.N.Y. March 29, 2010).

Bilski v. Doll, 556 U.S. 1268 (2009).

Burk, D.L. & Lemley, M.A. (2003). Policy Levers in Patent Law. *Virginia Law Review*, **89**(7), 1575–1696.

Business Software Alliance (2011). Amicus Curiae Brief in favor of Petitioner, *Microsoft v. i4i*, 131 S. Ct. 2238 (2011).

Cahoy, D. (2012). Inverse Enclosure: Abdicating the Green Technology Landscape. *American Business Law Journal*, **40**(4) 805–857.

Department of Health and Human Services (2010). *Gene Patents and Licensing Practices and Their Impact on Patient Access to Genetic Tests*. Retrieved from http://oba.od.nih.gov/oba/sacghs/reports/sacghs_patents_report_2010.pdf (accessed 19 September 2012).

Diamond v. Chakrabarty, 447 U.S. 303 (1979).

Diamond v. Diehr, 450 U.S. 175 (1981).

Dickinson, T. (2000). Statement before the Subcommittee on Intellectual Property, Competition, and the Internet, Committee on the Judiciary, U.S. House of Representatives Hearing on Gene Patents and Other Genomic Inventions, 106th Congress.

eBay, Inc. v. MercExchange, L.L.C., 547 U.S.388 (2006).

Ex parte Gutta, U.S. Board of Patent Appeals and Interferences Appeal 2008-4366 (2009).

Federal Trade Commission (2003). *To Promote Innovation: The Proper Balance of Competition and Patent Law and Policy*. Retrieved from http://www.ftc.gov/os/2003/10/innovationrpt.pdf (accessed 19 September 2012).

Gitter, D.M. (2013). "Biopharmaceuticals under the Patient Protection and Affordable Care Act: Determining the Appropriate Market and Data Exclusivity Periods" in Daniel Cahoy & Lynda J. Oswald (eds), *The Changing Face of American Patent Law and Its Impact on Business Strategy*. Cheltenham, UK and Bookfield, VT, USA: Edward Elgar Publishing, pp. 211–229.

Haken, J. (2005). Committee Print Regarding Patent Quality Improvement, House Subcommittee on Intellectual Property, Competition, and the Internet, Committee on the Judiciary, 109th Congress.

Heller, M.A. & Eisenberg, R.S. (1998). Can Patents Deter Innovation? The Anticommons in Biomedical Research. *Science*, **280**, 698–701.

In re Bilski, 545 F.3d 943 (Fed. Cir. 2008).

In re Durden, 763 F.2d 1406 (Fed. Cir.1985).

Lane, E.L. (2010). Keeping the LEDs on and the Electric Motors Running: Clean Tech in Court after eBay. *Duke Law and Technology Review*, **9**(1), 1–32.

Leahy-Smith America Invents Act, Pub. L. No. 112-29, 125 Stat. 284 (2011).

Marsnik, S.J. & Thomas, R.E. (2011). Drawing a Line in the Patent Subject Matter Sands: Does Europe Provide a Solution to the Software and Business Method Patent Problem? *Boston College International and Comparative Law Review*, **34**(2), 227–327.

McCubbins, M.D., Noll, R.G. & Weingast, B.R. (1989). Structure and Process,

Politics and Policy: Administrative Arrangements and the Political Control of Agencies. *Virginia Law Review*, **75**(2), 431–82.

McCubbins, M.D. & Schwartz, T. (1984). Congressional Oversight Overlooked: Police Patrols versus Fire Alarms. *American Journal of Political Science*, **28**(1), 165–79.

Menendez, R. (2011). Statement made in the U.S. Senate, 157th Congress. Retrieved from http://www.uspto.gov/aia_implementation/20110301-menendez _rmrks_s1052.pdf (accessed 19 September 2012).

Microsoft v. AT&T, 550 U.S. 437 (2007).

Microsoft v. i4i, 131 S. Ct. 2238 (2011).

National Institute for Health (2007). *NIH Policy for Sharing Data Obtained in NIH Supported or Conducted Genome-Wide Association Studies.* Retrieved from http://grants.nih.gov/grants/guide/notice-files/NOT-OD-07-088.html (accessed 19 September 2012).

National Research Council (2006). *Reaping the Benefits of Genomic and Proteomic Research: Intellectual Property Rights, Innovation, and Public Health.* Washington, D.C.: National Academies Press.

Obama, B. (2011). State of the Union Address. Retrieved from http://www.white house.gov/the-press-office/2011/01/25/remarks-president-state-union-address (accessed 19 September 2012).

Orozco, D. (2012). Administrative Patent Levers. *Penn State Law Review*, **117**(1), 1–51.

Paice v. Toyota, 85 U.S.P.Q.2d 1001 (2007).

Patent Act of 1952, as amended, 35 U. S. C. § 100 *et seq.*

Phelps, M.C. (2005). Hearing before the Subcommittee on Intellectual Property of the Committee of the Judiciary, U.S. Senate, 109th Congress. Retrieved from http://www.gpo.gov/fdsys/pkg/CHRG-109shrg24582/html/CHRG-109shrg24582 .htm (accessed 19 September 2012).

Samuelson, P. (1990). Benson Revisited: The Case Against Patent Protection for Algorithms and Other Computer Program-Related Inventions. *Emory Law Journal*, **39**(4), 1025–1154.

Thomas, R.E. (2008). Debugging Software Patents: Increasing Innovation and Reducing Uncertainty in the Judicial Reform of Software Patent Law. *Santa Clara Computer and High Technology Law Journal*, **25**(1), 191–241.

Thomas, R.E. & Aceves, C. (2013). "Coalition Formation and Battles to Effect Intellectual Property Policy Change in the Age of ACTA, AIA and the SHIELD Act" in Daniel R. Cahoy & Lynda J. Oswald (eds), *The Changing Face of American Patent Law and its Impact on Business Strategy.* Cheltenham, UK and Bookfield, VT, USA: Edward Elgar Publishing, pp. 15–41.

Tran, S. (2012a). Expediting Innovation. *Harvard Environmental Law Review*, **36**(1), 123–68.

Tran, S. (2012b). Patent Powers. *Harvard Journal of Law and Technology*, **25**(2), 595–659.

United Nations (2010). *Patents and Clean Energy: Bridging the Gap Between Evidence and Policy.* Retrieved from http://www.unep.ch/etb/events/UNEP%20 EPO%20ICTSD%20Event%2030%20Sept%202010%20Brussels/Brochure_EN_ ganz.pdf (accessed 19 September 2012).

USPTO (1999). *Revised Interim Utility Examination Guidelines.* Retrieved from http://www.uspto.gov/web/menu/utility.pdf (accessed 19 September 2012).

USPTO (2000). *Patent Pools: A Solution to the Problem of Access in Biotechnology*

Patents? Retrieved from http://www.uspto.gov/patents/law/patent_pools.pdf (accessed 19 September 2012).

USPTO (2006). *USPTO Partners with Open Source Community to Expand Patent Examiner Access to Software Code, Press Release.* Retrieved from http://www. uspto.gov/news/pr/2006/06-02.jsp (accessed 19 September 2012).

USPTO (2008). *USPTO Extends and Expands Peer Review Pilot, Press Release.* Retrieved from http://www.uspto.gov/web/offices/com/speeches/08-26.htm (accessed 19 September 2012).

Webbink, M.H. (2002). Hearing on Patent Reexamination and Small Business Innovation, House Subcommittee on Intellectual Property, Competition, and the Internet, Committee on the Judiciary, 107th Congress. Retrieved from http://judiciary.house.gov/legacy/webbink062002.htm (accessed 19 September 2012).

PART II

Revisions to patent application process

3. The America Invents Act, patent priority, and supplemental examination

Robert C. Bird*

Patent reform in the United States has been long overdue. Ignored decades ago as an obscure backwater of the law, the advancement of patent law was not seen as an important initiative. As recently as the late 1970s, patent law was perceived as weak, ineffective and unable to keep pace with rapid technological changes (Rooklidge & Barker, 2009, p. 154). Until the previous year, the most recent significant substantive amendment by Congress was the Patent Act of 1952 (Patent Act, 1952).

That perception has now fully matured into a rich and robust understanding of the value of intellectual assets. The competitive advantage of new technological innovations relies heavily on the protection and enforcement of intellectual property rights. Patent law enforcement was no longer a technicality left to lawyer-scientists, but developed into a high-stakes game of corporate survival.

As the perceived value of patents increased, so predictably did the increase of patent applications. The United States Patent and Trademark Office (PTO) is the entity before which all applicants must file their inventions to apply for patent protection in the United States. Unfortunately, the PTO is simply overwhelmed with applications (Aste, 2012). Only 6,000 patent examiners are employed to purge a backlog of over 700,000 patent applications that now languish before the PTO (Love, 2012). The amount of patent applications will only increase each year, potentially extending the already sluggish three-to-four-year process even further into the future (Ackerman, 2011).

Cumbersome rules, expensive processes and an overwhelmed government bureaucracy all but compelled Congress to act. On 8 September 2011, Congress passed the Leahy-Smith America Invents Act (AIA) (America Invents Act, 2011). The AIA was no mere technical amendment, but a significant revision and update of US patent law. Hopes were high that the AIA would substantially impact the patent filing process.

According to one government report, the AIA "arguably makes the most significant changes to the patent statute since the 19th century" (Schacht & Thomas, 2012). Other sources are less laudatory, merely calling the AIA the most important revision of the last 50 years (Perkins, 2012). Regardless of the time, there is little argument that the AIA represents a major shift in patent policy and administration that has not been witnessed in decades.

With any major shift in the law, the question remains whether the changes in the AIA are uniformly for the better. The bill received widespread support from a normally fractured and politicized Congress, earning overwhelming margins of 304–117 and 89–9 in the House and Senate respectively (Congressional Record, 2011; Congressional Record, 2011a). President Obama praised the AIA as "much-needed reform [that] will speed up the patent process so that innovators and entrepreneurs can turn a new invention into a business as quickly as possible" (White House, 2011).

With much publicity presaging its passage and the Act's obvious importance, scholars and commentators have been quick to analyze its provisions. By far the most popular subject, indeed one that "scholars and policymakers have focused with an almost laser-like exclusivity" (Rantanen & Petherbridge, 2011) has been the imposition of a first-to-file system for determining patent priority (e.g., Abrams & Wagner, 2012). This system, which awards a patent to whomever first filed an application for an invention, replaces giving priority to the first to invent, a 200-year-old tradition in the United States. A second system comprising a new supplemental examination process also merits attention. The supplemental examination process enables patentees to correct certain errors and omissions subsequent to the issuance of the patent. One purpose of the subsequent examination is to reduce the number of legal challenges based on the inequitable conduct rule, a contentious doctrine that commentators believe generates excessive litigation and uncertainty. This chapter will examine both the impact of the first-to-file system and the impact of the supplemental examination rule.

Part I introduces the major provisions of the AIA. Part II examines the impact of the newly adopted first-to-file system of patent priority on various interest groups in the patent system. Part III discusses the impact of the patent priority system in a global context. Part IV highlights concerns with another significant and new innovation arising from the AIA, a supplemental examination system of patents. Part V concludes.

I. AN INTRODUCTION TO THE AIA

The AIA was the culmination of several years of debate about the future direction of the US patent system and several failed attempts by Congress to reach consensus (Gutterman, 2011, § 26:13.30). Various issues were of significant concern in the legislative debates preceding the AIA. The difference between US and global patent laws might increase the difficulty of domestic inventors to acquire rights abroad. There was also an interest in improving patent quality and decreasing unnecessary litigation costs. Legislators also expressed concern over whether universities, individual inventors and small businesses were playing a sufficient role in US economic growth through patenting. The result was an Act that attempted to address these and other issues (Schacht & Thomas, 2012). The AIA, through a variety of mechanisms, modified standards for patent applicants, introduces new rules for potential patent litigants, and reinforces funding to the beleaguered PTO. A summary of significant, though by no means all, changes made by the AIA follows.

A.   Change to First-inventor-to-file System of Patent Priority

Prior to the passage of the AIA, the United States was the last industrialized nation to follow a first-to-invent priority system. Under the first-to-invent system, the patent office establishes priority by determining which applicant was the first to actually conceive of the invention. If two inventors filed applications for the same invention, the later applicant could challenge the earlier applicant through what is known as an interference proceeding. A rebuttable presumption would exist in favor of the first applicant, and the challenger would be tasked with offering evidence to show that her invention was conceived of prior to the first applicant (Recent Legislation, 2012).

The AIA changes this rule, which was once well established in the United States. Under the AIA, the US patent system joins the rest of the world in using a first-inventor-to-file system of priority. Under this system, the date on which the invention was actually invented is not dispositive when determining patent priority between two applicants. Instead, the inventor who first files an application with the patent office will be deemed to have first priority for the patent (Schacht & Thomas, 2012). The AIA also contains a grace period during which inventors have one year to decide whether to file patent application after a disclosure of the invention is made to the public (Perkins, 2012).

B.   Expansion of Prior Commercial Use Defense

The commercial use defense under the AIA is not entirely new, but rather an enlargement of a defense that was only applicable under limited circumstances. The commercial use defense originates from the American Inventors Protection Act of 1999 (AIPA, 1999). If an inventor obtained a patent, this defense allows an earlier commercial user to have a defense against patent infringement. Under the AIPA, this defense was only available to business method patents (AIPA, 1999). The AIA expands this defense to be available for any type of patentable invention. The prior commercial use must have occurred at least one year prior to the inventor's public disclosure of the invention, or the inventor's filing date, whichever is earlier. A successful defense does not invalidate the patent, is transferrable only under limited circumstances, and must be proven by clear and convincing evidence (Perkins, 2012; Herrington, Ilan, Jedrey & Prunella, 2011).

C.   Expansion of Inter Partes Proceedings and Modification of Post-grant Review Proceedings

The AIA introduces a new proceeding called a "post-grant review." This review allows challengers to contest the validity of a patent on a wide variety of grounds by filing a petition with the PTO. The petition must be filed within nine months of the issuance of the patent. If the PTO finds a novel question of law or concludes that it is more likely than not that one of the challenged claims against patentability would succeed, the challenge escalates to a post-grant review (Schneider, 2011). The review, heard by the Patent Trial and Appeal Board (PTAB), reviews the claim with full participation of both parties. The PTO must act quickly, making a final decision within one year of the commencement of the review with a six-month extension if the PTO can show good cause for the delay (Schacht & Thomas, 2012, p. 11). The losing party can appeal the decision to the United States Court of Appeals for the Federal Circuit (Diebner, 2011).

The challenger need only marshal a preponderance of the evidence to show unpatentability, a standard that is lower than patent challenges in court, which must be proven by clear and convincing evidence. However, the challenger must consider carefully when it is appropriate to file a post-grant review challenge. Under the AIA, the challenger must raise patentability issues known to it in that proceeding, or else it risks being prevented from doing so at a later time (Herrington et al., 2011).

In addition to introducing new post-grant review proceedings, inter partes proceedings have been expanded. Formerly known as inter partes reexamination proceedings, the AIA introduces a new system called "inter partes review." This system is procedurally similar to the post-grant review proceedings previously described, but with some important distinctions. The inter partes review can only occur after the post-grant review period (nine months) has concluded. Furthermore, the scope of any challenge is limited. Inter partes review only allows challenges to prior art involving patents or printed publications, meaning in effect only challenges to novelty or obviousness in the requirement of patentability. Patent challenges under these proceedings, however, can be made throughout the entire patent term (Schacht & Thomas, 2012; Herrington et al., 2011).

D. Reform of Patent Marking Rules

Patent marking is the physical labeling of an item with the patent identification numbers associated with it. The purpose of such marking is to prevent innocent infringement and to deliver constructive notice that the listed patents protect the product. Although no duty to mark exists, entities that improperly mark their products with inaccurate patent identification numbers could be held liable under false marking statutes. A patentee can receive for each offense a fine of up to $500 (McCaffrey, 2011; Crudo, 2011).

The AIA sustains the false marking statute, but modifies it such that no longer can any person privately enforce the statute. Instead, only individuals who have suffered a "competitive injury" that arises from the false marking can sue and such individuals will only receive damages sufficient to compensate for the injury. False marking cases based on expired patents are eliminated (Yoches et al., 2011). In spite of these rules, the US government can continue to bring false marking suits without competitive injury and recover the maximum fine (Schacht & Thomas, 2012).

E. Introduction of a New Supplemental Examination Procedure

The AIA establishes a new procedure after the issuance of a patent called a "supplemental examination" (America Invents Act, 2011, section 12). The patent owner, not a challenger, commences a supplemental examination proceeding. Such a request asks the PTO to "consider, reconsider, or correct information believed to be relevant in the patent." The purpose of the examination is to enable owners to correct omissions or misstatements made through inadvertence or negligence during the course of the underlying patent application.

A patent owner requests the procedure, and if the PTO believes that the new information would raise a substantial new question of patentability, it will order a reexamination. The reexamination provides protection to the patent owner from subsequent challenges. The AIA states that a "patent shall not be held unenforceable ... on the basis of conduct relating to information that had not been considered, was inadequately considered, or was incorrect in a prior examination of the patent" if the information was corrected during a supplemental examination procedure (America Invents Act, 2011, §12).

Congress recognized that the rule might encourage patent holders to simply wait until a challenger raises the inequitable conduct claim before requesting a supplemental examination. Toward that end, the AIA does not permit parties to request the examination after an inequitable conduct challenge has already been raised in a judicial dispute. The PTO also has the ability to cancel a patent claim if it concludes that "material fraud on the [Patent] Office may have been committed in connection with the patent that is the subject of the supplemental examination" (America Invents Act, 2011, §12).

F. Prohibition of Tax Strategy and Human Organism Patents

In recent years, there has been the rise of tax strategy patents, in which the inventor patents a financial structure or product that is supposedly used in a strategy or process to reduce an entity's tax burden. Such patents have come under increasing criticism for denying taxpayers equal access to the laws and interpretations of the Internal Revenue Code and increase the difficulty for tax advisors to render advice to clients (Chumney, 2009). The AIA eliminates the possibility of such patents, stating that any strategy for avoiding tax liability is insufficient to differentiate a claimed invention from prior art.

Patents claiming human beings have long been criticized, with claims that such patents could represent a badge of slavery that violates the Thirteenth Amendment to the US Constitution (Bagley, 2003). The PTO has similarly denied such patent applications (Halewood, 2008), and the AIA gives statutory footing to this prohibition. The AIA specifically states that no patent can be issued from a claim directed to or encompassing a human organism.

G. Filing and Oaths by Assignee of the Inventor

Under prior law, only the inventor could file a patent application, even if the inventor developed the invention as an employee with a contractual obligation to assign the invention to an employer. Under the AIA, an assignee of the right can now file the patent application instead. Inventors must still be named on the patent application and submit required oaths that the individual is the original inventor. However, a patent assignee who is filing can submit a substitute statement justifying the absence of such oaths when the inventor is unwilling or unable to make the oath for various reasons (Herrington et al., 2011).

H. PTO Funding and Fee-setting

Funding of the PTO was traditionally determined by Congress. The AIA now gives the PTO the authority to set and adjust its fee schedule without congressional approval. Fees will then be placed in a reserve fund that is available to the PTO and may only be used for PTO operations.

Funding changes go beyond PTO flexibility. The AIA establishes a new category of applicants called a "micro-entity." Small entities, a classification that has already existed in patent law, must only pay one-half of the usual fee in many cases. The PTO defines small entities as individual inventors, non-profits, and businesses with fewer than 500 employees, among other requirements (Chien, 2011; Business Credit and Assistance, 2012, §121.802; Patents, Trademarks and Copyrights, 2012, §1.27(a)-(b)). Micro-entities need only pay one-quarter of the full fee assessed by the PTO. A filer can qualify as a micro-entity if it already qualifies as a small entity, has not been an inventor on more than four previous applications, lacks an income less than three times the median household income in the prior year, and has no obligation to assign to an entity with the aforementioned income (Ahmann & Rodewald, 2012).

II.   THE AIA AND THE PATENT PRIORITY DEBATE

One of the most high-profile reforms the AIA brings is the change of patent priority system. The United States has traditionally utilized a "first-to-invent" system. Under this system, the PTO grants patent rights to the inventor who can prove the earliest date of invention of the new idea. Evidence is submitted to the PTO regarding the steps in the invention process and timing to support a particular invention date (Perkins, 2012). America has held on to the first-to-invent system with the most tenacity of any nation. Since 1998, when the Philippines decided once and for all to depart from a first-to-invent patent priority regime, the United States has stood virtually alone in using this method of patent priority (Sedia, 2007).

By far the more common approach has been the "first-to-file" patent priority system. Under this regime, the first inventor to file her application receives the patent. This priority system generally occurs without regard to the date that the invention was actually created (Perkins, 2012). The first-to-file approach is used virtually everywhere else in the world.

A. Patent Priority, Empirical Research and the Uncertain Impact of First-to-file

The beneficial impact of the first-to-file system may be less certain than some predict. Relevant analyses and empirical evidence lean toward the AIA's first-to-file regime being less helpful to innovation and competitiveness than some might expect. The AIA's impact may even be negative. As with any new statute, however, the expected benefit and harm may vary according to one's perspective.

One important perspective is the differential impact of the filing regime on small firms and individual inventors. The focus on small entities is of no minor importance. Small inventors arguably have a disproportionally beneficial effect on the innovation ecosystem. Small firms and individual inventors, while not benefitting from the significant resources of large corporations, are also not bound by its potentially restraining norms, bureaucracy and groupthink. Small inventors can create outside the proverbial box and therefore be more disruptive to the culture of innovation, hastening the process of technological change. Furthermore, small inventors have an important role to play in certain industries. In high technology and pharmaceuticals, for example, small firms and individual inventors serve as innovation inputs to larger enterprises (Abrams & Wagner, 2012). Small firms should be made an important consideration in the overall welfare effects of the AIA.

Leading the way on this issue is a key empirical study by Abrams and Wagner (2012), which shrewdly exploited Canada's switch in 1989 from a first-to-invent to a first-to-file system. Canada was the last major industrialized nation to do so. Using patent data available in Canada from 1978 to the present, the authors compared the patenting behavior of individual inventors before and after the 1989 change. The authors found a statistically significant decline in patenting behavior by individual inventors relative to firms after the adoption of the first-to-file system.

Abrams and Wagner speculate a variety of reasons why individual inventors patent less. One reason may be that the first-to-file system places a premium on marshaling the resources necessary, and performing the requisite inventive steps, to filing a patent. This could include a better understanding of the complex patent laws, access to skilled legal assistance, and the institutionalized resources to prepare patent filings more quickly. The result could be that firms that have invented second or third may still receive patent protection because they have won the race to the

Patent Office due to their bureaucratic competence and legal expertise. As Rantanen and Petherbridge state in their debate with Jay Kesan, "[a] firm with resources—and a large potential book of business—can get its patent applications drafted more quickly than a firm without them" (Rantanen, Petherbridge & Kesan, 2012, p. 232).

In addition, Abrams and Wagner note that individual inventors may become demoralized due to the perception that first-to-file favors companies with resources or appears to be more based on luck or bureaucracy than inventive creation. Finally, individual investors might join firms after the first-to-file rule is implemented to take advantage of collected resources. The individual inventors that join firms might already be the ones sophisticated enough to know that bureaucratic expertise is necessary for quick filing. Their movement to firms might amplify the remaining pool of more vulnerable or unknowledgeable individual inventors.

While the authors express appropriate caution regarding implications of their findings, other earlier works modestly challenge their result. Mossinghoff (2005) found that small firms do not receive an advantage from the first-to-invent system of patent priority and there may be some small disadvantage under certain conditions. Though reporting mixed evidence, Lemley and Chien (2003) conclude that small entities do not necessarily benefit from the first-to-invent system. Both of these studies use data gathered from interference proceedings that determine the priority rules for multiple patent applications.

Mitigating such harm might be the AIA's provisions directed squarely at small businesses. The AIA establishes a new microcategory of small applicants. As noted earlier, this category reduces fees for qualified applications by as much as 75 percent (Patent Act of 1952, § 123). In addition, the AIA establishes an ombudsman to manage the concerns of small business (America Invents Act, 2011, § 28) as well as requires a study examining international patent protection for small businesses (America Invents Act, 2011, § 31).

While such measures may be helpful, they are not likely to counteract broader challenges of limited resources and lack of patenting expertise. Regarding the micro-category exception, section 123(e) of Title 35 of the United States Code empowers the Director of the PTO to limit micro-entity qualification as needed to "avoid an undue impact on other patent applicants" and as "otherwise reasonably necessary and appropriate" (Patent Act of 1952, § 123(e)). Thus, reduced fees for micro applicants, to the extent they convey an advantage now, can potentially be eroded if future PTO policy changes.

The small business ombudsman provision and the study regarding international patent protection, while potentially helpful, have uncertain benefits. They do not deliver concrete changes to patent practice nor require any action taken as a result of the study or the appointment. As Rantanen and Petherbridge argue in their debate with Jay Kesan, these provisions pay "little more than lip service to the interests that are likely be trampled by the legislation" (Rantanen et al., 2012).

III. PATENT PRIORITY AND ITS GLOBAL IMPACT

While empirical evidence studying patent priority is important, it is also helpful to discuss the values that underlie a switch to first-to-file. One such value is that the change in patent priority to first-to-file may impact competitiveness of US companies relative to their foreign counterparts. The most obvious global impact may be the harmonization of the US patent filing system with the rest of the world. Patent laws have remained diversified across jurisdictions for three reasons: the legacy of the centuries-old principle of territoriality, the use of patent laws as a policy tool for economic growth, and varying cultural characteristics (Chun, 2011).

Harmonization of patent law has been the subject of discussion in the international arena for decades. Treaties such as the Agreement on Trade-Related Aspects of Intellectual Property Rights, better known as TRIPS (TRIPS, 1994), and the Patent Cooperation Treaty (PCT, 1970) are examples of such successful harmonization efforts. Yet, as a general rule, a lack of success in harmonization has been due to the inability to reconcile different perspectives on the objective of the global patent system (Kappos, 2011).

Adoption of the first-to-invent system by the United States is a significant step toward harmonization, especially because of the disproportionately large impact US patent rules have on global patent filers. The purported harmonization established by the US first-to-invent system is unfortunately not as complete as it could be. The AIA does not eliminate a one-year "grace period" whereby inventors can decide whether to disclose patent protection after disclosing the invention to the public (America Invents Act, 2011; 35 U.S.C § 102(b), 2012). This allows inventors time to decide whether patenting is even desirable and, if so, to complete the application. Publication in a journal, as well as sales and other technical disclosures, will commence the one-year grace period (Schacht & Thomas, 2012).

This limitation has encouraged criticism from commentators that the AIA's revision is not a true adoption of a first-to-invent system. As one explains, "[c]ontrary to the perception of US lawyers that [the AIA's revision] is a first to file [system], [it] is in fact a revised version of a first to invent. . . . [T]he period that the inventor can rely on the first to invent is limited to the 12 months from the filing date and the evidence to establish the first to invent is limited to a disclosure" (Takenaka, 2011, p. 5). Another author claims that the AIA's grace period in effect creates a "first to publish" rule. The grace period enables inventors to publicly disclose the nature of the invention, and because it qualifies as prior art for other applicants, in effect causes competitors to be locked out (Recent Legislation, 2012, p. 1292).

In addition to harmonization effects, or lack thereof, the change from first-to-invent to first-to-file may impose transition costs on domestic filers. Domestic filers may need to expend resources in order to understand and navigate the new system. The transition cost for foreign filers, by contrast, might be less than their domestic counterparts because of their already present familiarity with the first-to-file patent system in their home country. This disadvantage, such that it might exist, would be most prominent for small organizations and individual inventors that focus mainly or exclusively on domestic patenting operations. Their experience with first-to-file would be limited, thus requiring a learning curve.

The transition cost disadvantage, however, might be minimal when more sophisticated domestic and foreign filers are compared. Larger firms with greater market power may already be familiar with first-to-file rules in foreign patent systems. Accordingly, the transition from first-to-invent to first-to-file may be no greater than their non-US counterparts.

Once the transition period ends and firms of various sizes absorb the necessary costs to navigate a first-to-file system, the cost calculus might change. Assume that the first-to-file system creates administrative efficiencies for the PTO that the first-to-invent system would lack. If the PTO experiences such efficiencies, the PTO may be able to process more applications more quickly with the same resources. Amplifying this effect is the AIA's strengthening of resources usable by the PTO. The AIA allows the PTO to adjust its fees as necessary, thus potentially generating new revenues and the hiring of additional patent examiners.

The benefits of increased efficiency would be shared roughly equally amongst the patent applicants. For example, if the average time to process a patent declines from three years to two and one half years, the six-month benefit per patent is enjoyed equally by filers. With the largest number of filers to the PTO being of US origin, that would mean that the US filers would be the majority recipient of efficiency advantages over non-domestic competitors.

These advantages, however, can vary by context. As Hubbard (2012) notes, in fields where foreign inventors obtain more patents than their domestic counterparts, efficiencies will deliver the greatest surplus to foreign inventors. As Hubbard laments in the context of improving competitiveness for US filers, "the U.S. patent office cannot save a sinking ship by speeding the rate at which it is taking on water" (Hubbard, 2012).

Sensitivity can also vary distribution of the efficiency benefit. Start-up firms may be more sensitive to the efficiency benefit as well as the harm caused by any delays due to the lack of resources that can sustain an entrepreneurial venture over time. Larger firms may be less sensitive to increased efficiency due to their improved ability to shoulder bureaucratic delays (Sichelman & Graham, 2010). Thus, the shift to first-to-file may impact different US firms in different ways according to size, industry and other variables.

Global changes made to the AIA, regardless of patent priority, may negate any disadvantage to US firms that might arise as a result of the shift to a first-to-file regime. For example, the PTO can streamline and improve the patent process in industries where the US has the greatest advantage.[1] Two programs pre-dating the AIA already hint at such a targeted expedite practice. An Accelerated Examination Program begun by the PTO in 2006 promised faster resolution if the invention improved the environment, contributed to the conservation of energy resources, or contributed to countering terrorism (Patents, Trademarks and Copyrights, 2012). Four years later, the PTO introduced a program to expedite the patenting of green technologies that would "create green jobs, and promote U.S. competitiveness in this vital sector" (Patent and Trademark Office, 2009). The latter program has now ended.

The AIA concretizes and broadens this PTO power. The AIA gives the PTO the authority to prioritize patent applications "for products, processes, or technologies that are important to the national economy or national competitiveness" (America Invents Act, 2011, § 25; Patent Act of 1952 § 2(b)(2)(G)). This departs from the targeted programs issued by the PTO and enables widespread patent reprioritization according to industry and technology. Such broad discretion presents significant discretion for the PTO to target competitiveness-enhancing measures, especially generated in the United States, for priority treatment.

However, granting the PTO such discretion is not without its pitfalls. There is no certainty that the PTO can skillfully identify products, processes, or technologies that generate a net gain to US filers if targeted for priority examination. No guarantee exists that the PTO has such expertise or that such targeting would not have the exact opposite effect of facilitating foreign filings at the expense of domestic ones. There is also a possibility that, if the benefits to expedited patenting are significant enough, foreign filers will reposition their patents such that they too receive the benefit of the facilitated review. To the extent that this is possible, it would reduce the competitive advantage granted to domestic filers under a targeted program (Hubbard, 2012).

In addition, any attempt to deliver a benefit to US companies with the de facto exclusion of foreign filers would certainly raise claims of protectionism by foreign interests. There is nothing to stop foreign patent offices from enacting similar rules that disadvantage US filers to compensate for the protectionist advantage granted by PTO rules. Such targeting may even violate the TRIPS agreement. Article 27.1 of TRIPS requires member states to provide uniform patent rights across technologies (TRIPS, art. 27.1; Rose, 2012). The targeting of preference measures by the PTO may be just the type of behavior that the TRIPS agreement was intended to prevent, and may encourage other countries to see sanctions before the WTO (Hubbard, 2012).

While receiving significant attention with the passage of the AIA, the debate over first-to-file versus first-to-invent might be a less significant issue over the long run. Lemley and Chien (2003) were skeptical of whether such a change might have a real impact, concluding that no systematic bias exists in favor of one group or another in a first-to-file system. The AIA shift to a first-to-file system may not change this calculus, or at least the shift may not definitively define the allocated benefits in one direction or the other.

Furthermore, as explained, global changes made under the AIA may generate long-term benefits that overshadow costs related to patent priority. The micro-patent program offers reduced costs to small filers, though such discounts are by no means guaranteed. The targeted prioritization power given to the PTO by the AIA could, if used tactically, amplify any competitive advantages to domestic filers. This does not necessarily mean that advantages or disadvantages generated by a new first-to-file regime no longer exist. Rather, the impacts of other provisions under the AIA, while not generating as much academic discussion, might be the source of greater welfare effects than the change in patent priority. To say that adoption of a first-to-file system is "much ado about nothing" is probably not accurate. The system will change behavior and result in real impact. Instead, the adoption of a first-to-file system may be "much ado about less than we think" as other factors exert greater influence and underlying structures of patent protection that do significantly favor large firms over small remain firmly intact.

IV.   THE POTENTIAL AND RISK OF SUPPLEMENTAL EXAMINATION

The supplemental examination procedure appears on initial review to be relatively benign. A patent filer is able to correct good faith mistakes in the patent document without fear that third parties in litigation at a later date will exploit such errors. The AIA introduced the supplemental examination procedure mainly to address concerns over the doctrine of inequitable conduct, well established in patent law. When an inventor files for a patent, the prosecution of that patent involves an interaction between the applicant and the PTO. The public does not participate. The patent system thus substantially relies on candor and honesty by the patent filer, and filers have "a duty of candor and good faith ... to disclose to the [Patent] Office all information known to that individual to be material to patentability" (37 C.F.R. § 1.56(a), 2011). Breach of this duty constitutes inequitable conduct and renders all claims of the patent unenforceable for the life of the patent (Cotter, 2011).

The power of the doctrine of inequitable conduct is that an accused infringer can raise it during patent infringement litigation. The tactical advantages of raising such a defense are significant, as it places the patent owner on the defensive and subjects the motives of the patent filer to scrutiny. The result is that patent defendants have been charging inequitable conduct in almost every case, causing the doctrine to become, in the words of at least one court, an "absolute plague" (*Burlington Indus. Inc. v. Dayco, Corp.*, 1988). The supplemental examination procedure attempts to reduce the overuse of the defense.

The critique of the supplemental examination procedure is that it might suppress claims of inequitable conduct too much. The doctrine serves the policy purpose of protecting the integrity of the patent system. Patent owners who receive patent protection, though under improper pretenses, are subject to challenge throughout the life of the patent protection. This incentivizes the patent owner to carefully submit information in support of a prospective patent that is accurate and justifiable. Giving the power to assert the claim to a third party provides a potentially self-interested and aggressive enforcement mechanism. In spite of the plague cited by courts and commentators, inequitable conduct does actually happen and serious breaches of the duty of candor can occur. It can potentially mitigate, though by no means eliminate, questions of patent quality in the US patent system (Dolak, 2010).

Rantanen and Petherbridge (2011) claim that supplemental examination offers nothing less than "patent amnesty." According to these authors, it encourages applicants to engage in strategies that it would have never considered under the pre-AIA system. Information about prior art may not be disclosed in the initial patent application because of the opportunity to fix that disclosure (or avoid it altogether) through the supplemental examination and do so without risk of consequence. Such lack of disclosure or careless disclosure could weaken the patent system overall.

Two significant exceptions do exist to the blanket protection offered by supplemental examination.[2] The exceptions are present to prevent the previously mentioned advantage-taking behavior by the patentee. These exceptions, however, in practice appear to provide little disincentive for the patentee to reduce the quality or accuracy of its patent submission.

The first exception prohibits a patentee from utilizing a supplemental examination when an inequitable conduct allegation is already pled in a civil action. This is apparently intended to prevent patentees from using supplemental examination as a tactical and last-minute defense against inequitable conduct litigation. A patent applicant's own internal files, however, are not publicly accessible. It is therefore arguably unlikely that the factual basis will be uncovered before the discovery process in a civil action. Thus, patentees retain control of whether to immunize themselves before a challenger has an opportunity to learn about the inequitable contact and plead it (Rantanen & Petherbridge, 2011).

The second exception allows for criminal prosecution if "material fraud . . . may have been committed in connection with the patent that is the subject of the supplemental examination" (America Invents Act, 2011, § 25). The possibility of criminal prosecution can no doubt be worrying, but in practice such prosecution is unlikely to occur. Federal law already prohibits willfully making a false statement to a branch of government in many circumstances punishable by fines or up to five years in prison (18 U.S.C. § 1001, 2006). However, assessment of fines and imprisonment has been rare in the patent context (Schneck, 2004–05), and thus threat of its application is unlikely to occur in a post-AIA world.

In sum, the supplemental examination appears to be a non-adversarial mechanism by which patentees can correct inaccurate information in their applications without fear of sanction or litigation. The risk, however, is that the new procedure may have the opposite effect in practice. Patentees, emboldened by the amnesty, may have little incentive to avoid obfuscation in their patent applications.

The result might be an increase in low-quality or invalid patents granted by the PTO. This could suppress innovation by deterring inventors from patenting or popularizing new discoveries for fear of infringement liability or the inability to secure a license (Ackerman, 2011). Rantanen and Petherbridge (Rantanen, Petherbridge & Kesan, 2012) go as far as to say that "in the view of the AIA, a firm might obtain a patent containing claims it knows or strongly suspects are unpatentable by not providing the Patent Office with the facts giving rise to that knowledge or suspicion" (p. 231). Such a result may be a lamentable, though unintended, consequence of the AIA that may require future revision if dire predictions such as this one come to pass in practice.

V. CONCLUSION

The AIA represents the most significant change in patent law in over 50 years. An increasing backlog of applications before the PTO, the emergence of troubling new types of patents, and deficits in administrative proceedings made reforms to patent law long overdue. The result has been a revision that was intended to modernize the US patent system, increase its effectiveness, and improve its fairness to all participants.

Two changes merit particular attention. First, the change from a first-to-invent to a first-to-file system of patent priority has the potential to bring the United States in line with the patent systems of the rest of the world. Although promising, the harmonization with foreign patent systems is incomplete and the benefit to various US interests uncertain. Second, the supplemental examination procedure, while mitigating the excess of the inequitable conduct doctrine, has the potential to create problems of its own. The procedure can potentially encourage applicants to obtain patents using suspect means, and if the applicant feels the threat of being caught later, it can use the supplemental examination procedure to immunize itself from harm.

Although it has been some time since the previous major change in patent law, this does not necessarily mean that the patent community will need to wait another half century for further revision. The stakes for patent protection are as high as they have ever been. Increasingly greater value is found in patent protection, and firms are willing to spend even greater resources to protect their patent portfolios. As one attorney skeptically speculates, the AIA will not satisfy business and legal practitioners for long. "Within two or three years," one partner at a large intellectual property law firm predicts, "we will be talking about patent reform again. You can bank on it" (Seidenberg, 2011). This prediction is likely too optimistic, or perhaps pessimistic, depending on one's point of view. Nonetheless, if the AIA revisions do not generate their promised benefits to various patent interests, it will only be a matter of time before still new revisions are advocated to improve the patent process in the United States.

NOTES

* Copyright 2013, Robert C. Bird
1. Regardless of any targeted programs, patent law may already be heterogeneous and perhaps beneficially so (Burk & Lemley, 2002; 2003).
2. A third exception exists regarding actions filed by the patent holder that involve the prohibition of unfair methods of competition and other unfair acts related to importation to the United States. The exception operates in a substantially similar fashion to the litigation defense mentioned in the text.

REFERENCES

Abramowicz, M. & Duffy, J. (2009). Ending the Patent Monopoly. *University of Pennsylvania Law Review*, **157**(6), 1541–1611.

Abrams, D. & Wagner, R.P. (2012). Poisoning the Next Apple: How the America Invents Act Harms Inventors. *Stanford Law Review*, **65**. Retrieved from http://ssrn.com/abstract=1883821.

Ackerman, L.J. (2011). Prioritization: Addressing the Patent Application Backlog at the United States Patent and Trademark Office. *Berkeley Technology Law Journal*, **26**(1), 67–92.

Ahmann, W. & Rodewald, T. (2012). Patent Reform: The Impact on Start-ups. *Intellectual Property & Technology Law Journal*, **24**(1), 3–13.

America Invents Act, Pub. L. No. 112-29, 125 Stat. 284 (2011).

America Inventors Protection Act, Pub. L. No. 106-113, 113 Stat. 1536 (1999).

Aste, D.M. (2012). To Disclose or Not to Disclose: Why the United States Properly Adopted the European Model for Third-Party Protection During Patent Prosecution. *Case Western Reserve Journal of Law, Technology & the Internet*, **3**(1), 153–94.

Bagley, M.A. (2003). Patent First, Ask Questions Later: Morality and Biotechnology in Patent Law. *William and Mary Law Review*, **45**(2), 469–547.

Burk, D.L. & Lemley, M.A. (2002). Is Patent Law Technology Specific? *Berkeley Technology Law Journal*, **17**(4), 1155–1206.

Burk, D.L. & Lemley, M.A. (2003). Policy Levers in Patent Law. *Virginia Law Review*, **89**(7), 1575–1696.

Burlington Indus. Inc. v. Dayco, Corp., 849 F.2d 1418 (Fed. Cir. 1988).

Business Credit and Assistance, 13 C.F.R. §121.802 (2012).

Chien, C.V. (2011). Predicting Patent Litigation. *Texas Law Review*, **90**(2), 283–329.

Chumney, W. (2009). Patents Gone Wild: An Ethical Examination and Legal Analysis of Tax-Related and Tax Strategy Patents. *American Business Law Journal*, **46**(3), 343–406.

Chun, D. (2011). Patent Law Harmonization in the Age of Globalization: The Necessity and Strategy for a Pragmatic Outcome. *Journal of the Patent and Trademark Office Society*, **93**(2), 127–66.

Congressional Record (2011, June 23). 157 Cong. Rec. H4505.

Congressional Record (2011a, Sept. 8). 157 Cong. Rec. S5442.

Cotter, T.F. (2011). An Economic Analysis of Patent Laws' Inequitable Conduct Doctrine. *Arizona Law Review*, **53**(3), 735–79.

Crudo, R.A. (2011). A Patently Public Concern: Using Public Nuisance Law to Fix the False Patent Marking Statute after the Leahy-Smith America Invents Act. *George Washington Law Review*, **80**(2), 568–601.

Diebner, G.F. (2011). Legislative Developments in Patent Law 2011 – The "America Invents Act." *Practising Law Institute: Patents, Copyrights, Trademarks, and Literary Property Course Handbook Series*, 1058, 503–11.

Dolak, L.A. (2010). Inequitable Conduct: A Flawed Doctrine Worth Saving. *Wake Forest Journal of Business and Intellectual Property Law*, **11**(1), 1–31.

Gentolia, J. (2011). *The Implications of the America Invents Act on Innovation in America, Venturestab*. Retrieved from http://www.venturestab.com/2011/10/the-implications-of-the-america-invents-act-on-innovation-in-america/.

Gutterman, A.S. (2011). *Legal Compliance Checkups: Business Clients*. Eagan, Minnesota: Clark Boardman Callaghan.

Halewood, P. (2008). On Commodification and Self-Ownership. *Yale Journal of Law & The Humanities*, **20**(2), 131–62.

Herrington, D.H., Ilan, D., Jedrey, N.E. & Prunella, M. (2011). Congress Makes Substantial Changes to Patent Law with the America Invents Act. *Intellectual Property and Technology Law Journal*, **23**(2), 3–7.

Hubbard, W. (2012). Competitive Patent Law. *Florida Law Review*, forthcoming, Retrieved from http://ssrn.com/abstract=1980383, 1–65.

Kappos, D.J. (2011). Patent Law Harmonization. *Landslide*, **3**(6), 16–18.

Lemley, M.A. & Chien, C.V. (2003). Are the US Patent Priority Rules Really Necessary? *Hastings Law Journal*, **54**(5), 1299–1333.

Love, B.J. (2012). Interring the Pioneer Invention Doctrine. *North Carolina Law Review*, **90**(2), 379–458.

McCaffrey, C. (2011). The Virtues of Virtual Marking in Patent Reform. *Northwestern University Law Review*, **105**(1), 367–401.

Mossinghoff, G.J. (2005). The First-to-Invent Rule in the U.S. Patent System has Provided No Advantage to Small Entities. *Journal of the Patent and Trademark Office Society*, **87**(6), 514–20.

Patent Act of 1952, 35 U.S.C. §§ 1-376 (1952) (as amended).

Patent Cooperation Treaty. 28 U.S.T. 7645, 1160 U.N.T.S. 231 (1970).

Patent and Trademark Office (2009). The U.S. Commerce Department's Patent and Trademark Office (USPTO) will pilot a program to accelerate the examination of certain green technology patent applications. Retrieved from http://www.uspto.gov/news/pr/2009/09_33.jsp.

Patents, Trademarks and Copyrights, 37 C.F.R. §1.102(c) (2012).

Perkins, J. (2012). Patent Law Change: A First Look at the "America Invents Act." *DCBA Brief*, **24**(January), 30–34.

Rantanen, J. (2006). Slaying the Troll: Litigation as an Effective Strategy Against Patent Threats. *Santa Clara Computer and High Tech Law Journal*, **23**(1), 159–210.

Rantanen, J. & Petherbridge, P. (2011). Toward a System of Invention Registration: The Leahy-Smith America Invents Act. *Michigan Law Review First Impressions*, **110**(November), 24–32.

Rantanen, J., Petherbridge L. & Kesan, J.P. (2012). America Invents, More or Less? *University of Pennsylvania Law Review PENNumbra*, **160**(March), 229–52.

Recent Legislation (2012). Patent Law – Patentable Subject Matter – Leahy-Smith America Invents Act Revises New Patent Law Regime – Leahy-Smith America

Invents Act, Pub. L. No. 112-29, 125 Stat. 284 (2011) (To Be Codified in Scattered Sections of 35 U.S.C.). *Harvard Law Review*, **125**(5), 1290–97.

Rooklidge, W.C. & Barker, A.G. (2009). Reform of a Fast-Moving Target: The Development of Patent Law Since the 2004 National Academies Report. *Journal of the Patent and Trademark Office Society*, **91**(3), 153–99.

Rose, S.A. (2012). Semiconductor Chips, Genes, and Stem Cells: New Wine for New Bottles? *American Journal of Law and Medicine*, **38**(1), 113–57.

Schacht, W.H. & Thomas J.R. (2012, Jan. 24). The Leahy-Smith America Invents Act: Innovation Issues. *Congressional Research Service*, 7-5700, R42014.

Schneck, T. (2004–05), Patenting Human Life, A Multidimensional Problem. *Lincoln Law Review*, **32**(1), 1–28.

Schneider, J.E. (2011). Senate Passes Leahy-Smith America Invents Act, Patent Reform Heads to President, *Fulbright Alert*, Fulbright & Jaworski, LLP. Retrieved from http://www.fulbright.com/index.cfm?fuseaction=publications.detail&pub_id=5097&site_id=494

Sedia, A.J. (2007). Storming the Last Bastion: The Patent Reform Act of 2007 and its Assault on the Superior First-to-Invent Rule. *DePaul Journal of Art, Technology & Intellectual Property Law*, **18**(1), 79–125.

Seidenberg, S. (2011). A New Mother of Invention. *ABA Journal*, **97**(12), 16–17.

Sichelman, T. & Graham, S.J.H. (2010). Patenting by Entrepreneurs: An Empirical Study. *Michigan Telecommunications and Technology Law Review*, **17**(1), 111–80.

Stephens, N.W. (2012). From Forest Group to the America Invents Act: False Patent Marking Comes Full Circle. *Iowa Law Review*, **97**(3), 1003–27.

Takenaka, T. (2011). Harmony with the Rest of the World? The American Invents Act. *Journal of Intellectual Property Law and Practice*, **7**(1), 4–7.

TRIPS, Agreement on Trade-Related Aspects of Intellectual Property Rights, Including Trade in Counterfeit Goods (1994). art. 27.1, 33 I.L.M. 1197.

White House blog (2011, Sept. 16), President Obama Signs America Invents Act, Overhauling the Patent System to Stimulate Economic Growth, and Announces New Steps to Help Entrepreneurs Create Jobs, Press Release. Retrieved from http://www.whitehouse.gov/the-press-office/2011/09/16/president-obama-signs-america-invents-act-overhauling-patent-system-stim.

Yoches, R.E., Lim, E.H., Schultz ,C.S., Thayer, L.J., Arner, E.H. & McNeill, R.M. (2011). How Will Patent Reform Affect the Software and Internet Industries? *The Computer and Internet Lawyer*, **28**(12), 5–14.

4. Inequitable conduct after *Therasense* and the America Invents Act

T. Leigh Anenson and Gideon Mark*

This chapter examines the dramatic constriction of the inequitable conduct defense to patent infringement accomplished in 2011 by the issuance of the United States Court of Appeals for the Federal Circuit (Federal Circuit) decision in *Therasense, Inc. v. Becton, Dickinson & Co.* and the enactment of the America Invents Act (AIA). The chapter questions whether *Therasense* and the AIA have unduly narrowed the inequitable conduct defense and thus undermined the core goals of patent law. Those core goals include the encouragement of innovation, full and early disclosure, and investment in research and development (*Pfaff v. Wells Elecs., Inc.*, 1998). The chapter concludes that *Therasense* and specific features of the AIA, particularly its adoption of new post-issuance review proceedings and a new "best mode" amendment, will likely operate in tandem to sharply curtail the availability of the inequitable conduct defense and impair the operation of the US patent system.

I. INEQUITABLE CONDUCT BACKGROUND

Inequitable conduct in acquiring a patent before the US Patent and Trademark Office (PTO) is a judicially created defense to patent infringement. No US statute expressly provides for the defense. The 1952 Patent Act (the last major revision of US patent law prior to the AIA) and its legislative history are both silent concerning the grounds and standard of proof for an inequitable conduct defense (Daniel, 2008). Instead, the doctrine has its roots in the equitable defense of unclean hands that was applied in a trio of pre-1950 Supreme Court cases (*Precision Instrument Mfg. Co. v. Auto. Maint. Mach. Co.*, 1945; *Hazel-Atlas Glass Co. v. Hartford Empire Co.*, 1944; *Keystone Driller Co. v. Gen. Excavator Co.*, 1933). The doctrine was first clearly articulated by the Supreme Court in

Precision, which held that courts could dismiss patent infringement suits based on inequitable conduct committed during the patent's prosecution.

Supreme Court precedent emphasized the critical role played by the defense in promoting patent quality and the public interest that is predominant in an effectively functioning patent system. Because patents are a departure from the norm of market competition, the doctrine of inequitable conduct rests on the recognition that part of the quid pro quo for the acquisition of a patent monopoly is an insistence that the circumstances surrounding the application be free from fraud or other inequitable conduct. Therefore, the inequitable conduct defense serves multiple important policy purposes. They include protecting the integrity of the patent system by ensuring applicant candor, encouraging patent applicants to internalize costs of the patent system, avoiding patent monopolies that stem from inequitable conduct, and punishing patentees who behave inequitably toward the public during the patent acquisition process (*Therasense, Inc. v. Becton, Dickinson & Co.*, 2011; Petherbridge, Rantanen & Mojibi, 2011).

A. Elements

Traditional inequitable conduct analysis in patent cases involves two elements. The accused patent infringer must show by clear and convincing evidence that: (1) an individual associated with the filing and prosecution of a patent application made an affirmative misrepresentation of a material fact, failed to disclose material information, or submitted false material information to the PTO; and (2) did so with the intent to deceive the PTO.

Prior to *Therasense*, courts commonly followed PTO Rule 56 (37 CFR § 1.56), originally adopted as part of the Rules of Practice in 1949 and then substantially reformulated in 1977 and 1992, in determining whether information was material (*J.P. Stevens & Co. v. Lex Tex Ltd.*, 1984). Rule 56 as originally adopted prohibited fraud but said nothing about inequitable conduct. The definition of fraud in this context was unclear (Milliman-Jarvis, 2012). The 1977 amendment transformed Rule 56 from a provision enabling the PTO to strike applications for fraud to one that formally established a duty of candor and good faith by patent applicants and their attorneys to disclose information they were aware of that was material to the examination of the application. The 1977 amendment adopted a "reasonable examiner" standard by defining information as "material" if there was a substantial likelihood that a reasonable examiner would consider it important in deciding whether to allow the application to issue as a patent. In the ensuing years, the Federal Circuit regularly referred to this standard as the one to use in cases raising claims of inequitable conduct (*Dayco Prods., Inc. v. Total Containment, Inc.*, 2003). Pursuant to this test a false statement or nondisclosure could be material for purposes of an inequitable conduct determination even if the invention in question would otherwise be patentable (*Digital Control, Inc. v. Charles Mach. Works*, 2006).

The 1992 amendment continued to impose a duty to disclose material information, but it provided a more detailed definition of materiality. The amended Rule 56 (which remained in effect for the next 20 years) imposed a duty on individuals associated with the filing and prosecution of an application to disclose to the PTO all information known to be material to patentability as defined in the rule. Information was material if it was not cumulative to information already of record or made of record in the patent application and it either established, by itself or in combination with other information, a prima facie case of unpatentability of a claim or refuted, or was inconsistent with, a position the applicant took in opposing an argument of unpatentability relied upon by the PTO or asserting an argument of patentability.

When it adopted the 1992 amendment the PTO considered and rejected the adoption of a but-for test of materiality. It did so because it concluded that use of such a narrow standard would not enable the PTO to obtain the information it required to properly evaluate patentability (*Therasense, Inc. v. Becton, Dickinson & Co.*, 2011). Rule 56's materiality standard, as adopted in 1977 and refined in 1992, also was consistent with the materiality standard applied in a range of analogous contexts. As the *Therasense* dissent noted, the use of a but-for standard has been rejected in the context of, *inter alia*, fraudulent registration of copyrights and trademarks (*Eckes v. Card Prices Update*, 1984; Nimmer & Nimmer, 2010), proxy solicitations regulated under section 14(a) of the Securities Exchange Act of 1934 (*TSC Indus., Inc. v. Northway, Inc.*, 1976), criminal prosecutions under the federal mail and fraud statutes (18 USC §§ 1341, 1343), and common law fraud (Restatement (Second) of Torts, 1977).

The revised Rule 56, like the prior versions, continued to omit use of the term "inequitable conduct." The PTO has justified this omission on the ground that inequitable conduct covers too broad a spectrum of conduct to be subject to mandatory striking of a patent application (O'Connor, 2010).

The other element of inequitable conduct is intent. In *Precision*, the Supreme Court's only major discussion of inequitable conduct, the Court failed to delineate the requisite level of intent, although it did refer to, *inter alia*, willful conduct. The requisite level of intent has varied considerably since *Precision*, ranging on the spectrum from negligence to gross negligence to recklessness to specific intent (Irving, Stevens, Lee & Simpson,

2010; Goldman, 1993). Because direct evidence of intent to deceive is rare, a finding of intent pre-*Therasense* was often based on the totality of the circumstances, including circumstantial evidence (Auth & Rockman, 2010).

B. Effect

The inequitable conduct defense has frequently been referred to as the "atomic bomb" of patent litigation because its success renders both the entire patent and related patents permanently unenforceable while also generating claims under the antitrust and securities laws (Kass & Browand, 2011), either as counterclaims or in follow-on cases, such as antitrust class actions filed by direct and indirect purchasers (Gordon & Stack, 2011). The draconian nature of the defense, in combination with its low threshold of proof, made it appealing to accused patent infringers. One study, cited by *Therasense*, estimated that 80 percent of patent infringement suits contain an allegation of inequitable conduct (Committee Position Paper, 1988). However, other estimates of the frequency with which the defense is asserted are considerably lower, ranging from less than 20 percent (Brown, 2009) to approximately 25 percent (Cotropia, 2009) to 16–35 percent (Mack, 2006) to 40 percent (Mammen, 2009).

Patent applicants often attempt to negate the defense by providing the PTO with voluminous prior art references—many of which are trivial or useless (Scheinfeld & Bagley, 2011)—and concurrent patent applications for the same technology in other countries (Qualters, 2011). This deluge no doubt has contributed to the PTO's backlog of patent applications. In September 2011, approximately 670,000 applications were awaiting their first action (USPTO Performance & Accountability Report, 2012a). The foregoing numerous negative and unintended consequences of the inequitable conduct doctrine often produced a description of it as a plague on the courts and the US patent system.

The Supreme Court has provided no guidance concerning inequitable conduct since it issued its opinion in *Precision* in 1945. The lower courts have grappled with the contours of the defense in this vacuum. *Therasense* represented the Federal Circuit's second attempt in two decades to reduce inequitable conduct claims in patent cases. The Federal Circuit, of course, is the near-exclusive appellate court for patent cases (Gugliuzza, 2012). The court's prior attempt to reduce inequitable conduct claims occurred in *Kingsdown Med. Consultants, Ltd. v. Hollister, Inc.* In that case the court did not address materiality, but it overturned precedent (*Driscoll v. Cebalo*, 1984) which held that a showing of gross negligence was sufficient to establish the intent prong of the defense. *Kingsdown* held that the patentee's conduct must indicate sufficient culpability to require a finding of specific intent to deceive (*Kingsdown Medical Consultants, Ltd. v. Hollister, Inc.*, 1988). In the subsequent years, however, Federal Circuit panels routinely ignored the case (Peng, Lewis, Herzfeld, MacAlpine & Irving, 2011) and the requisite culpability was watered down to a "should have known" standard, which was tantamount to gross negligence (*In re Bose Corp.*, 2009).

Until *Therasense*, some courts also employed a sliding scale approach to materiality and intent that allowed a lesser showing of either element based on a stronger showing of the other (*American Hoist & Derrick Co. v. Sowa & Sons, Inc.*, 1984). In theory, use of a sliding scale was restricted to situations in which there was clear and convincing proof of both materiality and intent. But in practice, use of the scale often produced findings of inequitable conduct with little or no independent support for a finding of intent (Kass & Browand, 2011). As noted by the Federal Circuit, use of a sliding scale conflated and diluted the standards for both intent and materiality (*Therasense, Inc. v. Becton, Dickinson & Co.*, 2011). The foregoing factors prompted the Federal Circuit to consider *Therasense en banc*.

II. *THERASENSE*

The Federal Circuit's decision in *Therasense* imposed significant limitations on the elements of the inequitable conduct defense. These limitations included, but were not limited to, elevated standards for intent and materiality.

A. Procedural History

Therasense owned US Patent No. 5,820,551 (the '551 patent), which involves disposable blood-glucose test strips for diabetes management. Therasense had prosecuted the original application for the patent for more than 13 years, beginning in 1984, during which time it was repeatedly rejected over US patent No. 4,454,382 (the '382 patent), also owned by Therasense. Following amendment of the claim, the examiner finally allowed the '551 patent to issue. In March 2004, Therasense sued several defendants, including Becton, Dickinson & Company, alleging infringement of the '551 patent. Following trial, the federal district court held that the '551 patent was unenforceable due to inequitable conduct because Therasense did not disclose to the PTO allegedly inconsistent statements that had previously been made to the European Patent Office regarding the European counterpart to the '382 patent.

Therasense appealed to the Federal Circuit, where a three-judge panel affirmed the holding of unenforceability. Therasense then successfully petitioned for rehearing *en banc*. Eleven judges participated in the decision, which was 6–1–4 (four dissenting votes and one concurrence). The majority opinion, which vacated the judgment and remanded for further proceedings (*Therasense, Inc. v. Becton, Dickinson & Co.*, 2012), noted that the court granted *en banc* review because it recognized the problems created by the expansion and overuse of the inequitable conduct doctrine (*Therasense, Inc. v. Becton, Dickinson & Co.*, 2011).

B. Majority Opinion

The majority opinion highlighted four key points. First, to prevail on its inequitable conduct defense, an accused infringer must show by clear and convincing evidence that the applicant knew of the reference, knew that it was material, and made a deliberate decision to withhold it. In the absence of direct evidence of intent, a specific intent to deceive must be the single most reasonable inference able to be drawn from the evidence. The intent requirement is not satisfied by a finding that a misrepresentation or omission constitutes negligence or even gross negligence.

Second, as a general rule, the materiality required to establish inequitable conduct is "but-for" materiality. In making this materiality determination courts must apply the preponderance of evidence standard used by the PTO, rather than the clear and convincing standard applied by courts to determine patent invalidity. An undisclosed reference is material if the PTO would not have allowed a claim had it been aware of the undisclosed prior art (*Aventis Pharma S.A. v. Hospira, Inc.*, 2012; *Therasense, Inc. v. Becton, Dickinson & Co.*, 2011). This but-for standard set a higher bar for establishing materiality than the PTO's own definition under Rule 56. Indeed, the Federal Circuit specifically declined to adopt the then-current version of Rule 56 in defining inequitable conduct because, according to the court, reliance on that standard had resulted in the precise problems the court sought to address by taking the case *en banc*.

Third, there is an exception to but-for materiality in cases of affirmative egregious misconduct, such as the filing of an unmistakably false affidavit. In these cases the misconduct is material regardless of the effect the misconduct had on the PTO. It is effectively material per se. Fourth, intent and materiality are distinct requirements and district courts should not use a sliding scale to determine the existence of inequitable conduct. Instead, courts should assess the evidence of materiality independent of their analysis of intent (*American Calcar, Inc. v. American Honda Motor Co.*, 2011; *Therasense, Inc. v. Becton, Dickinson & Co.*, 2011).

Therasense also reaffirmed that a district court's factual findings concerning materiality and intent are subject to appellate review for clear error, and left intact the rule that whether a district court's determination that conduct was inequitable was entrusted to the district court's equitable discretion and reviewable on appeal for abuse of discretion (Cotter, 2011).

C. PTO Proposed Rulemaking

Two months after the Federal Circuit issued its decision in *Therasense* the PTO issued a notice of proposed rulemaking with respect to Rule 56.

The proposed amended rule modified the duty of disclosure by limiting the scope of materiality in a manner consistent with the "but-for" standard announced in *Therasense*. The proposed amended rule provided that information is material to patentability if it is material under the standard set forth in *Therasense*, and information is material to patentability under *Therasense* if: (1) the PTO would not allow a claim if it were aware of the information, applying the preponderance of the evidence standard and giving the claim its broadest reasonable construction; or (2) the applicant engages in affirmative egregious misconduct before the PTO as to the information (Revision of the Materiality to Patentability Standard, 2011).

D. Negative Impact

Therasense and amended Rule 56 are likely to restrict the availability of the inequitable conduct defense in patent infringement actions, to a degree that undermines the goals of the US patent system. The most significant aspect of the case is the elevation of materiality to a "but-for" standard. As indicated, this means prior art is but-for material only if the PTO would not have allowed the claim if it had been aware of the undisclosed art. This rejection of Rule 56 broke with many years of federal precedent, departed from principles of materiality commonly applied by courts in other contexts, divided the Federal Circuit, and prompted the dissent to characterize the new standard as draconian (*Therasense, Inc. v. Becton, Dickinson & Co.*, 2011). More broadly, as the dissent noted, the majority departed from a line of Supreme Court precedent, as set forth in the trilogy of *Precision, Hazel-Atlas* and *Keystone* (*Therasense, Inc. v. Becton, Dickinson & Co.*, 2011). In that trilogy the Supreme Court recognized the importance of both uncompromising candor to the PTO by patent applicants and a flexible approach to equitable claims—something that is wholly lacking in but-for materiality.

The "egregious misconduct" exception was designed by the *Therasense* majority to mitigate the harshness of its new materiality standard. The court explained that by creating an exception to punish affirmative egregious acts without penalizing the failure to disclose information that would not have changed the patent issuance decision, it was striking the necessary balance between encouraging honesty before the PTO and preventing unfounded accusations of inequitable conduct (*Therasense, Inc. v. Becton, Dickinson & Co.*, 2011). But the exception does not apply in cases of mere nondisclosure or failure to mention prior art references. Neither of these events renders an affidavit unmistakably false—the one example of egregious misconduct that the court provided. In short, the exception will be rare, and will do little to mitigate the rigidity of the new but-for standard.

Difficulty in establishing materiality post-*Therasense* is not the only obstacle confronted by accused patent infringers seeking to utilize the inequitable conduct defense. Another obstacle is presented by *Therasense*'s holding about intent. As indicated, in the absence of direct evidence of deceitful intent a court may find specific intent only if it is the single most reasonable inference to be drawn from the evidence. Post-*Therasense*, courts have been very reluctant to infer intent based on circumstantial evidence (Thurlow & Elbert, 2011). In the first six months after the *en banc Therasense* decision was issued, district courts rendered final decisions in 14 cases involving inequitable conduct. The district court found the specific intent required by *Therasense* in only one of the cases, and it found inequitable conduct in none of them (Thurlow & Elbert, 2011).

Finally, *Therasense* also operates to effectively raise the standard for pleading inequitable conduct. The current standard was established by the Federal Circuit two years prior to *Therasense*, when it held in *Exergen Corp. v. Wal-Mart Stores, Inc.* (2009) that inequitable conduct must be pleaded with particularity under Rule 9(b) of the Federal Rules of Civil Procedure by identifying the specific who, what, when, where, and how of the material misrepresentation or omission committed before the PTO (*SAP America, Inc. v. Purple Leaf, LLC*, 2012; *Exergen Corp. v. Wal-Mart Stores, Inc.*, 2009).

Therasense did not squarely address the pleading requirements for an inequitable conduct defense (*Bayer Cropscience AG v. Dow Agrosciences LLC*, 2012), but it did raise the standard in substance insofar as all of the elements of the new inequitable conduct standard now must be pleaded with particularity (Thurlow & Elbert, 2011). Accordingly, while *Exergen* alone had no significant downward impact on the number of cases alleging inequitable conduct (Peng et al., 2011), *Exergen* in combination with *Therasense* will have a substantial chilling effect. The heightened pleading burden in tandem with the heightened substantive burden will operate to foreclose many assertions of the inequitable conduct defense.

Until addressed by the US Supreme Court, the Federal Circuit's harsh restrictions on use of the inequitable conduct defense will be operative for the foreseeable future. These restrictions, particularly *Therasense*'s adoption of but-for materiality, will function to reduce the incentive for patent applicants to be candid with the PTO and thereby undermine one of the primary goals of the US patent system. *Therasense* also is likely to have other negative effects, including a reduction in patent quality, insofar as the PTO will tend to become even more poorly informed about inventions and relevant art than it is already (Rantanen & Petherbridge, 2011–12). As will be shown below, the adoption of the AIA will serve to exacerbate *Therasense*'s negative effects.

III. AMERICA INVENTS ACT

Congress enacted the AIA after the Federal Circuit issued its decision in *Therasense*. The AIA is generally regarded as the most significant revision to the US patent regime since the 1952 enactment of the Patent Act, which recodified the entirety of US patent law (Rantanen, Petherbridge & Kesan, 2012). The AIA might even be the most significant change to US patent laws since the 1836 Patent Act, which established the modern American system of patent examination.

The AIA was the culmination of efforts to reform the US patent system that had been under way since the early 2000s. The first version of what became the AIA was introduced in June 2005, and subsequent versions were introduced in the following years (Matal, 2011–12). The failure of these early efforts resulted in frequent intervention by the Federal Circuit and Supreme Court to resolve significant patent issues. In addition to *Exergen* in 2009 and *Therasense* in 2011, the intervention encompassed the Federal Circuit decision in *In re Seagate Technology, LLC* in 2007 (raising the standard for finding willful patent infringement), as well as Supreme Court decisions concerning the standard for granting injunctions in patent cases (*eBay, Inc. v. MercExchange, L.L.C.*, 2006), the obviousness standard (*KSR Int'l Co. v. Teleflex Inc.*, 2007), the standard for granting declaratory judgment concerning the validity of an issued patent (*MedImmune, Inc. v. Genentech, Inc.*, 2007), the scope of extraterritoriality of an issued patent (*Microsoft Corp. v. AT&T Corp.*, 2007), the scope of eligible subject matter under 35 USC § 101 (*Bilski v. Kappos*, 2010), and the standard of review for patent invalidity (*Microsoft Corp. v. i4i Ltd. Partnership*. 2011).

While the AIA does not expressly address inequitable conduct, several of the statute's provisions may operate to significantly restrict the use of the defense. These provisions relate to post-issuance review and the best mode of using the invention. Both changes are discussed below, along with their adverse implications for the inequitable conduct defense.

A. Post-issuance Review

The first set of AIA provisions affecting inequitable conduct pertains to post-issuance review. These provisions include post-grant review, *inter partes* review, and supplemental examination.

1. Background
The proceedings available after the grant of a patent are conducted through the PTO to reconsider issued patents and can result in confirmation, cancellation, withdrawal, or modification of patent claims. Prior to passage of the AIA, the only post-issuance review options were *ex parte* reexamination (adopted in 1980) and *inter partes* reexamination (adopted in 1999). Only the patentee and the PTO participate in the former, whereas the patentee, PTO and the third-party requester all participated in the latter. In both cases the PTO Director could order a reexamination after a requester raised a substantial new question of patentability for the claims for which it sought reexamination (35 USC §§ 303(a), 312(a)). The ambiguity of this standard resulted in routine rubber-stamping of requests (Janis, 1997). Ninety-two percent of *ex parte* reexamination requests and 95 percent of *inter partes* reexamination requests were granted through September 2011 (USPTO, 2011a, 2011b).

Both procedures have been used infrequently. Nearly 4,500 patents are issued every week, whereas *ex parte* reexamination has applied, on average, to only 380 patents per year (Carrier, 2011) and the PTO received only 1,389 requests for *inter partes* reexamination during the period November 1999 to September 2011 (USPTO, 2011b).

The two review options have been criticized on multiple grounds. One ground is lack of timeliness and resulting uncertainty. *Ex parte* reexaminations take an average of two years and *inter partes* reexams took as long as three years (Iancu & Haber, 2011). A second ground is perceived bias. In *ex parte* reexams the requester does not participate in the proceeding (unless she is the patentee). This defect is magnified by the PTO's susceptibility to well-recognized externalities that favor sustaining patent claims (Rantanen, Petherbridge & Kesan, 2012; Masur, 2011). Not surprisingly, then, during the period July 1981–September 2011 all claims were canceled in *ex parte* reexams only 11 percent of the time (USPTO, 2011a).

(Conversely, claims were canceled or narrowed in *inter partes* reexams 89 percent of the time (USPTO, 2011b).) A third ground is that neither option is available to adjudicate a wide range of invalidity controversies. *Inter partes* reexamination allowed challenges only on grounds of novelty or non-obviousness (Carrier, 2011). Fourth, participation of the requester in *inter partes* reexams was limited, insofar as no cross-examination of the patentee or his witnesses was permitted. Fifth, *inter partes* reexamination was subject to strong estoppel provisions that operated as a major disincentive to use the proceeding, especially when coupled with the inability of a requester to cross-examine the patentee (Carrier, 2011; USPTO, 2004).

The pre-AIA regime of post-issuance review has been substantially modified with the introduction of a series of new procedures designed to minimize litigation costs and increase certainty. The new procedures took effect on September 16, 2012, one year from the date of enactment of the AIA. *Ex parte* reexamination procedures remain intact, notwithstanding their various defects (Blum, 2012). *Inter partes* reexamination has been substantially changed and redesignated as "*inter partes* review." New post-grant review and supplemental examination procedures have also been created. Each of these features is analyzed below.

2.   Post-grant review

Post-grant review is new under the AIA and can be requested no later than nine months following the grant or re-issuance of a patent issued under the new first-to-file rules. Post-grant review is available on any ground relating to the statutory requirements for patentability, including invalidating prior art, prior public use, lack of enablement, lack of written description, lack of utility, lack of obviousness, and lack of novelty (AIA, § 6(d)).

Formerly, a party seeking reexamination was required to show that cited prior art raised "a substantial new question of patentability." Under the AIA, a petition may be granted if (1) the information therein, if unrebutted, makes it more likely than not that at least one of the claims challenged in the petition is unpatentable, or (2) the petition raises novel or unsettled legal questions that are important to other patents or applications. While a party may seek post-grant review (or *inter partes* review) or instead opt to sue in district court, neither PTO proceeding may be instituted by a party that has filed a declaratory judgment action challenging the validity of the patent in court.

Post-grant reviews are adjudicated by three-judge panels of the new Patent Trial and Appeal Board (PTAB), which replaces the Board of Patent Appeals and Interferences within the PTO. The refusal to open a proceeding is not appealable. Both post-grant review and *inter partes* review use a preponderance of evidence standard and permit limited discovery with poorly defined boundaries. In post-grant review the parties can take discovery that is limited to evidence directly related to factual assertions advanced by either party, whereas discovery in *inter partes* review includes depositions of witnesses submitting affidavits or declarations, as well as what is "otherwise necessary in the interest of justice" (AIA, § 6).

The new materiality standard established in *Therasense* may affect inequitable conduct allegations that a patent challenger contemplates asserting in an infringement action filed after a post-grant review (or *inter partes* review). For example, a post-grant review that succeeds in invalidating some but not all claims may be used to prove the materiality of a reference that a patentee failed to cite in the original prosecution of her patent (Walters & Verkuil, 2012). How often will this occur? Post-grant review presents the potential to shift numerous patent validity disputes from the federal courts to the PTO, given the opportunity to challenge a patent based on any invalidity theory, a lower standard of proof and the absence of any presumption of validity. But post-grant review is unlikely to be widely used, given the high cost of analyzing potential threats from thousands of patents. More likely, such review will be used in targeted fashion by companies focusing on emerging patent portfolios of strategic competitors. The nine-month window for seeking post-grant review also is likely to restrict the use of review as a non-litigation option, particularly for accused infringers, insofar as opportunities for such review can be avoided by asserting patent rights following the expiration of the window (Bui, 2011).

Perhaps the greatest disincentive to frequent use of post-grant review may be provided by its robust estoppel effect. If the post-grant review results in a final written decision by the PTAB that is adverse to the petitioner, she is estopped from asserting invalidity before the PTO, International Trade Commission, or in a federal court on any basis that was raised or reasonably could have been raised during the review that led to the final decision. This differs considerably from the estoppel effect attaching to *inter partes* reexamination pre-AIA, which followed exhaustion of all appeals. Under the AIA estoppel is attainable within 12 to 18 months, in contrast to the roughly six years an appeal from an *inter partes* reexamination took to navigate the PTO and obtain a final decision from the Federal Circuit (Signore, Kunin & Parthum, 2012).

The AIA's robust estoppel effect also is present in *inter partes* review, but it could be particularly costly in post-grant review where the grounds on which a petitioner may assert invalidity are unrestricted and there is no exemption from the scope of estoppel for newly discovered prior art. The lack of restriction offers significant opportunities to find that a basis for invalidity either was raised or reasonably could have been raised, thereby triggering the estoppel effect.

As discussed below, the AIA's new supplemental examination procedure offers a major opportunity for patentees to prevent prior art references or other information from being used as the basis for subsequent allegations of inequitable conduct. This opportunity makes it likely that patent owners will seek supplemental examination of patents for prior art references cited in post-grant or *inter partes* review, in order to immunize the patents from exposure to later charges of inequitable conduct if that information was used by the PTAB to invalidate (Walters & Verkuil, 2012).

3. *Inter partes* review

The AIA's new *inter partes* reviews will permit few if any occasions to assert an inequitable conduct defense. *Inter partes* review replaces *inter partes* reexamination and applies to all issued patents—not merely those patents issued on or after 29 November 1999, as in the case of *inter partes* reexamination. There are other important differences between the two procedures. *Inter partes* review allows the patentee to respond to the petition and explain why the review should not proceed, whereas in *inter partes* reexamination a response by the patentee was only allowed after the examiner instituted reexamination. Further, unlike *inter partes* reexamination, a petition for *inter partes* review may only be filed after the later of the termination of a post-grant review or nine months following issuance or re-issuance of the patent. *Inter partes* review thus is available to requesters seeking to challenge the validity of a patent after the nine-month window for filing post-grant review has closed (AIA, § 6(a)).

Inter partes review introduces a new standard to commence review that replaces the former "substantial new question of patentability" standard. This standard also differs from the new test applicable in post-grant reviews. The presentation of a novel or unsettled legal question is not a valid ground for granting *inter partes* review. Rather, the petitioner must show that the information presented in her petition, together with any response from the patentee, establishes that there is a reasonable likelihood that the petitioner would prevail with respect to at least one of the claims challenged in the petition. Another difference between *inter partes* review and post-grant review is that in the former, a patent may only be challenged on the ground that it lacks novelty in violation of 35 USC § 102 or that it was obvious in violation of 35 USC § 103 (AIA, § 6).

The refusal to open an *inter partes* review is not appealable. *Inter partes* reviews are adjudicated by three-judge panels of the new PTAB. Their decisions are appealable directly to the Federal Circuit. Prior to enactment of the AIA, litigation did not preclude *inter partes* reexamination and, absent a discretionary stay, the proceedings could advance in tandem. *Inter partes* reexaminations were used by parties to create a record to bolster their positions in ongoing litigation. For example, litigants would use the process to support an inequitable conduct defense (Davidson, 2011). The situation is different now. It will be more difficult to obtain *inter partes* review than it was to obtain *inter partes* reexamination pre-AIA, because the standard for obtaining review has been raised. The prior standard of "substantial new question of patentability" was met in 95 percent of *inter partes* reexamination requests. The new standard should yield a lower percentage.

Moreover, *inter partes* review is unavailable where there is litigation concerning the patent and either more than one year has passed since the petitioner was served with the patent infringement complaint or the petitioner filed a civil action challenging the validity of a claim of the patent before filing the petition for *inter partes* review (Iancu & Haber, 2011). As noted, *inter partes* reexamination was rare pre-AIA. *Inter partes* review is apt to be even rarer, thus further restricting the option to litigants to bolster their inequitable conduct defenses.

4. Supplemental examination

The AIA's new supplemental examination procedures are quite likely to restrict the inequitable conduct defense as well. Under the new procedures, a patent owner may request supplemental examination of a patent any time after its issuance to consider, reconsider or correct information believed to be relevant to the patent. The new procedure took effect in September 2012, applies to any patent issued before, on or after that date, and provides for reexamination if the Director concludes that the reference presented in the request presents a substantial new question of patentability. If he so concludes, then reexamination proceeds primarily according to the current *ex parte* reexamination rules, with a couple of differences. The most important difference is that the current restriction limiting *ex parte* reexaminations to consideration of prior art patents and printed publications is inapplicable in supplemental examinations and "information" is not limited or defined by the AIA. Supplemental examinations can be based on any information believed relevant to the patent. Accordingly, a patent owner can utilize supplemental examinations to call to the attention of the PTO prior art patents and printed publications, as well as non-print prior art and non-prior art information previously held by the Federal Circuit to be material in inequitable conduct cases (Dolak, 2012).

Supplemental examination is not available if allegations of inequitable conduct have been pled with particularity in court proceedings (AIA,

§ 12(a)). If defendant alleges in court that certain conduct constitutes inequitable conduct, the patentee loses the ability to cure the defect through supplemental examination. In general, however, this new post-issuance proceeding will permit a patentee to effectively inoculate a patent against all but the most egregious charges of inequitable conduct, by resubmitting the patent for reexamination based on corrected information. Once that corrected information is considered, the patent cannot later be held unenforceable on the basis of conduct relating to such information. The legislative history of the AIA also indicates that supplemental examination can serve to prevent a patent from subsequently being held invalid (Matal, 2012). The proceeding is available only to patent owners (AIA, § 12(a)), who will be able to cure intentional failures to disclose prior art that would otherwise be grounds for a finding of inequitable conduct. Pursuant to *Therasense*, survival of a patent in a supplemental examination is likely to be perceived as effectively establishing that corrected errors in disclosure were not but-for material and thus not proper grounds for a finding of unenforceability on the basis of inequitable conduct (Golden, 2012).

In order to benefit from supplemental proceedings, a patentee will be required to preempt any allegations by a defendant and postpone any attempt to enforce the patent until the supplemental proceedings conclude. The AIA specifically requires the patentee to seek and conclude the supplemental examination before attempting enforcement (AIA, § 12). Where that occurs, supplemental examinations can be used as free passes by patentees who deceive the PTO. As such, supplemental examinations create a patent amnesty program. Amnesty is created not merely for issued patents. It also is created for any other patent that, if it had been examined in light of information relevant to the patentability of the claimed invention reasonably available during the initial examination, might not have been issued or might have been issued in a much narrower form (Rantanen & Petherbridge, 2011). Post-grant review is unlikely to negate the powerful impact of supplemental examinations, because such examinations are likely to affect a much broader body of patents (Rantanen, Petherbridge & Kesan, 2012).

Likewise, while the potential impact of the amnesty is reduced because the Director may cancel the affected claims and make a confidential referral to the Attorney General for possible prosecution if the Director becomes aware of material fraud on the PTO during the course of a supplemental examination (AIA, § 12), this reduction in impact is liable to be extremely limited. The Director had the power to encourage prosecution of those who engage in material misconduct long before the AIA was enacted, but the power was almost never exercised (Rantanen & Petherbridge, 2011). There is no reason to assume the situation will change following enactment. Moreover, the AIA's legislative history indicates that § 12 was not intended to expand the PTO's investigatory duties, and even if the PTO makes a referral to the Attorney General it must conclude the supplemental examination (Matal, 2012). Finally, insofar as the statute of limitations for the criminal law most likely applicable (18 USC § 1001, which establishes liability for false statements in matters involving the US government) is five years, prosecution for most material misconduct would be time-barred by the time a patent is scrutinized in a supplemental examination or *ex parte* reexamination.

Supplemental examinations are overtly designed to reduce patentees' exposure to inequitable conduct claims (Tran, 2012). The net result is likely to be an increase in the cost of competition, higher barriers to market entry, decreased innovation, lower-quality patents, and a decline in the economic competitiveness of the US (Rantanen & Petherbridge, 2011). In summary, the AIA's added provisions for supplemental examination and post-grant review, together with its modification of *inter partes* review, will substantially constrict the defense of inequitable conduct.

B. Best Mode

Similar to the AIA's post-issuance review provisions, the AIA's new "best mode" provision also will operate to constrain the use of the inequitable conduct defense. At least since the 1800s, US patent law has required an inventor to disclose the best means contemplated by the inventor of carrying out her invention as of the filing date of the patent application (Patent Act of 1952, § 112). This "best mode" requirement has applied to all inventions, beginning with the 1952 Patent Act. Failure to disclose the best mode furnished grounds for rejecting the application in the PTO and for declaring the patent invalid or unenforceable in subsequent litigation (Petherbridge & Rantanen, 2012). The requirement has several justifications, one of which is to ensure that the public is placed on a level playing field with the patentee upon expiration of the patent (*Christianson v. Colt Indus. Operating Corp.*, 1989).

Best mode has endured in the US despite being subject to criticism on several grounds. It has been argued that best mode has failed to level the field because it is subjective—only the best mode contemplated by the inventor must be disclosed, even if the best mode, in an objective sense, is not revealed to the public (Vacca, 2011–12). Best mode also fails to meet its goal because the rapid pace of technological change may negate the best mode before the patent term ends. It also has been argued that best mode increases litigation costs while providing modest benefits, and, because the rule is unique to the US, it places at a disadvantage foreign applicants who apply for patents in their home countries and then must amend their US applications to comply with the best mode requirement (National Research Council, 2004; Chisum, 1997).

The AIA did not substantively change the best mode requirement (except insofar as the requirement now encompasses the best mode contemplated by the inventor *or joint inventor*), but it did amend 35 USC § 282 to eliminate failure to disclose the best mode as a ground for asserting invalidity of the patent, unenforceability or cancellation of any or all claims in a patent. Thus, under the AIA, patent applicants must disclose the best mode to receive a patent. Nevertheless, if a patent is obtained despite a failure to so disclose, no challenge to the patent rights can be made based on such a failure. The prohibition on invalidating a patent claim for failure to disclose best mode encompasses *ex parte* reexamination and post-grant review.

It is not completely clear whether inequitable conduct based on intentional concealment of the best mode remains a viable defense in civil litigation. Nothing in the AIA explicitly excludes such a defense in litigation. Indeed, whereas the AIA only excludes failure to disclose the best mode as a direct basis for invalidity or unenforceability, defendants generally did not assert such a failure in pre-AIA litigation. Rather, they asserted inequitable conduct before the PTO as the direct basis for a finding of unenforceability. But such a distinction is unlikely to prevail, because the AIA does not distinguish between direct and indirect bases for validity and unenforceability. Moreover, Congress, when it enacted the AIA, was aware that best mode violations were frequently styled as inequitable conduct claims, and this probably explains why the AIA excludes failure to disclose the best mode as a basis for both invalidity and unenforceability (Vacca, 2011–12). In short, the failure to disclose best mode most likely has been eliminated as a defense in both PTO proceedings and civil litigation.

Prior to enactment of the AIA, best mode was not a primary defense and it was rarely successful (*Bayer AG v. Schein Pharms.*, 2002). Now it has been eliminated as a defense altogether. While the best mode requirement has been nominally retained, it has been rendered meaningless in any proceeding in which the issue of compliance with the requirement might arise (Armitage, 2012). This aspect of the AIA may create an incentive for inventors to actively conceal the best mode (Villasenor, 2011), as long as the risk of detection by the PTO is sufficiently low. In fact, the risk of detection by the PTO is virtually nonexistent, because the patent examiner will almost never have evidence sufficient to permit her to conclude that the inventor, at the time of filing the application, knew of a better mode of practicing the claimed invention (Vacca, 2011–12).

The effective elimination of best mode and its concomitant constriction of the inequitable conduct defense undermine the quid pro quo basis of patent law, which is that the patent applicant should play fair and square with the patent system. It is unfair if the applicant can receive from the public the right to exclude, while at the same time maintaining part of the invention as a trade secret by concealing from the public the preferred embodiment of the invention (*Amgen, Inc. v. Chugai Pharm. Co.*, 1991; *Wahl Instruments, Inc. v. Acvious, Inc.*, 1991). In short, the AIA limits the inequitable conduct defense at cross-purposes with fundamental objectives of the US patent system.

IV. CONCLUSION

Through a combination of judicial and political action, *Therasense* and the AIA appear to have unduly narrowed the inequitable conduct defense. The Federal Circuit limited the defense explicitly and in substance by restricting its elements and establishing a more lenient disclosure obligation. Congress constrained the defense implicitly and largely through procedures. In addition to the removal of best mode violations as a basis for inequitable conduct, the AIA's provisions for post-issuance review provide patentees with a safe harbor from allegations of inequitable conduct while estopping patent challengers from asserting the defense. As further detailed in this chapter, the restrictions imposed collectively by *Therasense* and the AIA will tend to undermine the purposes of patent law. At a minimum, the undue contraction of the inequitable conduct defense will minimize the incentive for patent applicants to make full and early disclosure to the overall detriment of the US patent system.

NOTE

* The authors thank Lynda Oswald and Dan Cahoy for the invitation to present the research for this chapter at the Patent Law Scholars Colloquium 2012, hosted by the University of Michigan Stephen M. Ross School of Business and the Penn State University Smeal College of Business, and to the other participants for helpful comments. Special thanks to John Calvert, Senior Advisor, Office of Innovation Development, at the US Patent & Trademark Office, for his participation and contribution. Copyright 2013, T. Leigh Anenson and Gideon Mark.

REFERENCES

America Invents Act, Pub. L. No. 112-29, 125 Stat. 284 (2011) (codified in scattered sections of 35 USC).

American Calcar, Inc. v. American Honda Motor Co., 651 F.3d 1318 (Fed. Cir. 2011).

American Hoist & Derrick Co. v. Sowa & Sons, Inc., 725 F.2d 1350 (Fed. Cir. 1984).

Amgen, Inc. v. Chugai Pharm. Co., 927 F.2d 1200 (Fed. Cir. 1991).

Armitage, R. A. (2012). Understanding the America Invents Act and its Implications for Patenting. *AIPLA Q.J.*, **40**(1), 1–133.

Auth, D. & Rockman, J.M. (Aug. 16, 2010). Federal Circuit Considers Inequitable Conduct En Banc, *New York Law Journal*.

Aventis Pharma S.A. v. Hospira, Inc., 2012 WL 1155716 (Fed. Cir. Apr. 9, 2012).

Bayer AG v. Schein Pharms., 301 F.3d 1306 (Fed. Cir. 2002).

Bayer Cropscience AG v. Dow Agrosciences LLC, 2012 WL 1253047 (D. Del. Apr. 12, 2012).

Bilski v. Kappos, 130 S. Ct. 3218 (2010).

Blum, S. (2012). Note, Ex Parte Reexamination: A Wolf in Sheep's Clothing. *Ohio St. L.J.*, **73**(2), 395–435.

Brown, B. (2009). Comment, Inequitable Conduct: A Standard in Motion. *Fordham Intell. Prop. Media & Ent. L.J.*, **19**(Winter), 593–628.

Bui, H.H. (2011). An Overview of Patent Reform Act of 2011: Navigating the Leahy-Smith America Invents Act Including Effective Dates for Patent Reform. *J. Pat. & Trademark Off. Soc'y*, **93**(4), 441.

Carrier, M.A. (2011). Post-Grant Opposition: A Proposal and a Comparison to the America Invents Act. *U.C. Davis L. Rev.*, **45**(Nov.), 103–35.

Chisum, D.S. (1997). Best Mode Concealment and Inequitable Conduct in Patent Procurement: A Nutshell, a Review of Recent Federal Circuit Cases and a Plea for Modest Reform. *Santa Clara Computer & High Tech. L.J.*, **13**(May), 277–319.

Christianson v. Colt Indus. Operating Corp., 870 F.2d 1292 (7th Cir. 1989).

Committee Position Paper (1988). The Doctrine of Inequitable Conduct and the Duty of Candor in Patent Prosecution: Its Current Adverse Impact on the Operation of the United States Patent System. *AIPLA Q.J.*, **16**(1), 74–87.

Cotropia, C.A. (2009). Modernizing Patent Law's Inequitable Conduct Doctrine. *Berkeley Tech. L.J.*, **24**(Spring), 723–83.

Cotter, T.F. (2011). An Economic Analysis of Patent Law's Inequitable Conduct Doctrine. *Ariz. L. Rev.*, **53**(Fall), 735–79.

Daniel, B.D. (2008). Heightened Standards of Proof in Patent Infringement Litigation: A Critique. *AIPLA Q.J.*, **36**(4), 369–417.

Davidson, B.M. (2011). Reexamining Reexaminations. *Los Angeles Lawyer*, **34**(December), 26–31.

Dayco Prods., Inc. v. Total Containment, Inc., 329 F.3d 1358 (Fed. Cir. 2003).

Digital Control, Inc. v. Charles Mach. Works, 437 F.3d 1309 (Fed. Cir. 2006).

Dolak, L.A. (2012). America Invents the Supplemental Examination, but Retains the Duty of Candor: Questions and Implications. *Akron Intell. Prop. J.*, **6**.

Driscoll v. Cebalo, 731 F.2d 878 (Fed. Cir. 1984).

eBay, Inc. v. MercExchange, L.L.C., 547 US 388 (2006).

Eckes v. Card Prices Update, 736 F.2d 859 (2d Cir. 1984).

Exergen Corp. v. Wal-Mart Stores, Inc., 575 F.3d 1312 (Fed. Cir. 2009).

Golden, J.M. (2012). Patent Law's Falstaff: Inequitable Conduct, the Federal Circuit, and *Therasense*. *Wash. J. L. Tech. & Arts*, **7**(Spring), 353–78.

Goldman, R.J. (1993). Evolution of the Inequitable Conduct Defense in Patent Litigation. *Harv. J.L. & Tech.*, **7**(Fall), 37–99.

Gordon, G.G. & Stack, S.A. (2011). Aligning Antitrust and Patent Law: Side Effects from the Federal Circuit's Cure for the Inequitable Conduct "Plague" in *Therasense*. *Antitrust*, **26**(1), 88–93.

Gugliuzza, P.R. (2012). Rethinking Federal Circuit Jurisdiction. *Geo. L.J.*, **100**(June), 1437–1505.

Hazel-Atlas Glass Co. v. Hartford Empire Co., 322 US 238 (1944).

Iancu, A. & Haber, B. (2011). Post-issuance Proceedings in the America Invents Act. *J. Pat. & Trademark Off. Soc'y*, **93**, 476.

In re Bose Corp., 580 F.3d 1240 (Fed. Cir. 2009).

In re Seagate Technology, LLC, 497 F.3d 1360 (Fed. Cir. 2007).

Irving, T.L., Stevens, L.L., Lee, S.M.K. & Simpson, A.N. (2010). The Evolution of Intent: A Review of Patent Law Cases Invoking the Doctrine of Inequitable Conduct from Precision to Exergen. *U. Dayton L. Rev.*, **35**(Spring), 303–27.

Janis, M.D. (1997). Rethinking Reexamination: Toward a Viable Administrative Revocation System for U.S. Patent Laws. *Harv. J.L. & Tech.*, **11**(Fall), 1–122.

J.P. Stevens & Co. v. Lex Tex Ltd., 747 F.2d 1553 (Fed. Cir. 1984).

Kass, L.T. & Broward, N.T. (June 6, 2011). 'Therasense': Vaccine for a Plague, *National Law Journal*.

Keystone Driller Co. v. Gen. Excavator Co., 290 US 244 (1933).

Kingsdown Medical Consultants, Ltd. v. Hollister, Inc., 863 F.2d 867 (Fed. Cir. 1988) (en banc).

KSR Int'l Co. v. Teleflex Inc., 550 US 398 (2007).

Mack, K. (2006). Note, Reforming Inequitable Conduct to Improve Patent Quality: Cleansing Unclean Hands. *Berkeley Tech. L.J.*, **21**, 147–75.

Mammen, C.E. (2009). Controlling the "Plague": Reforming the Doctrine of Inequitable Conduct. *Berkeley Tech. L.J.*, **24**(Fall), 1329–97.

Masur, J. (2011). Patent Inflation. *Yale L.J.*, **121**(Dec.), 470–532.

Matal, J. (2011–12). A Guide to the Legislative History of the America Invents Act: Part I of II. *Fed. Cir. B.J.* **21**, 435–513.

Matal, J. (2012). A Guide to the Legislative History of the America Invents Act: Part II of II. *Fed. Cir. B.J.*, **21**, 539–653.

MedImmune, Inc. v. Genentech, Inc., 549 US 118 (2007).

Microsoft Corp. v. AT&T Corp., 550 US 437 (2007).

Microsoft Corp. v. i4i Ltd. Partnership. 131 S. Ct. 2238 (2011).

Milliman-Jarvis, D. (2012). The State of Ethical Duties after *Therasense*. *Geo. J. Legal Ethics*, **25**(Summer), 695–713.

National Research Council of the National Academies (2004). *A Patent System for the 21st Century* (Merrill, S.A. et al. eds.).

Nimmer, M.B. & Nimmer, D. (rev. ed. 2010). *Nimmer on Copyright*. New York: Matthew Bender & Co.

O'Connor, S.M. (2010). Defusing the "Atomic Bomb" of Patent Litigation: Avoiding and Defending Against Allegations of Inequitable Conduct after McKesson et al. *J. Marshall Rev. Intell. Prop. L.*, **9**(Winter), 330–97.

Patent Act of 1952, Pub. L. No. 593, 66 Stat. 792.

Patent Act of 1836, ch. 357, 5 Stat. 117.

Peng, Z., Lewis, S., Herzfeld, D., MacAlpine, J. & Irving, T. (2011). A Panacea for Inequitable Conduct Problems or *Kingsdown* Version 2.0? The *Therasense* Decision and a Look into the Future of U.S. Patent Law Reform. *Va. J.L. & Tech.*, **16**(Fall), 373–99.

Petherbridge, L. & Rantanen, J. (2012). The Pseudo-Elimination of Best Mode: Worst Possible Choice? *UCLA L. Rev. Discourse*, **59**, 170–77.

Petherbridge, L., Rantanen, J. & Mojibi, A. (2011). The Federal Circuit and Inequitable Conduct: An Empirical Assessment. *S. Cal. L. Rev.*, **84**(Sept.), 1293–1352.

Pfaff v. Wells Elecs., Inc., 525 U.S. 55 (1998).

Precision Instrument Mfg. Co. v. Auto. Maint. Mach. Co., 324 U.S. 806 (1945).

Qualters, S. (2011, May 26). 'Therasense' a Strong Candidate for High Court Review, Patent Lawyers Say; Decision Raising the Bar for Inequitable Conduct Defense Departs from Position of PTO, DOJ, *Nat'l Law Journal*.

Rai, A.K. (2011). Who's Afraid of the Federal Circuit?. *Yale L.J. Online*, **121**, 335–45.

Rantanen, J. & Petherbridge, L. (2011). Toward a System of Invention Registration: the Leahy-Smith America Invents Act, *Mich. L. Rev. First Impressions*, **110**(Nov.), 24–32.

Rantanen, J. & Petherbridge, L. (2011–12). *Therasense v. Becton Dickinson*: A First Impression. *Yale J.L. & Tech.*, **14**, 226.

Rantanen, J., Petherbridge, L. & Kesan, J.P. (2012). America Invents, More or Less? *U. Pa. L. Rev. PENNumbra*, **160**, 229.

Restatement (Second) of Torts §§ 538, 546 (1977).

Revision of the Materiality to Patentability Standard for the Duty to Disclose Information in Patent Applications (2011, July 21). 76 Fed. Reg. 43,631.

SAP America, Inc. v. Purple Leaf, LLC, 2012 WL 2237995 (N.D. Cal. June 15, 2012).

Scheinfeld, R.C. & Bagley, P.H. (2011, July 27). Inequitable Conductors: All Aboard the 'Therasense' Train, *New York Law Journal*.

Signore, P., Kunin, S. & Parthum, J. (2012). Practice Implications of the Leahy-Smith America Invents Act, *in* Westlaw Journal Expert Commentary Series, Patents in the 21st Century: The Leahy-Smith America Invents Act, 1–41.

Therasense, Inc. v. Becton, Dickinson & Co., 649 F.3d 1276 (Fed. Cir. 2011) (en banc).

Therasense, Inc. v. Becton, Dickinson & Co., 2012 WL 1038715 (N.D. Cal. Mar. 27, 2012).

Thurlow, P.G. & Elbert, M. (2011, Nov. 16). Inequitable Conduct: Analysis of Post-Therasense Decisions and the Supplemental Examination Provision of the America Invents Act. *Bloomberg Law Reports – Intellectual Property*, **5**(48).

Tran, S. (2012). Patent Powers. *Harv. J.L. & Tech.*, **25**(Spring), 595–647.

TSC Indus., Inc. v. Northway, Inc., 426 U.S. 438 (1976).

USPTO (2004). Report to Congress on Inter Partes Reexamination, retrieved from http://www.uspto.gov/web/offices/dcom/olia/reports/reexam_report.htm.

USPTO (2011a). Ex Parte Reexamination Filing Data – Sept. 30, 2011, retrieved from http://www.uspto.gov/patents/EP_quarterly_report_Sept_2011.pdf.

USPTO (2011b). Inter Partes Reexamination Filing Data – Sept. 30, 2011, retrieved from http://www.uspto.gov/patents/IP_quarterly_report_September_2011.pdf.

USPTO (2012a, Jan. 3). Performance & Accountability Rep. FY2011, Fig. 8, retrieved from http://www.uspto.gov/about/stratplan/ar/2011/index.jsp.

USPTO (2012b, Jan. 6). Changes to Implement the Inventor's Oath or Declaration Provisions of the Leahy-Smith America Invents Act; Proposed Rules, 77 Fed. Reg. 982.

Vacca, R. (2011–12b). Patent Reform and Best Mode: A Signal to the Patent Office or a Step Toward Elimination? *Alb. L. Rev.*, **75**, 279–304.

Villasenor, J. (2011). The Comprehensive Patent Reform of 2011: Navigating the Leahy-Smith America Invents Act. *Brookings Policy Brief*, **184**(September), 1–8.

Wahl Instruments, Inc. v. Acvious, Inc., 950 F.2d 1575 (Fed. Cir. 1991).

Walters, E.S. & Verkuil, C.R. (2012). Patent Litigation Strategy: The Impact of the America Invents Act and the New Post-Grant Patent Procedures, retrieved from http://www.mofo.com/files/Uploads/Images/120307-Patent-Litigation-Strategy .pdf.

Wyatt, E. (2011, Sept. 9). Fighting Backlog in Patents, Senate Approves Overhaul, *New York Times*, p. B4.

5. The patenting of a profession— accounting in the crosshairs

Wade M. Chumney, David L. Baumer and Roby B. Sawyers*

Patents have the potential to constrain professionals in the exercise of autonomous responsibility in their practices. Furthermore, the ability of a profession to serve the public good may also be affected by patenting, which could alter the willingness of professionals to disseminate and put into practice new learning. (Thomas, 1999, p. 1176)

While the argument that patents may constrain professionals by infringing on the ability of practitioners to serve their clients is not new, concern over the application of business method patents to the accounting profession is a more recent phenomenon. Concerns raised by the American Institute of CPAs (AICPA) and other groups resulted in proposals to place limits on the patentability of tax strategies. These groups have argued that tax strategy patents preempt Congress's legislative control of the Internal Revenue Code and its interpretations. They also argue that tax strategy patents make it difficult for tax advisors to render advice to clients, potentially increase the costs of tax advice to clients, and may mislead taxpayers into thinking that a patented tax strategy is valid in the eyes of the IRS (AICPA, 2011). Tax strategy patents have been widely discussed in the academic literature as well (Burk & McDonnell, 2007; Beale, 2008; Sawyers, Baumer & Chumney, 2009; Chumney, Baumer & Sawyers, 2009; Aprill, 2010).

Chumney et al. (2009) argued that if the courts validate tax strategy and other business method patents, there are no barriers to the issuance of additional patents that carve out essential chunks of the professions themselves, including the practice of accounting. These concerns have been confirmed in litigation. In January 2006 a patentee alleged infringement of an estate planning technique in which non-qualified stock options were used to fund a grantor-retained annuity trust (*Wealth Transfer Group, L.L.C. v. Rowe*, 2006). More recently, a patent issued to Silicon Economics, Inc. (SEI) led to an action seeking damages and clarification of its ownership interest in its invention by SEI against the Financial Accounting Standards Board (FASB) (*Silicon Economics, Inc. v. Financial Accounting Foundation and Financial Accounting Standards Board*, 2010). Even though SEI did not file an infringement suit against FASB the patent that was issued to SEI by the US Patent and Trademark Office (PTO) claimed exclusive rights to business methods that are at the core of the practice of accounting. In August 2011, SEI's suit against FASB was dismissed for lack of jurisdiction (Justia US Law).

In September 2011, Congress addressed the issuance of tax strategy patents in Section 13 of the America Invents Act, titled "Tax Strategies Deemed Within the Prior Art." This section states: "For purposes of evaluating an invention under section 102 or 103 of title 35, United States Code, any strategy for reducing, avoiding, or deferring tax liability, . . . shall be deemed insufficient to differentiate a claimed invention from the prior art" (Leahy-Smith America Invents Act, 2011). While this legislation prospectively prohibits *new* tax strategy patents, it does not prohibit existing tax strategy patents or other accounting-related patents (or business method patents in general). Likewise, software-related innovations that relate to the preparation of tax filings are still likely patentable (Armon, 2011). The recent US Supreme Court decision in *Bilski v. Kappos* (2010) and subsequent guidance issued by the PTO may provide additional limits on business method patents, but much ambiguity remains. In the meantime, the ongoing proliferation of business method patents threatens to diminish the discretion and authority of accounting practitioners by prohibiting the use of certain methods and procedures that would otherwise be utilized.

In the next section, we provide context for examining accounting-related patents by examining the history of patent law, requirements as to what constitutes patentable subject matter, and the evolution of those requirements culminating in the allowance of business method patents. Following the discussion of context, we discuss and analyze several accounting-related business method patents. After a discussion of the potential consequences associated with the existence of accounting-related patents, we propose a "Learned Profession" defense as a solution to the problems and provide a short conclusion. In the proposal for a Learned Profession defense, we discuss why professions are "different" from other businesses and thus should not be constrained by business method patents. We note that the medical profession has experienced an interface with patent law and the results were significant. Indeed, by passing the Physicians' Immunity Statute in 1996, Congress has barred patent holders from recovering damages against medical professionals for infringing on patents related to medical procedures (Patent Act of 1952, § 287(c)).

I.   THE PATH TO ACCOUNTING-RELATED PATENTS

In order to understand the present situation concerning accounting-related patents, one must first understand the history that led to their existence. Recognition of the need for patent law is longstanding and actually pre-dates the United States government. The power of the federal government to enact legislation to protect inventors is enumerated in Article 1 Section 8 of the Constitution, and Congress passed the first Patent Act in 1790 (Patent Act of 1790). Fundamentally, a patent is a right granted by the federal government to an inventor enabling him or her to exclude others from making, using, selling, or importing the invention within the United States without the inventor's consent. Patents are filed with the PTO and generally last for a term of 20 years from the date of filing (Patent Act of 1952, § 154(a)(2)).

For an invention to receive patent protection it must be novel, useful, and nonobvious. Once a patent is granted, a patent holder may seek injunctive relief and monetary damages against an infringing party. Monetary damages consist of either the patentee's lost profits or royalty-based damages. Additionally, the court has discretion to award up to three times the amount of actual damages if the infringement is determined to be willful (Patent Act of 1952, § 284).

Throughout the last two centuries there has been significant litigation over the issue of what is considered patentable *subject matter*. In the past 30 years, the Supreme Court and the Court of Appeals for the Federal Circuit (CAFC) have issued a number of opinions that have had the effect of radically expanding the scope of what constitutes patentable subject matter. Prior to 1981, inventions that made use of software were routinely denied patents in Supreme Court decisions (*Gottschalk v. Benson*, 1972). However, beginning with the landmark decision *Diamond v. Diehr* (1981), the Supreme Court issued a series of rulings that have effectively expanded the scope of patentable subject matter.

A particularly contentious expansion of patentable subject matter occurred in an area that has often been referred to as "business method" software patents. In *Diamond v. Diehr*, the Supreme Court maintained that a patent should not be issued for computer software that merely solves an equation or algorithm, but when additional steps exist that integrate the algorithm into a particular process, the invention may be patentable. Since *Diamond v. Diehr*, patent law has evolved such that use of software and use of mathematical algorithms are no longer poison pills. The evolution of patent law continued in the 1998 *State Street* case, when the CAFC ruled that the transformation of data through computer software that produces "a useful, concrete and tangible result" is a process that is potentially eligible to be patented. In *State Street*, the patentee owned software that solved various value, cost and tax issues in connection with a web and spoke mutual fund. According to the court, "[t]his investment configuration provides the administrator of a mutual fund with the advantageous combination of economies of scale in administering investments coupled with the tax advantages of a partnership" (*State Street Bank & Trust Co. v. Signature Financial Group, Inc.*, 1998, p. 1370) .

In the wake of *State Street*, courts had to deal with the issue of whether a patented process implemented through software merely solved an equation or algorithm or whether the software could be reduced to "a practical application" that produced "a useful, concrete and tangible result" (*In re Alappat*, 1994, p. 1544).

State Street was a seminal case that created a new category of patents—business method patents. Business method patents have been defined as patents for those methods of processing data and uniquely designed for or used in practicing, administrating, or managing an enterprise; techniques used in athletics, instruction, or personal skill; and any computer-assisted implementations of such methods and techniques (Freed & Reynolds, 2001). Court acceptance of business method patents has laid the foundation for the application and issuance of patents involving accounting-related innovations, a foundation still supported by the Supreme Court. The issue of disallowing business method patents completely was discussed in *Bilski* by both the majority opinion by Justice Kennedy and in a concurring opinion by Justice Stevens. Both rejected the opportunity to eliminate business methods as patentable subject matter, by rejecting the "machine-or-transformation" test as the sole test for determining the patentability of a process (*Bilski v. Kappos*, 2010).

II. ACCOUNTING-RELATED PATENTS

United States Patent and Trademark Office Class 705 includes patents dealing with "apparatus and corresponding methods for performing data processing operations, in which there is a significant change in the data or for performing calculation operations wherein the apparatus or method is uniquely designed for or utilized in the practice, administration, or management of an enterprise, or in the processing of financial data." In 2006, over 10,000 applications were filed for business method patents (categorized as Class 705) by the PTO, and there have been at least 7,400 patent applications filed in this category every year since 2000 (Toupin,

2006). In fact, the number of applications in Class 705 has increased every year since 2002, with 17,231 applications being filed in 2010 (USPTO, 2011).

Presently, accounting-related patents compose only a small fraction of business method patents. Subclass 30 (Accounting) includes 975 issued patents (as of 30 June 2012) based on computerized arrangements for "recording, analyzing, verifying or reporting of funds or other quantitatively innumerable factors used in a business." Although the earliest patent issued in this subclass dates back to 1938, 684 of the patents in this subclass were applied for and issued since January 1, 1999, following the 1998 *State Street* decision.

Although many of the patents in Class 705/30 are innocuous enough, several patents appear to go beyond the invention of "an apparatus and corresponding method(s) for performing data processing operations," to include the patenting of intellectual ideas that had, up to that time, been actively debated in the scholarly and professional literature. In addition to the increase in rate of issuance, it seems clear that some of these patents are not peacefully coexisting with the accounting profession as more and more chunks of the profession are being carved out by inventors of new data manipulations.

Patent Number 7,620,573—Financial Accounting Methods and Systems to Account for Assets and Liabilities

A recent example of this confused interface between patents and professions became apparent through the filing of a lawsuit in May 2010 by Silicon Economics, Inc. (SEI), the holder of Patent No. 7,620,573 (Jameson, 2009) against the Financial Accounting Standards Board (FASB) seeking damages and clarification of its ownership interest in its invention. In November 2009, SEI was granted a patent titled "Financial accounting methods and systems to account for assets and liabilities." According to the lawsuit, "the SEI invention involves an equation derived from the present value equation of finance and credit/debit posting procedures to calculate instantaneous end-of-period asset and liability incomes and windfalls. These incomes, together with operating income, yield more accurate recurring net income measurements, since asset and liability value trends are included, while windfalls are excluded." In the lawsuit, SEI claims that this patent (as well as others the company has received) "significantly improves on existing accounting practices," and that "SEI's EarningsPower Accounting (EPA) provides significantly more accurate financial statements than FASB's Fair-Value Accounting" (*Silicon Economics, Inc. v. Financial Accounting Foundation*, 2011).

In the patent, the inventors argue that financial statements prepared in accordance with Generally Accepted Accounting Principles (GAAP) are deficient and that investors and other interested parties such as lenders dismiss accounting income and look for other measures of performance to evaluate companies. The patent then claims to invent a "going-concern earning-power view of income" that includes, among other things, present value calculations of expected future earnings and probabilistic expectations of future events. Going-concern earning power income includes operating income as well as a new section of the income statement termed "market income," which is the "present value of the mathematically expected appreciation and depreciation of assets and liabilities."

The SEI invention introduces two new types of accounts called "market income" and "market moves" that are associated with each asset and liability. Changes in asset and liability values are posted to the market moves accounts rather than expense and revenue accounts. Liability market income accounts and liability market moves accounts are analogous to expense accounts, while asset market income and asset market moves accounts are analogous to revenue accounts. If an asset value has increased, the asset is debited and the corresponding market moves account is credited. If an asset value has decreased, the asset is credited and the corresponding market moves account is debited. If a liability value has increased, the liability is credited and the corresponding market moves account is debited. If the liability value has decreased, the liability account is debited and the market moves account is credited. The patent goes on to explain how a present value calculation of a multi-year contract could be used to create a new asset with the corresponding credit to a revenue account (if repeatable) or a market moves account (if not repeatable) based on the estimated probability of repetition.

On 17 August 2011 the SEI lawsuit against Financial Accounting Foundation and Financial Accounting Standards Board was dismissed for lack of standing after the plaintiff failed to show actual injury (*Silicon Economics, Inc. v. Financial Accounting Foundation*, 2011). What is troubling about this suit is that the plaintiffs were issued a patent whose subject matter involved theories of accounting, income measurement and economics. Had the suit not been dismissed, both US and international accounting policymakers such as the FASB, the Securities and Exchange Commission (SEC) and the International Accounting Standards Board (IASB) could have been constrained in their ongoing development of a conceptual framework of accounting.

Patent Number 7,302,409—Accounting System for Absorption Costing

Managerial accounting is not immune to the patenting of subject matter, as seen in this patent issued in November 2007 claiming the creation of "an accounting system for an income statement under absorption costing (full costing), with a means for identifying the break-even point in a break-even chart, using a 45-degree line . . ." (Hayashi, 2007). The invention further includes "a means for identifying the individual break-even point for each individual income statement of manufacturing management accounting departments in the company. . . ."

In the patent specification, it is noted that the use of absorption costing has caused difficulties in creating break-even charts and that the invention cures some of the weaknesses in preceding theories with the following original ideas: (1) not using the quantity of goods but the amount of money in the chart; (2) using only sales for the horizontal axis in the chart; and (3) simplifying the chart by confining the two applied manufacturing overheads in beginning and year-end inventories to one parameter called the net carryover manufacturing overhead in inventories.

Again, it appears that the substance of this invention is the creation of break-even charts that are a fundamental tool used in the practice of managerial accounting. Enforcement of this patent against companies and accounting professionals has the potential of reducing the value of accounting information provided by accountants to their CFOs or CEOs. Issuance of a patent for this analysis seems to carve deep inroads into the practice of accounting.

Patent Number 6,311,166—Method for Analyzing Effectiveness of Internal Controls in a Model of an Accounting System

This patent was issued in October 2001 to Price Waterhouse World Firm Services BV (Amsterdam, NL) and claims a "method of assessing control risk in a model-based reasoning system used for analyzing financial accounting systems by decomposing and quantifying the risk factors in the model so that the risk factors can be used to determine the areas in the accounting system where sufficient control is lacking and to determine which controls are key and thus should be subject to detailed testing" (Nado et al., 2001).

The invention suggests that it is "an extremely difficult task to anticipate errors that can occur, to determine subsequent effects and to evaluate the effectiveness of controls for detecting errors." The invention appears to extend a previous model-based reasoning system developed by Price Waterhouse called "Comet" that was used in audits to develop a series of flowcharts used as a platform for the quantitative analysis of control risk.

Analyzing internal controls is a fundamental part of the audit process and Section 404 of the Sarbanes Oxley Act of 2002 requires that each annual report of a company contain: (1) a statement of management's responsibility for establishing and maintaining an adequate internal control structure and procedures for financial reporting; and (2) management's assessment, as of the end of the company's most recent fiscal year, of the effectiveness of the company's internal control structure and procedures for financial reporting. Section 404 also requires the company's auditor to attest to, and report on, management's assessment of the effectiveness of the company's internal controls and procedures for financial reporting in accordance with standards established by the Public Company Accounting Oversight Board. As with the previously discussed patents, this patent appears to limit the methods by which companies and their auditors can analyze the effectiveness of their internal control systems.

Patent Number 6,567,790—Establishing and Managing Grantor Retained Annuity Trusts (GRAT) Funded by Nonqualified Stock Options

US Patent No. 6,567,790, issued on 20 May 2003 (Slane, 2003), describes an estate planning method for minimizing transfer tax liability in connection with the transfer of non-qualified stock options to a family member utilizing a grantor retained annuity trust (GRAT). The creator of Patent No. 6,567,790, Mr. Robert Slane, claimed an invention (called a SOGRAT) that funds a GRAT with stock options. According to its inventors, the method maximizes the transfer of wealth from the grantor of the GRAT to a family member by minimizing the amount of estate and gift tax paid. In a typical GRAT, the grantor establishes and funds an irrevocable trust with appreciated assets and receives a payment of a fixed annuity amount for a specified number of years (which the grantor is expected to outlive). At the end of the term of years, the remaining trust assets pass to the named beneficiaries (typically family members). The key is that the grantor's transfer of property to the GRAT is treated as a gift to the remainder beneficiaries and the value of the gift is discounted equal to the present value of the remainder interest as determined using IRS valuation tables. Sawyers et al. (2009) demonstrate that GRATs were used by tax practitioners for many years before the patent application and that the funding of a GRAT with stock options was not a novel, useful and nonobvious invention. However, this did not stop the holders of the patent from filing a lawsuit in January 2006 alleging the infringement of the technique (*Wealth Transfer Group v. Rowe*, 2006).

Rather than encourage or extend innovation, each of the patents discussed above appear to limit and preempt innovation in various aspects of the accounting profession: (1) financial accounting (determining accurate and relevant measures of net income); (2) managerial accounting (identifying a break-even point for companies utilizing absorption costing); (3) auditing (analyzing the effectiveness of internal controls); and (4) tax (estate planning tools).

On the other hand, inroads into the practice of accountancy made by business method patents have been blunted by Congress and the courts. In the recently enacted America Invents Act, Congress dictated that any strategy for reducing, avoiding, or deferring tax liability is deemed prior art and in two of the four patents discussed above, the plaintiff/patentees either settled or had their infringement claims dismissed. In the Appendix, we describe other recently issued business method patents that appear to intrude into the practice of accounting.

III. ACCOUNTING-RELATED PATENTS AND PATENTABLE SUBJECT MATTER

Whether or not the subject of a patent is patentable subject matter is the first threshold that must be crossed when determining patent validity. Pursuant to Section 101, "[w]hoever invents or discovers any new and useful process, machine, manufacture, or composition of matter, or any new and useful improvement thereof, may obtain a patent therefore, subject to the conditions and requirements of this title" (Patent Act of 1952, § 101). Thus, there are four statutory categories of invention that qualify for patent protection: process, machine, manufacture, or composition of matter. However, in the *State Street* decision, which is the subject of continued debate, the CAFC opined that:

> The question of whether a claim encompasses statutory subject matter should not focus on which of the four categories of subject matter a claim is directed to— process, machine, manufacture, or composition of matter—but rather on the essential characteristics of the subject matter, in particular, its practical utility. (*State Street Bank & Trust Co. v. Signature Financial Group, Inc.*, 1998)

There are three categories of judicial exceptions to patentable subject matter that do not receive patent protection, unless they are directed toward a practical application: abstract ideas (such as mathematical algorithms), natural phenomena, and laws of nature (*Diamond v. Diehr*, 1981; *Gottschalk v. Benson*, 1972).

The Supreme Court in *Diamond v. Diehr* noted that "[t]ransformation and reduction of an article to a different state or thing is the clue to the patentability of a process claim that does not include a particular machine" (*Diamond v. Diehr*, p. 184). This two-prong requirement of *Diehr* may be problematic for accounting-related patents. Accounting-related patents do not appear to have the aforementioned quality of "transformation and reduction of an article to a different state or thing" (*Diamond v. Diehr*, p. 184). It could be argued that what is being transformed in the case of accounting-related patents that utilize computers is simply the allocation of memory on the computer's hard drive. An analogy can be made to using a pencil to transform what is written on a notepad. In *Gottschalk v. Benson*, the Supreme Court found such processes to be unpatentable, noting "[t]he mathematical procedures can be carried out in existing computers long in use, no new machinery being necessary" (*Gottschalk v. Benson*, p. 72). And, as the court noted, they can also be performed without a computer. In describing the unpatentable procedure utilized in *Flook*, the court stated, "[t]he computations can be made by pencil and paper calculations" (*Parker v. Flook*, 1978).

The second prong of the *Diehr* case appears to require that the machine utilized in process patents be a particular machine. To mirror the language found in *Benson*, accounting-related patents "can be carried out in existing computers long in use, no new machinery being necessary" (*Gottschalk v. Benson* at 67, 1972) which is a fatal flaw. Many accounting-related patents utilize only a general purpose computer in their implementation. Consequently, allowing one to obtain a patent on these would arguably have the same effect as allowing one to patent mental processes alone.

Each of the accounting-related patents discussed earlier suffer from the same defect. The US Supreme Court in *Diamond v. Diehr* stated that the "[t]ransformation and reduction of an article to a different state or thing is the clue to the patentability of a process claim that does not include particular machines." None of the accounting-related patents discussed in this chapter result in transformation of an article to a different state and nor are they tied to a particular machine.

These accounting-related patents do, however, produce a "useful, concrete, and tangible" result, which is the criterion elucidated by the CAFC in the *State Street Bank* decision (*State Street Bank & Trust Co. v. Signature Financial Group, Inc.*, 1998). However, in a recent dissent in a patent case that was decided on other grounds, Justice Breyer, joined by Justices Stevens and Souter, explicitly rejected the "tangible, concrete results" criterion:

[T]he Federal Circuit's decision in *State Street* . . . does say that a process is patentable if it produces a "useful, concrete, and tangible result." [citation omitted] But this Court has never made such a statement and, if taken literally, the statement would cover instances where this Court has held to the contrary. The Court, for example, has invalidated a claim to the use of electromagnetic current for transmitting messages over long distances even though it produces a result that seems "useful, concrete, and tangible." [citation omitted] Similarly, the Court has invalidated a patent setting forth a system for triggering alarm limits in connection with catalytic conversion despite a similar utility, concreteness, and tangibility. [citation omitted] And the Court has invalidated a patent setting forth a process that transforms, for computer-programming purposes, decimal figures into binary figures—even though the result would seem useful, concrete, and at least arguably (within the computer's wiring system) tangible. [citation omitted] (*Laboratory Corp. of America Holdings v. Metabolite Laboratories, Inc.*, 2006, pp. 136–37).

These three justices were joined by Justice Kennedy in a concurrence filed in 2006, in which they criticized the "potential vagueness and suspect validity" of some business method patents (*eBay Inc. v. MercExchange, L.L.C.*, 2006, p. 396). It is obvious that the Supreme Court has some interest in reviewing its Section 101 patentable subject matter jurisprudence.

However, prior to its recent decision in *Bilski v. Kappos*, it had been nearly 30 years since the Supreme Court had addressed the issue of patentable subject matter. In this much anticipated May 2010 decision, scholars interested in business method patents were treated to some insights from the Supreme Court as to what is patentable. However, while the "useful, concrete, and tangible result" mantra from *State Street* was rejected, much ambiguity remains (*Bilski v. Kappos*, 2010).

The ambiguity in the *Bilski* opinion was that the Court refused to limit patentable subject matter to whether the process was tied either to: (1) a particular machine or apparatus; or (2) it transforms a particular article into a different state or thing (the "machine or transformation" test). Justice Kennedy was of the opinion that there could be "Information Age" inventions that did not satisfy the "machine or transformation" test but nevertheless should be entitled to patent protection. Kennedy also noted that the dictionary definition of process did not exclude business methods, though he noted that business method patents raise special problems in terms of vagueness. Other safeguards mentioned by Kennedy against profligate issuance of business method patents were strict enforcement of the ban on issuing patents for abstract ideas and making sure business method patents were novel under Section 102 and nonobvious under Section 103 of the Patent Act. Accordingly, while the *Bilski* decision may provide some limits on accounting-related business method patents, it is not clear that they are no longer valid (*Bilski and Warsaw v. Kappos*, 2010).

A. USPTO Standards in the Wake of *Bilski*

Shortly after the *Bilski* opinion was issued, the PTO published "Interim Guidance for Determining Subject Matter Eligibility for Process Claims in view of Bilski and Warsaw v Kappos" (Federal Register/Vol. 75, No. 143/ Tuesday, July 27, 2010). The main thrust of these interim regulations was enthusiastic endorsement of the Supreme Court decision, which the PTO interpreted to mean that the machine or transformation test was the main clue to the patent eligibility of a claim. In particular, the PTO Guidance lists as a factor weighing against patent eligibility claims that are mere statements of a general concept that would effectively grant a monopoly over the concept. The PTO guidance also provides examples of general concepts that are not patentable. The first ineligible category of unpatentable concepts includes, but is not limited to, "basic economic practices and theories (e.g., hedging, insurance, financial transactions, marketing)." This broad exclusion from patentability would seem to include the hedging patent in *Bilski* and the SEI patent, which "involves an equation derived from the present value equation of finance and credit/debit posting procedures to calculate instantaneous end-of-period asset and liability incomes and windfalls." Very recently, the PTO issued additional guidance on the issue of patentable subject matter based on the recent US Supreme Court decision in *Mayo Collaborative Services v. Prometheus Laboratories, Inc.* (2012), which did not contradict *Bilski*. The July 2, 2012, PTO memo entitled "Interim Procedure for Subject Matter Eligibility Analysis of Process Claims Involving Laws of Nature" is technical and complicated, but appears to represent additional efforts of the PTO and US Supreme Court to rein in the scope of patentable subject matter.

IV. POLICY ARGUMENTS AGAINST THE ISSUANCE OF ACCOUNTING-RELATED PATENTS

There are a number of arguments that weigh against the issuance of accounting-related patents.

A. Societal Costs Exceed Benefits

The rationale for patents has always been that innovation benefits society and that less than socially optimal amounts of innovation will likely occur if business rivals can copy expensive innovations made by others. However, societal benefits are less likely for accounting and other business method processes relative to inventions that have historically received patent protection (i.e., technology-based patents), and the costs are likely to be greater. For example, benefits arising from the ability to patent tax strategies must be balanced by the societal costs of sequestering certain tax strategies for the benefit of a few taxpayers. Likewise, any benefits from patenting methods of computing financial accounting income reduce the ability of accounting standard-setting bodies such as the FASB and IASB and the accounting profession more broadly to develop and require a common set of accounting measures and standards to be used by companies in their publicly available financial statements. The case has not been made that the public good is served by patenting these accounting-related strategies and methods.

B.   Patents That Preempt Do Not Encourage Innovation

Although there is legitimate debate about refining and improving accounting practices, it is not clear that new methods merit the issuance of patents, thus preventing others from additional experimentation. Innovation in the accounting profession and business in general was occurring long before there were business method patents. Competition for new clients and competition among firms means that accounting professionals have incentives to develop new and innovative strategies to reduce audit costs or develop innovative tax strategies without the protection of a patent.

C.   Increased Costs to Accounting Professionals

If accounting-related business method patents become prevalent, many ordinary client planning and consulting decisions will become complicated by the possible patent implications of the decision, which could add significantly to the cost of doing business. Firms and their employees, in the normal processes of doing business, should not be surprised by the discovery of heretofore unknown patents requiring exhaustive due diligence searches every time they recommend a new accounting method, audit technique or tax strategy.

D.   Diminution of Information Flow

Accounting-related patents are troublesome in that they may interrupt academic and professional debate about accounting issues resulting in a diminution of information flow (Beale, 2008). Presentations and dialogue regarding accounting issues and interpretations of the tax law among professionals and academics at meetings and conferences could be constrained due to concerns over patent infringement or due to concerns that "patent prospectors" might appropriate and patent new ideas being discussed as their own. Additionally, the discourse that normally occurs in accounting journals could be inhibited as accounting professionals and academics might prefer the potential benefits of patent protection of their ideas over the recognition of another publication. The reduction in the flow of information that normally occurs among accounting practitioners could eventually lead to externalities such as limitations in the flow of information to both the public and government officials (Beale, 2008).

E. Public Choice and Rent-seeking

If patents are used to extract payment from users, a type of rent-seeking may result in which unjustified profits are obtained through manipulation of government laws, rules, and practices. Economists have identified many prominent examples of the pejorative term "rent-seeking," which takes place when a barrier to entry erected by government enables incumbent firms to earn extra-normal profits (rents) not dissipated by new entry. A number of rent-seeking examples can be cited, such as producers of agricultural products who convince Congress to erect quotas and tariffs so that they can be protected from global competition. The deleterious effects of rent-seeking come about because the costs are spread across a wide group (generally all of society) but the rents or profits are concentrated among a few (Tollison & Cogleten, 1995). By design of the Framers, inventors who obtain patents are protected from imitation or duplication in order to promote more innovation and, as a result, earn rents for a limited period of time (US Constitution, Article I, § 8). However, where the patented innovation is an accounting method or tax strategy, the societal value of the innovation is questionable.

F. Learned Profession Defense

Even though the case was dismissed, the May 2010 filing of the SEI suit against FASB demonstrates that the challenge to accounting professionals as a result of business method patents is no longer hypothetical or avoidable. Earlier a taxpayer was sued by the owner of an estate tax strategy patent, though the case was settled. Even with the limitations imposed by the Supreme Court in *Bilski* and the new PTO guidelines, there are few conceptual barriers to continued assaults on the practices of various professions through the issuance of business method patents. Furthermore, the fact that such patents exist may have an oppressive effect on professionals, regardless of whether or not litigation takes place. Certainly, the *SEI v. FASB* encounter illustrates that even without an infringement suit *per se*, patents that make claims as to professional practices can create uncertainty and raise the cost of due diligence.

In the medical profession, however, Congress has already intervened and declared that patent infringement lawsuits against medical practitioners for practicing their profession are unenforceable (Patent Act of 1952, § 287 (c)). Historically, patents on medical procedures were rarely granted or enforced in the United States (McCormick, 1994). However, by 1996 as many as 15 medical procedures were patented every week (Yang, 1995). This resulted in the leaders of the medical profession coming forward to restrict patents on medical procedures, on the basis that they threatened innovation (Chartrand, 1995).

> The response of the medical profession may serve as a good predictor of the reaction of other professions that are newcomers to the patent system. . . . Whether business and other professionals will, like physicians, possess the wherewithal to persuade Congress to create particularized patent-free spheres of activity remains to be seen. Few occupations are as well-organized, imbued with a sense of profession and capable of employing the rhetoric of public service as the practice of medicine (Thomas, 1999, p. 1177).

The approach taken by the Physicians' Immunity Statute in 1996 was to shrink liability by barring patent holders from obtaining damages or injunctions against medical practitioners for infringing patents on medical procedures. But this approach has several notable limitations. First, it raises questions regarding compliance with the Agreement on Trade Related Aspects of Intellectual Property (TRIPS). Second, the statute has a narrow reach, due to its: (1) failure to protect processes if they also involve patented drugs, devices, or products; and (2) prospective nature, covering only patents issued after the date of enactment. Finally, determination of the application of the immunity provision is a question of fact that is not resolved on summary judgment; thus, it does not protect the practitioner from the costs associated with preparing a full defense (Aprill, 2012).

The aforementioned limitations associated with the Physicians Immunity Statute support an alternative to the limited liability approach in order to adequately protect professionals. The authors contend that there is a fundamental distinction between a patentable invention and professional innovation. Although there is no uniform definition of a profession, Kritzer (1999) makes a distinction between three different definitions of a profession: the lay, historical, and sociological. The lay definition is very broad and is generally used to make a distinction from an amateur. It is used to describe almost any means of livelihood as long as they are committed to a set of standards of performance. This conception is very broad. The historical definition focuses upon trained expertise and selection by merit. This view corresponds with the dictionary definition: Webster's New World Dictionary (1979) defines a profession as a "vocation or occupation requiring advanced education and training, involving intellectual skills, as medicine, law, theology, engineering, teaching, etc." Neither of these two views establishes a narrow enough definition for our purposes.

Kritzer's (1999) third view, the sociological definition, takes the perspective of the various stages of economic development. Its understating of a professional is that of specific occupational groups that are at a minimum defined as "exclusive occupational groups applying somewhat abstract knowledge to particular cases" (Abbott, 1988, p. 8). Additionally, professions add the notions of altruism, regulatory autonomy through peer review processes, and autonomy via the service recipient (Kritzer, 1999). Furthering this concept of profession, Millerson (1964) lists six essential features of a profession: (1) a profession involves a skill based on theoretical knowledge; (2) the skill requires training and education; (3) the professional must demonstrate competency by passing a test; (4) integrity is maintained by adherence to a code of conduct; (5) the service is for the public good; and (6) the profession is organized. Additionally, in accounting, as in medicine and law, there is a fiduciary relationship between professionals and their clients, which assumes that professionals will place interests of clients above their own, unlike most third party transactions whereas, within limits, each party is not required to look out for the interests of the other party.

Combining these characteristics with their abstract knowledge-based expertise has enabled professions to generally assert claims of independence that other occupational groups have been generally unsuccessful at advancing (Larson, 1977). West (2003, p. 41) focuses on the level of occupational authority recognized by a group and defines a profession as "occupational groups that enjoy largely unchallenged authority in connection with the technical aspects of the services they deliver." "Professions are characterized by an elevated occupational authority, typically involving an exclusive and state-sponsored mandate to provide certain services and define the nature of those services" (West, 2003, p. 64). Accountants exercise a substantial degree of authority within the accounting domain (as do lawyers and doctors), particularly over financial reporting matters and audits of financial statements.

Being in a profession can be considered as having a "license to experiment"—and the post-*State Street* trend in business method patents runs counter to this notion. There should be a clear delineation between development of intellectual skills known by those in a profession, and inventions of a new process, machine, manufacture, or composition of matter. Advancements of portions of a profession are not inventions, but rather the ordinary professional development of intellectual skills and mental steps. As such, they should not qualify as patentable subject matter.

If methods to calculate accounting income, analyze the effectiveness of internal controls, calculate break-even points and reduce estate taxes can be patented, there is effectively no limit to the scope of accounting-related business patents that infringe on the rights of accounting professionals. It is time to implement a "Learned Profession" defense to the validity of business method patents that claim portions of any vocation or occupation that falls within this definition of a profession. Although one legal dispute between the owner of an accounting-related patent and practitioners has been decided favorably for accountants, there are a number of issued patents that claim practices that are fundamental to practice of accounting (see Appendix).

V. CONCLUSION

The growing number of accounting-related business method patents issued since the *State Street* decision threaten the innovation, continual learning and knowledge growth characteristic of the accounting profession. We argue that accounting-related patents have significant costs to society, are not necessary to encourage innovation, result in increased costs to accounting professionals, and result in a potential diminution of information flow. We suspect that accounting-related business method patents may interrupt fruitful academic and professional discourse surrounding the accounting issues and thus limit or preempt innovation. The foundation for business method patents appears to be shrinking as Congress, the Supreme Court, and the PTO have recently acted in ways that limit patentable subject matter. In *Bilski* the Supreme Court was reluctant to limit business process patents to those that were either tied to a particular machine or resulted in transformation of an article to a different state or thing because "Information Age" innovations might be sacrificed. By proposing a Learned Profession defense we are not precluding issuance of patents for Information Age inventions that are not tied to a particular machine or transformation. We are, however, very much concerned about business method patents that unduly burden professionals, especially accountants.

NOTE

*   Copyright 2013, Wade M. Chumney, David L. Baumer and Roby B. Sawyers.

REFERENCES

Abbott, A. (1988). *The System of Professions: An Essay on the Division of Expert Labor*. Chicago: University of Chicago Press.

AICPA (2011). *AICPA Position on Patents for Tax Planning Methods*. Retrieved from http://www.aicpa.org/Advocacy/Issues/DownloadableDocuments/Tax StrategyPatents/Issue_Paper_Tax_Strategy_Patents_111th_Congress.pdf.

Aprill, E.P. (2010). The Supreme Court's Opinions in *Bilski* and the Future of Tax Strategy Patents. *Journal of Taxation*, **113**(2), 81–93.

Aprill, E.P. (2012). The Path to the Tax Patent Prohibition. *Columbia Journal of Tax Law*, **3**(1), 1–3.

Armon, O. (2011). *The Leahy-Smith America Invents Act*. Retrieved from http://www.law.berkeley.edu/files/bclt_New_Patent_Law_Explained_Panel_1-Litigation_Changes.pdf.

Beale, L.M. (2008). Tax Patents: At the Crossroads of Tax and Patent Law. *University of Illinois Journal of Law, Technology and Policy*, **2008**(1), 107–47.

Bilski v. Kappos, 130 S. Ct. 3218 (2010).

Black, F. (1980). The Magic in Earnings: Economic Earnings versus Accounting Earnings. *Financial Analysts Journal*, **36**(6), 19–24.

Burk, D.L. & McDonnell B.H. (2007). Patents, Tax Shelters, and the Firm. *Virginia Tax Review*, **26**, 981–1004.

Chartrand, S. (1995). Why is This Surgeon Suing? *New York Times*, June 8, p. Dl.

Chisum, D. (2004). *Principles of Patent Law*. New York: Foundation Press.

Chumney, W.M., Baumer, D.L. & Sawyers R.B. (2009). Patents Gone Wild: An Ethical Examination and Legal Analysis of Tax-Related and Tax Strategy Patents. *American Business Law Journal*, **46**(3), 343–406.

Diamond v. Diehr, 450 U.S. 175 (1981).

eBay Inc v. MercExchange, L.L.C., 547 U.S. 388 (2006).

Freed, J.M. & Reynolds, T.C. (2001). The New Patent Landscape. *Computer and Internet Law*, **18**(12), 1–8.

Gottschalk v. Benson, 409 U.S. 63 (1972).

Hayashi, Y. (2007). *U.S. Patent No. 7,302,409*. Washington, DC: US Patent and Trademark Office.

In re Alappat, 33 F.3d 1526 (Fed. Cir.1994).

Jameson, J. (2009). *U.S. Patent No. 7,620,573*. Washington, DC: US Patent and Trademark Office.

Justia US Law, at http://law.justia.com/cases/federal/district-courts/california/candce/5:2010cv01939/227209/34

Kritzer, H.M. (1999). The Professions are Dead, Long Live the Professions: Legal Practice in a Postprofessional World. *Law & Society Review*, **33**(3), 713–59.

Laboratory Corp. of America Holdings v. Metabolite Laboratories, Inc. 548 U.S. 124 (2006).

Larson, M.S. (1977). *The Rise of Professionalism: A Sociological Analysis*. Berkeley, CA: University of California Press.

Leahy-Smith America Invents Act, Pub. L. No. 112-29, 125 Stat. 284 (2011) (codified as amended in scattered sections of 35 U.S.C.).

Mayo Collaborative Services v. Prometheus Laboratories, Inc., 566 U.S. ___ (2012).

McCormick, B. (1994). Just Reward or Just Plain Wrong? Specter of Royalties from Method Patents Stirs Debate. *American Medical News*, Sept. 5, p. 3.

Millerson, G. (1964). *The Qualifying Associations: A Study in Professionalization.* London: Routledge and Kegan Paul.

Nado, R.A., Chams, M.M., Delisio, J.L., Hamscher, W.C. & Halliday, R.W. (2001). *U.S. Patent No. 6,311,166.* Washington, DC: US Patent and Trademark Office.

Parker v. Flook, 437 U.S. 584 (1978).

Patent Act of 1790, 1 Stat. 109 (1790).

Patent Act of 1952, 35 U.S.C. §§ 1-376 (1952 (as amended)).

Sawyers, R.B., Baumer, D.L. & Chumney, W. (2009). When Worlds Collide: Applying the Nonobviousness and Novelty Requirements of Patent Law to Tax Strategy Patents. *ATA Journal of Legal Tax Research*, **7**, 1–15.

Silicon Economics, Inc. v. Financial Accounting Foundation and Financial Accounting Standards Board, CV 10-01939, (N.D. Cal. 2010).

Silicon Economics, Inc. v. Financial Accounting Foundation and Financial Accounting Standards Board, Civil Action No. 11-163, (D. Del. 2011).

Slane, R.C. (2003). *U.S. Patent No. 6,567,799.* Washington, DC: US Patent and Trademark Office.

State Street Bank & Trust Co. v. Signature Fin. Group, Inc., 149 F.3d 1368 (Fed. Cir. 1998).

Thomas, J.R. (1999). The Patenting of the Liberal Professions. *Boston College Law Review*, **40**(5), 1139–85.

Tollison, R.D. & Cogleten, R.D. (1995). *The Economic Analysis of Rent Seeking.* Cheltenham, UK: Edward Elgar Publishing.

Toupin, J. (2006). *Hearing on Issues Relating to the Patenting of Tax Advice Before the Subcommittee on Select Revenue Measures of the House Committee on Ways and Means*, 109th Cong. 8 (2006) (statement of James Toupin, General Counsel, US Patent and Trademark Office).

US Constitution, Art. 1 § 8.

US Patent and Trademark Office (2010). Notices, *Federal Register*, **75**(143), July 27, 43922–28.

USPTO (2011). Class 705 Application Filing and Patents Issued Data. Retrieved from http://www.uspto.gov/patents/resources/methods/applicationfiling.jsp. USPTO (2012).

2012 Interim Procedure for Subject Matter Eligibility Analysis of Process Claims Involving Laws of Nature, memorandum from Andrew Hirshfield, Deputy Commissioner from Patent Examination Policy, Retrieved from http://www.uspto.gov/patents/law/exam/2012_interim_guidance.pdf (July 3, 2012).

Wealth Transfer Group L.L.C. v. John W. Rowe, No. 3:06-cv-00024 (D. Conn 2006).

Webster's New World Dictionary: Second College Edition (1979). (2d ed.), Cleveland, OH: Williams Collins Publishers.

West, B.P. (2003). *Professionalism and Accounting Rules.* Routledge New Works in Accounting History. New York: Routledge.

Yang, W.W. (1995). Patent Policy and Medical Procedure Patents: The Case for

Statutory Exclusion from Patentability. *Boston University Journal of Science and Technology*, **5**(1).

APPENDIX

A number of recent patents have been issued that appear to seriously intrude into the practice of accounting.

Patent Number: 8,036,980
Patent Title: Method and system of generating audit procedures and forms
Abstract: The present invention provides a computer-implemented method for assessing risks associated with an audit. A user is presented with a plurality of audit items and a set of risk levels associated with the audit items and may also be presented with a plurality of prompts designed to elicit a set of responses from the user. The set of user responses being associated with a set of risks associated with the audit. The set of risk levels being associated with a set of assertions associated with the audit items and may include first and second risk levels of different degrees. The method further includes processing a set of responses received from the user in response to the items presented. The method includes automatically generating a suggested audit approach that is based at least in part on the processed responses. The method may also determine a set of procedures that are based on the responses. The set of procedures are presented to the user based on the suggested audit approach. The user is presented for selection with a set of audit approaches comprising the suggested audit approach and an alternative audit approach.

Patent Number: 7,925,553
Patent Title: System and method for preparing a tax liability projection
Abstract: A system for tax planning with legislation conformance options comprises one or more processors coupled to a memory. The memory stores instructions executable by the processors to implement a tax planner configured to receive data exported from a tax return preparation tool. The tax planner receives input indicating whether a tax projection to be prepared using the data is to include an impact of specified tax legislation. If the input indicates that the tax projection is to include the impact of the specified legislation, the tax planner is configured to include the impact of the specified legislation in the tax projection without requiring data to be re-exported from the tax return preparation tool. If the input indicates that the tax projection is to exclude the impact of the specified

legislation, the tax planner is configured to prepare the tax projection without including the impact of the specified legislation.

Patent Number: 7,885,867
Patent Title: Enhanced method and computer program product for providing supply chain execution processes in an outsourced manufacturing environment
Abstract: A method and computer program product for facilitating supply chain processes in an outsourced manufacturing environment is provided. The method includes a customer focus team system providing logistical administrative services for a contract manufacturer on behalf of a manufacturing enterprise. The customer focus team is assigned to the contract manufacturer based upon geographic proximity. The logistical administrative services include facilitating transfer and replenishment of components needed during manufacture, ensuring ongoing inventory demand issues are addressed and resolved, and obtaining and providing metrics on outsourced supply chain parts and activities. The logistical administrative services also include assisting the contract manufacturer during shortfalls of supplies, collaborating with commodity team councils relating to acquisition of critical parts, and providing assistance on matters related to import, export, and tax issues. The method also includes a commodity council team assigned to a supplier based upon geographic proximity and providing logistical administrative support services to the supplier.

Patent Number: 7,813,949
Patent Title: Method and system for flexible budgeting in a purchase order system
Abstract: A system and method of budgeting in a purchase order system are disclosed. The method of budgeting includes allocating a budget according to one or more planning levels and selecting or defining one or more keys, each key corresponding to one or more planning levels.

Patent Number: 7,797,183
Patent Title: Method and system for calculating an environmental score for a business unit
Abstract: A method and system for calculating an environmental score are described and generally related to calculating a score for a separately accountable business unit, where the score is indicative of external costs for the business unit. A computer system for calculating a score for a separately accountable business unit, the score being indicative of a level of unaccounted-for external environmental cost of economic activities of

the separately accountable business unit, the system includes accessing means for accessing accounts data indicative of recognized costs for the separately accountable business unit, accounts processing means for processing the accounts data by adding external environmental costs to the recognized costs and for calculating the score for the separately accountable business unit using the processed accounts data.

Patent Number: 7,752,090
Patent Title: System and method for reversing accounting distortions and calculating a true value of a business
Abstract: A method for reversing accounting distortions of financial information, comprising the steps of obtaining a set of financial information regarding an entity, the financial information including accounting distortions and notes detailing said accounting distortions; analyzing the financial information and notes to determine an accurate economic model; and using said accurate economic model to automatically determine the true profitability of an entity and comparatively value a plurality of expectations with respect to the financial information.

Patent Number: 7,716,094
Patent Title: Estimated tax reminder and payment facilitation service
Abstract: An estimated tax reminder system generates and sends reminders to taxpayers of their estimated tax obligations. The system determines the estimated tax obligation for a taxpayer and receives filing status information for the taxpayer reflecting whether or not a payment has been made for the taxpayer. In an embodiment, a computer program product accepts payment instructions for fulfilling estimated tax obligations and carries out the instructions.

Patent Number: 7,711,602
Patent Title: Systems and methods for supply chain management
Abstract: The present invention is directed to systems and methods for supply chain management. An order for one or more products is received from a buyer or a seller. For each product in the received order, a buyer and a seller are determined. In some instances, multiple buyers and/or sellers may be determined. A product shipment configuration and a logistics plan are generated. A transporter is determined. The generated product shipment configuration is transmitted to a buyer, a seller, a transporter or combinations thereof. The generated logistics plan is transmitted to a buyer, a seller, a transporter or combinations thereof. In some embodiments, event data related to the generated logistics plan is received. In some such embodiment, exception reports are generated from

the received event data. These processes, or subsets thereof, can in certain instances be implemented on a system processor in communication with a system data store, or be stored in the form of executable instructions on one or more computer readable media.

Patent Number: 7,693,733
Patent Title: Method of and system for analyzing, modeling and valuing elements of a business enterprise
Abstract: An automated system and method for analyzing, modeling and valuing elements of a business enterprise on a specified valuation date. The performances of the elements are analyzed using search algorithms and induction algorithms to determine the value drivers associated with each element. The induction algorithms are also used to create composite variables that relate element performance to enterprise revenue, expenses and changes in capital. Predictive models are then used to determine the correlation between the value drivers and the enterprise revenue, expenses and changes in capital. The correlation percentages for each value driver are then multiplied by capitalized value of future revenue, expenses and changes in capital, the resulting numbers for each value driver associated with each element are then added together to calculate a value for each element.

Patent Number: 7,624,049
Patent Title: Financial accounting methods and systems to account for assets and liabilities
Abstract: A method to calculate true ex-ante operating income, via a present value calculation and posting in a double-entry bookkeeping framework based upon credits and debits, is disclosed. The ultimate object is a true ex-ante net income accounting measurement that better serves financial statements users.

Patent Number: 7,523,053
Patent Title: Internal audit operations for Sarbanes Oxley compliance
Abstract: A system provides audit opinions on an enterprise's organizations, processes, risks, and risk controls. The system first evaluates the enterprise's set of risk controls. The audit opinions of the set of risk controls are used to evaluate the set of risks associated with the set of risk controls. The audit opinions of the set of risks and of the set of risk controls are in turn used to evaluate the set of processes associated with the set of risks. Finally, all of these audit opinions are used to evaluate the set of organizations associated with the set of processes. The system streamlines the evaluation of risk by determining suggested audit opinions. Suggested audit

opinions for a given item can be determined from audit opinions previously determined and associated with the given item. Rules can be defined for a given item to specify how to determine the suggested audit result.

Patent Number: 7,412,413
Patent Title: Computerized financial services method
Abstract: A method of determining a measure of residual income in relation to a company or investment, comprises first determining the forecast earnings or cash flow stream (E) of the company or investment for at least one time period (t) in the future, and deducting from this a charge (CC) for the mean cost of capital employed. The charge (CC) for the cost of capital employed is based not upon balance-sheet values, but rather upon a value of enterprise value (EV). The value of enterprise value (EV) is determined by adding the value of debt (VOD) and adjustments (ADJ), if any, to the current market capitalization (MC) of the company or investment. A measure (EV+) of residual income (RI) is thereby obtained as EV+=E-CC. A warranted enterprise value can be obtained by summing the present values of the residual income for a plurality of future years, with the present value of the difference between the terminal value and the present enterprise value, and the present enterprise value itself. Various subsidiary metrics can be developed from the residual income measure obtained. Instead of using enterprise value, the market capitalization (MC) can be used. In this case the interest rate used to calculate the cost of capital is the cost of equity capital only, and the cash flow/earnings used are taken after deduction of interest paid.

Patent Number: 6,959,287
Patent Title: Method and system for conducting a target audit in a high volume transaction environment
Abstract: A target audit methodology to provide a transaction-based detail of errors in an environment with a high volume of transactions. The primary components comprise a distributed computer network, such as the global Internet, coupled to numerous databases and a workstation. A Random Sample Query is used to pull a statistically valid sample from a general population of transactions to identify initial transaction errors. The initial transaction errors are analyzed to determine parameters for identifying other similar errors with a high probability of occurrence within the total population of transactions. A Possible Error Query is designed to retrieve these specific error types and is processed against the population of transactions. The results of the Possible Error Query are assigned financial impact and detailed for the client by individual transaction in an invoice.

PART III

Changes to the scope of enforcement and infringement

6. Unexpected hazards of a specialized patent court: lessons from joint infringement doctrine

Lynda J. Oswald*

There are a number of reasons why a legislature might create a specialized court to address the highly technical issues raised by patent law, including fostering uniformity in outcomes, coherent evolution of doctrine and policy, and development of judicial expertise and competency. The US Congress created the US Court of Appeals for the Federal Circuit (Federal Circuit or CAFC) in 1982 with the goal of achieving just these objectives. Unlike the other US federal appellate courts, whose jurisdiction is defined by geography and covers a broad spectrum of federal issues, the Federal Circuit has nationwide jurisdiction over a narrow range of subject matter, including appeals in patent cases.

Critics argue that the creation of this specialized court has had its downside as well, including over-activism and potential capture of the court by the patent bar and its constituencies. However, there is an additional, more subtle, but nonetheless important, risk to a specialized court. Because the Federal Circuit has limited jurisdiction and hears a narrow range of cases, it is much less likely to look at traditional common law doctrines, such as tort and agency law, across numerous dimensions, as would the regional federal courts of appeal with broader jurisdiction. In particular, because the Federal Circuit is not applying traditional common law principles in a variety of settings, its decisions can warp those traditional rules to fit the unique and complex patent law issues before the court. The result is that fundamental common law doctrines can become distorted and ultimately lost and patent law can become distanced from traditional legal doctrine in a manner neither contemplated nor intended by Congress. Patent law can take on a life of its own, divorced from the principles, doctrines, and norms that typically underlie US law.

The Federal Circuit itself has recognized the dangers inherent in a specialized court. Chief Judge Randall Rader, for example, noted in a 2001 speech that while the specialized nature of the Federal Circuit has dramatically increased the pace of common law development of patent law, it has also "retarded [its] development in some important ways," because "there is less percolation, less chance for experimentalism, less chance ... for the 'laboratory of federalism'—various district courts and circuits, each resolving similar issues in the same way and providing the Supreme Court with a prism through which they view the law and choose the best solutions for the future" (Rader, 2001, p. 4).

Although Judge Rader was speaking of the development of the common law of patent, his remarks also resonate within the relationship of patent law to traditional common law doctrines, such as tort and agency. This chapter examines this phenomenon through the lens of joint infringement (also known as "divided infringement").[1] The US Patent Act of 1952 does not address the liability of multiple parties whose collective action is necessary to support direct infringement of a multi-step process or method patent claim. Instead, joint infringement evolved as a common law patent doctrine to address the problem of concerted action by multiple actors to infringe a patent.

The incidence of joint infringement appears to be growing in recent years. Not only have a number of joint infringement cases been presented to the Federal Circuit in recent years, but the complexity of modern supply chains and the multi-step nature of modern inventions (particularly business methods and software) create incentives for actors to divvy up steps of patent infringement in an effort to avoid liability. Moreover, the nature of the patents involved makes it easier for them to do so effectively and economically.

The federal courts have recognized, however, that allowing parties to evade infringement liability merely by divvying up their actions among multiple actors can be grossly unfair to patent rights holders. Thus, the federal courts have stepped into the statutory void, devising a common law cause of action for such instances: joint infringement. The courts' formulation of this common law patent doctrine was initially grounded in direct patent infringement and morphed over time from an agency law standard to a tort-like standard of cooperation or connection (that resembled but was not explicitly based in joint tortfeasor law) and back again to a standard of control or direction that drew heavily upon (but again was not explicitly based in) the original agency law standard. Then, on 31 August 2012, the Federal Circuit issued a 6-5 en banc decision in *Akamai Technologies, Inc. v. Limelight Networks, Inc.* that turned joint infringement doctrine on its head by moving joint infringement out of the direct infringement category and into the indirect infringement category of induced infringement. In doing so, the Federal Circuit cast aside well-settled common law doctrines of patent, tort, and agency in favor of a contorted statutory reading that finds little support in precedent, policy, or theory.

At some level, it seems that the Federal Circuit is acting in an outcome-determinative manner, without giving sufficient thought to the theoretical underpinnings of the legal rules that it is creating and to the manner in which those rules fit into the larger picture of traditional common law principles. Of even more concern, the Federal Circuit is setting policy and law by creating a joint infringement doctrine that is not grounded in either precedent or statutory language. Returning explicitly and openly to the foundations of the tort and agency law doctrines that purportedly underlie joint infringement doctrine would enable the Federal Circuit to articulate liability rules that are more principled, more grounded in traditional US legal doctrine, and more consistent with the overall patent law scheme. The lessons that can be drawn from the joint infringement scenario thus provide important insight into how a specialized patent court should structure its decision-making process to ensure that its patent law decisions are consistent with the underlying legal doctrines of the jurisdiction in which it operates. This chapter opens the conversation on evaluating the relationship of patent law to traditional common law doctrines in the context of joint infringement and lays the foundation for further research that should be done in this area.

I. SETTING THE STAGE: THE FEDERAL CIRCUIT AND PATENT LAW

To understand the complexities of the direct infringement doctrine, one must understand the nature of the Federal Circuit itself and its unique role as a specialized appellate court, as well as the basic structure of US patent law.

A. The Federal Circuit: The Goal of Uniformity

Patent cases begin in the federal district courts. Prior to 1982, appeals of patent cases were taken from the federal district courts to the regional circuit courts of appeal. In addition, appeals from decisions of the US Patent and Trademark Office (PTO) were taken to the Court of Customs and Patent Appeals (CCPA). Because each of the regional circuits can set its own precedents, interpretation of patent law could, and did, vary significantly from circuit to circuit, leading to "forum-shopping" by litigants. Moreover, there was a lack of uniformity between the regional circuits, the CCPA, and the PTO on patent law issues. Although the US Supreme

Court has the authority to resolve circuit "splits" and other differences in interpretation among the various appellate courts, it accepted very few patent cases in this era. Hence, there was no uniform voice speaking on patent law issues.

In 1982, Congress established the Federal Circuit as a specialized appellate court for patent cases, with a stated goal of "increas[ing] doctrinal stability in the field of patent law" (S. Rep. No. 97-275, 1981). Many interested parties at the time hoped that this increased stability would lead to stronger patent law doctrines that in turn would lead to stronger patents themselves (Merges, 1992).

Unlike the regional appellate courts, the Federal Circuit's jurisdiction is based solely on subject matter; geography plays no role. The Federal Circuit has nationwide jurisdiction over specific subject matters, including international trade, government contracts, patents, trademarks, federal personnel, veterans' benefits, and public safety officers' benefit claims. Appeals come to the Federal Circuit from a wide variety of venues, including the federal district courts, other specialized courts, such as the US Court of International Trade, and certain administrative agencies, including the Board of Patent Appeals and Interferences (BPAI) and the Trademark Trial and Appeals Board.[2] Patent cases in particular can come to the Federal Circuit through a multitude of avenues, including from the federal district courts, the BPAI, the Court of Federal Claims, and the International Trade Commission (ITC).

The Federal Circuit can have up to 12 active judges. There is currently one vacancy on the court, so there are 11 active judges and four senior judges.[3] Appeals are generally heard by a panel of three judges, although the Federal Circuit has in recent years chosen to hear a number of cases en banc.

Overall, intellectual property cases accounted for 45 percent, or almost half, of the Federal Circuit's caseload in FY 2011. Trademark appeals were a small sliver, comprising 2 percent of the total caseload. Patent cases were the largest single category; 43 percent of the Federal Circuit's caseload consisted of patent cases originating from the district courts, the PTO, and the ITC. The next largest category of cases pertained to personnel actions and comprised only 20 percent of the total caseload (US Court of Appeals for Federal Circuit, 2011). In short, patents form a large and important segment of the Federal Circuit's workload each year.

Various metrics indicate that indeed the creation of the Federal Circuit has led to a more robust patent system. In the 30 years prior to the creation of the Federal Circuit, the regional circuit courts had affirmed 62 percent of the trial courts' findings of infringement. The Federal Circuit, by contrast, affirmed 90 percent of such findings in its first eight years (Koenig,

1980; Harmon, 1991). Moreover, post-creation of the Federal Circuit, inventors have been more likely to file for patents, and patent holders more likely to litigate to protect their patents. The number of US patent applications by US inventors has grown steadily from 33,890 in 1982 to 108,624 in 2011 (US Patent and Trademark Office, Dec. 2011). In 1981, 831 patent suits were begun in federal court (Administrative Offices of the US Courts, 1981); in 2011, 3,872 such suits were filed (US Courts, 2011, at Table C-2).

Because the creation of a federal appellate court with such limited jurisdiction is a novelty within the US legal system, commentators have watched the court's activities carefully, concerned that the court's specialized jurisdiction would create "an isolated and sterile jurisprudence" (Nard & Duffy, 2007). Commentators have used several different measures for evaluating whether the Federal Circuit has indeed become entrenched and stagnant in its decision-making. Some have approached the issue from the perspective of uniformity, looking specifically at how the court internally has handled issues such as the doctrine of equivalents (Petherbridge, 2009) or claim interpretation (Wagner & Petherbridge, 2004). Cotropia examined the percentages of dissents and en banc reviews that the Federal Circuit engaged in from 1998 to 2009 as compared with select other circuits, finding that the Federal Circuit had the second highest percentage of dissents, but that it engaged in a relatively low number of en banc hearings (Cotropia, 2010). Vacca, by contrast, examined the proportion of patent en bancs (specifically excluding non-patent en bancs) held by the Federal Circuit from 1982–2010 as compared with en banc reviews held by each of the regional circuit courts, and concluded that "the Federal Circuit appears to decide more cases en banc than does any other circuit" (Vacca, 2011). Vacca ultimately concluded that the Federal Circuit uses en banc reviews to mimic the substantive rulemaking of administrative agencies.

The studies thus indicate that the Federal Circuit is indeed "different" from the regional circuit courts, but the extent and significance of that difference is still open to debate. The court's application of traditional common law doctrine in joint infringement cases provides yet another lens for evaluating the efficacy of the court's specialized jurisdiction.

B. US Patent Law: A Brief Background

The current version of the US Patent Act—the Patent Act of 1952, as amended—recognizes four classes of patentable inventions: machines, manufactures, compositions of matter, and processes (Patent Act of 1952, § 101). Most patents will contain multiple claims, only one of which need be violated in order for direct infringement to occur. However, under the "all elements rule," each element of the claim at issue must be found in the equivalent device, either literally or figuratively; i.e., infringement requires that each and every element of a claim be performed. In the first three of the four patent categories listed above, infringement occurs when a single claim is performed by any actor who makes, uses, sells, offers for sale, or imports into the US the patented invention (Patent Act of 1952, § 171(a)).

The fourth category—process patents (which includes method patents)—is where the joint infringement problem arises. Often, a process or method patent claim will contain multiple steps. For example, steps (1), (2), and (3) may all need to be performed in order for the claim to be infringed. If a single party performs all three steps, that party is a direct infringer. Suppose, however, that no single party performs all the steps. Rather, Party A performs step (1); Party B performs step (2); and Party C performs step (3). No single party has infringed the patent claim, yet the combined actions of all three parties result in a making or use of the patented claim. For those three parties to be direct infringers, their actions must somehow be combined into a single act. However, the Patent Act has no specific mechanism for addressing the liability of multiple parties whose collective action is necessary to support infringement of a multi-step process or method patent claim; hence, the judicial creation of joint infringement doctrine.

II. COMMON LAW TORT LIABILITY AND STATUTORY PATENT INFRINGEMENT RULES

Joint infringement is complicated to analyze in part because of the multitude of liability rules wrapped into the notion of patent infringement. US patent law has a statutory basis but much of the legal doctrine in the area arises from court decisions. In particular, patent *infringement* doctrine has both common law and statutory foundations. Although direct and indirect infringement are defined in the Patent Act (as discussed below), traditional tort law doctrine plays an explicit and significant role in fleshing out patent infringement liability.

Joint infringement scenarios typically take one of two forms. First, one party may perform some of the steps of the claim and then arrange, via an implicit or explicit agreement, for another party to complete the necessary steps. Second, the very nature of the claim at issue may require performance by two or more parties, as in *Akamai*, where the combined actions of the accused infringer and its customers were required to implement a method for improved storage of webpage content. Courts have traditionally been reluctant to allow an accused infringer to escape liability merely because it deliberately passed off parts of the claim to other parties to perform. The difficulty, of course, lies in determining when the actions of multiple parties should be combined, and when those actions are too attenuated to allow the various actors to be treated as a single entity for purposes of patent infringement liability.

At its most fundamental level, a patent is a property interest of the patent holder and infringement of the patent is a tortious taking of that property (*Carbice Corp. of Am. v. Am. Patents Dev. Corp.*, 1931). Thus, liability rules underlying general tort and agency law doctrine have informed the rules underlying patent infringement liability generally (and joint patent infringement in particular), at least to the extent that that infringement liability is not set forth in the statutory language.

The analysis is complicated by the proliferation of terms (e.g., "direct," "indirect," "secondary," and "vicarious") in the tort liability field generally and the patent infringement liability field specifically. The vocabulary surrounding these terms is imprecise and often overlapping, and the rules often intertwine in unexpected manners. It is necessary to understand these complex relationships, however, to understand the development and future direction of joint infringement rules, as well as to understand and gauge the role and efficacy of the Federal Circuit as a specialized patent court.

A. Traditional Tort Principles of Liability

General tort law principles recognize, in addition to the direct liability of the actor actually responsible for the wrongdoing, an indirect or secondary liability that can be imposed upon a party who did not directly commit the wrongdoing at issue, but whom the law nonetheless holds liable for the injuries incurred by the plaintiff. Two primary theoretical justifications are offered for such secondary liability: (1) it promotes efficiency (i.e., it provides a mechanism for shifting costs to those in the best position to prevent future harm and to compensate for existing harm); and (2) it satisfies moral imperatives (i.e., those who intend to bring about a harm to another should be held liable even if another party was the direct cause of the harm incurred) (Bartholomew & Tehranian, 2006). Balanced against these justifications for secondary liability is a concern that liability not be imposed on inappropriate parties or in a manner that would impede the stream of lawful commerce (Lemley, 2005).

Under traditional US tort law, secondary liability typically takes the forms of: (1) vicarious liability and (2) contributory liability (Bartholomew & Tehranian, 2006). *Vicarious liability* refers to the situation where a party is held liable for another's wrong "irrespective of [the party's] own participation in that wrong" (Gardner, 2007). Vicarious liability flows from the relationship between the defendant and the wrongdoer. It does not depend upon notions of fault or wrongdoing and most often arises as the result of the defendant's ability to control or direct the actions of the direct wrongdoer (Bartholomew & Tehranian, 2006), such as in a principal-agent relationship (Restatement (Second) of Agency, 1958, § 220(1)).

Contributory liability, on the other hand, implicates notions of fault, intent, or culpability (Bartholomew, 2009). It rests upon evidence that the contributory tortfeasor knowingly assisted the direct tortfeasor in engaging in a tortious act; the net result is that the direct and contributory wrongdoers can be held jointly and severally liable for the wrongdoing.

Both vicarious and contributory liability focus on ways in which to hold a third party secondarily liable for harm created by another. *Joint tortfeasor liability*, by contrast, looks to the direct liability of two or more co-wrongdoers. "Joint tort" and "joint tortfeasors" are difficult concepts to define and the rules in this area are unclear (Prosser et al., 1984, § 46). The leading tort law treatise notes that "[t]he original meaning of a 'joint tort' was that of vicarious liability for concerted action." The "common purpose" and "mutual aid in carrying it out" leads to a "joint enterprise" that renders each involved liable for the whole injury done. The agreement between the parties need not be explicit; rather, "a tacit understanding" between them will suffice, subject to an important caveat: "One who innocently, and carefully, does an act which happens to further the tortious purpose of another is not acting in concert with the other" (Prosser et al., 1984, § 46). These rules have important application in the area of joint infringement, as discussed in Part III below.

B.   Patent Infringement Liability Rules

Patent law has its own vocabulary and taxonomy norms when it comes to liability (and that vocabulary and those norms do not necessarily match those used even in other intellectual property law areas, such as copyright). With the patent law field, the distinction is most often drawn between *direct* and *indirect* infringement liability. Further, the patent statute subdivides indirect liability into two forms: (1) inducement of infringement and (2) contributory infringement.

Although the original US patent statute, the Patent Act of 1790, defined the scope of a patent, it had no specific provision regarding infringement. Rather, the 1790 Act left the parameters of infringement to the judiciary to flesh out and define. It was not until the Patent Act of 1952 was adopted that the statutory definitions of direct and indirect infringement were provided. At that point in time, the common law notion of direct infringement was well developed, and the statutory definition of direct infringement in the 1952 Act was little more than a restatement of existing judicial doctrine on the matter (S. Rep. No. 82-1979, 1952). Indirect patent infringement, by contrast, has continued to evolve over the past six decades through the case law.

1.   Direct patent infringement

Direct patent infringement occurs when an authorized person makes, uses, sells, offers to sell, or imports into the United States a patented invention (Patent Act of 1952, § 271(a)). Direct infringement is a strict liability offense: the infringer need not have had the intent to infringe, nor need the infringer even know of the patent (Oswald, 2003). Independent creation is not a defense to liability. Knowledge and intent become relevant in the direct infringement context only in the remedy phase, where evidence of willful infringement permits a court to award enhanced damages and/or attorneys' fees (Patent Act of 1952, § 284).

2.   Indirect patent infringement

While direct patent infringement is a fairly straightforward matter, the development of indirect infringement liability followed a chaotic path. Notions of indirect infringement initially evolved in the case law, starting in the late 1800s. The courts recognized that if patent infringement liability were limited to direct infringement, parties who were indirectly involved in infringing activities but whose culpability may well exceed that of direct infringers could escape all liability (Adams, 2006). The courts thus fashioned a single category of indirect infringement—*contributory infringement*—which was defined to be "any other activity [other than direct infringement] where, although not technically making, using or selling, the defendant displayed sufficient culpability to be held liable as an infringer" (*Hewlett-Packard, Co. v. Bausch & Lomb, Inc.*, 1990, p. 1469). Interestingly, the courts grounded this new liability in "a theory of joint tortfeasance, wherein one who intentionally caused, or aided and abetted, the commission of a tort by another was jointly and severally liable with the primary tortfeasor" (*Hewlett-Packard Co. v. Bausch & Lomb, Inc.*, 1990, p. 1469). During this early time period, the courts also determined that contributory infringement, as a form of indirect infringement, necessarily hinged upon the existence of direct infringement by another party; without evidence of a direct infringement by a third party, there could be no contributory infringement by a defendant (*Saxe v. Hammond*, 1875).

Initially, common law contributory infringement liability was conceived of narrowly and encompassed only those who did not directly infringe but who nonetheless assisted others in directly infringing by supplying a component part specially adapted to infringement (Adams, 2006). Eventually, a second line of cases emerged that addressed those instances in which the components had non-infringing uses but were used for infringing purposes—and so was born the *inducement of infringement* doctrine (Oswald, 2006).

The Patent Act of 1952 codified both direct and indirect patent infringement notions. The Act formally separated the case law's original notion of a single type of indirect infringement into the two different causes of action that had gradually emerged in the opinions. Today, section 271(b) of the Act addresses inducement of infringement and Section 271(c) addresses contributory infringement.

Under Section 271(c) of the Patent Act, *contributory infringement* embraces the sale of a component or other product that has no substantial noninfringing use. The "classic" example of a contributory infringement arises when a supplier sells a part that is necessary for and used in a patented product or process and that has no other use. Congress viewed contributory infringement as a fairness measure. In codifying this form of liability, legislators noted that contributory infringement is "an expression of both law and morals" because it is intended to prevent one party from benefitting from another's patent while escaping liability (S. Rep. No. 82-1979, 1952).

Inducement of infringement liability is found in Section 271(b) of the Patent Act, which provides: "Whoever actively induces infringement of a patent shall be liable as an infringer." Inducement liability typically arises when a defendant sells an article to another party, who uses it to directly infringe a patent, or when a defendant makes an extraterritorial sale of an item covered by a US patent that is then imported into the United States. Historically, induced infringement, like contributory infringement, required direct infringement by another party. As noted below in Part III, however, the Federal Circuit's recent en banc decision in *Akamai* calls this premise into question.

Unlike direct infringement and contributory infringement, induced infringement has a specific *scienter* requirement found in the statutory language, which applies to those who "actively" induce another to infringe. Even after codification, the federal courts struggled with articulating the intent element necessary to support a finding of inducement of patent infringement. In 2006, the Federal Circuit sat en banc in *DSU Medical Corp. v. JMS Co.* to resolve an intra-circuit split on this issue and held that proof of inducement under § 271(b) requires that the patent holder show "the alleged infringer's actions induced infringing acts *and* that he knew or should have known his actions would induce actual infringements" (*DSU*

Medical Corp. v. JMS Co., 2006). In 2011, the Supreme Court further clarified the standard of knowledge for inducement of infringement in *Global-Tech Appliances, Inc. v. SEB, S.A.*, holding that induced infringement "requires knowledge that the induced acts constitute patent infringement" and that "knowledge" can be demonstrated by the doctrine of willful blindness (*Global-Tech Appliances, Inc. v. SEB, S.A.*, 2011, p. 2068).

Until 31 August 2012, most commentators believed that induced infringement had only a tangential role to play in joint infringement cases, as joint infringement was usually viewed as a form of direct, not indirect, liability. As discussed in Part III below, however, the *Akamai* en banc has moved joint infringement to the realm of induced infringement, creating doctrinal confusion along the way.

III. JOINT INFRINGEMENT

Joint infringement liability is an odd, common law graft onto the statutory patent infringement liability scheme. It occupies a curious space in the taxonomy of patent infringement—a space made even more curious by the *Akamai* en banc decision in August 2012. The Patent Act generally contemplates infringement arising from the actions of a single actor. Moreover, historically, both forms of indirect infringement required direct infringement by another party as a predicate, a requirement that effectively forestalled addressing most joint infringement scenarios as ones of contributory or inducement liability.

The relationship between the alleged participants in the joint infringement is key to understanding their potential liability. On the one hand, the courts have long rejected the notion that an accused infringer could avoid liability merely by deliberately passing over one or more steps of the claimed process or method to a third party. On the other hand, because of the strict liability nature of direct infringement, the courts have looked for some connection—e.g., some sort of cooperative or collusive behavior—between the alleged joint infringers; mere proximity or association between the parties is insufficient. The difficulty, of course, lies in determining where specific behavior lies along the continuum between mere proximity and explicit collusion. Joint infringement cases pose numerous factual scenarios: e.g., (1) one actor may direct or control the actions of another; (2) two or more actors may work together on equal terms with a common objective but without a "mastermind"; or (3) two or more actors may each engage in activities that, when combined, infringe a patent, but do so without intent or knowledge that their combined activities work an infringement. Which of these activities should lead to liability?

These categories of behavior similarly have lent themselves to various formulations of joint infringement "standards" or tests. These formulations have evolved and changed over time, but can be placed into four broad categories: (1) joint infringement based on agency; (2) joint infringement based on cooperation or "some connection"; (3) joint infringement based on "control or direction"; and, most recently, (4) joint infringement as a form of inducement (and hence, an indirect infringement).

The first two categories formed the original bases for joint infringement liability articulated by the federal courts prior to the creation of the Federal Circuit. The third category, the "control or direction" standard, was created by the Federal Circuit and was the leading theory of joint infringement liability prior to the *Akamai* en banc. These categories are simplifications of a very messy set of case decisions, however, and should be viewed with a healthy dose of caution. The courts have not applied these theories clearly and consistently, and the cases do not break down temporally into neat categories; rather, the theories overlap and intertwine, both over time and in terms of analysis.

A. Evolution of Joint Infringement Doctrine

As noted in Part II.B above, Section 271 of the Patent Act of 1952 codified preexisting common law notions of infringement. However, joint infringement did not make it into the statutory scheme of the 1952 Act and so its development must be traced through court opinions. The history of the development of joint infringement doctrine has been discussed in detail by several commentators (e.g., Lemley et al., 2005; Gupta, 2012; Lowrie et al., 2011). Only a brief summary is provided here, with the objective of setting the stage for discussion of the Federal Circuit's recent en banc decision in *Akamai*.

1. Initial joint infringement doctrine: agency law
The *Restatement (Third) of Agency* defines agency as "the fiduciary relationship that arises when one person (a 'principal') manifests assent to another person (an 'agent') that the agent shall act on the principal's behalf and subject to the principal's control, and the agent manifests assent or otherwise consents to so act" (Restatement (Third) of Agency, 2006, § 101). Traditionally, vicarious liability under an agency theory generally implicates some measure of direction or control over the actors actually engaging in the infringing acts, regardless of whether those actors are called employees or independent contractors. An agency relationship arises only where both parties consent to the agent acting on

the principal's behalf and subject to the principal's control. Agency law thus falls under the vicarious tort liability umbrella discussed earlier in Part II.A.

Not surprisingly, early courts turned to the familiar doctrine of agency to address joint infringement scenarios as the doctrine is an easy fit for those instances in which the accused infringer directed another party to complete one or more steps of the claim on its behalf (*Crowell v. Baker Oil Tools, Inc.*, 1944). These courts recognized that an accused infringer should not escape liability merely by placing an agent or independent contractor between it and the infringing acts (*Free Standing Stuffer, Inc. v. Holly Dev. Co.*, 1974). A finding that one of the parties involved acted as an agent of the other created direct infringement liability in the principal, in effect rendering the infringement legally attributable to the actions of a single actor, rather than the combined effect of the actions of multiple actors. This approach enabled the courts to impose joint infringement liability without having to devise new legal doctrine and kept patent doctrine within the familiar confines of traditional common law doctrine.

However, some early courts stretched agency doctrine to reach results they felt were dictated by inherent notions of fairness and equity. In *Mobil Oil Corp. v. W.R. Grace & Co.*, decided in 1973, for example, the trial court found W.R. Grace & Co. liable as a direct infringer where the company performed all but the final heating step of the patented processes and sold the resulting products to its customers, who completed the process. Grace was liable, the court found, because it knew at the time it sold the products to its customers that the final step "would in fact be promptly and fully completed by those customers," and that "in this respect, [Grace], in effect, made each of its customers its agent in completing the infringement step" (*Mobil Oil Corp. v. W.R. Grace & Co.*, 1973, p. 253). *Mobil* was not a true example of agency, however, as Grace did not actually control or direct the customers who completed the final step; it merely provided the means by which the customers could undertake that step.

2.   Joint infringement based on explicit cooperation or "some connection"

The second phase of joint infringement cases imposed liability upon joint defendants where they deliberately divvied up the steps and relied upon each other to perform some of the steps in an effort to avoid infringement liability. Unlike agency theory, however, where the principal directed the actions of the agent, the "some connection" theory contemplated actors that were co-equals. For example, in *Hill v. Amazon*, decided in 2006, the trial court rejected the notion that the plaintiff must show an agency relationship or that the accused joint infringers "worked in concert" and held instead that only "some connection between the parties is required to make out a case of direct infringement of a method claim when one party does not perform all of the steps of the method" (*Hill v. Amazon*, 2006, p. *17). Similarly, in *Faroudja Laboratories, Inc. v. Dwin Electronics*, decided in 1999, the trial court stated that the requisite connection for joint infringement could be shown where the entities "worked in concert with other entities to complete the process of infringement" or were in direct contact (*Faroudja Laboratories, Inc. v. Dwin Electronics*, 1999, p. *17). This standard was adopted by several other lower courts, such as in *Marley Mouldings Ltd. v. Mikron Indus., Inc.*, decided in 2003, where the trial court explained that direct infringement liability was appropriate "because that party, through its connection with the entity performing only part of the process, is in actuality performing the combination of each and every step of the claimed method" (*Marley Mouldings Ltd. v. Mikron Indus., Inc.*, 2003, p. *9).

3. Joint infringement based on "control or direction": the emergence of Federal Circuit doctrine and the revival of vicarious liability doctrine

Initially, joint infringement doctrine developed among the federal trial courts and the regional courts of appeal. The Federal Circuit was not created until 1982 and so, prior to that date, there was no appellate court with specialized patent expertise speaking with a single voice on the complicated issue of joint infringement.

The Federal Circuit's initial forays into joint infringement were restrained. In fact, the early Federal Circuit seemed to actively avoid application of joint infringement theories, even in cases where it was clearly applicable (*Fromson v. Advance Offset Plate, Inc.*, 1983; *Metabolite Labs., Inc. v. Lab. Corp. of Am. Holdings*, 2004). Then, in 2006, the Federal Circuit suggested in dicta in *On Demand Machine Corp. v. Ingram Industries, Inc.* that not only was joint infringement possible, but that the standard was less rigorous than other courts had thought, requiring only a minimal connection (i.e., "participation" but not necessarily "cooperation" between the parties).[4] The following year, however, the Federal Circuit addressed what was to be the first in a rapid series of joint infringement cases, establishing the "control or direction" standard that harkened back to traditional agency theory. Two cases in particular— *BMC Resources v. Paymentech*, decided in 2007, and *Muniauction, Inc. v. Thomson Corp*, decided in 2008—were important in establishing this new standard.

BMC Resources, Inc. v. Paymentech, Inc. was important because it established two key principles: (1) joint infringement rests upon "control or direction" and (2) for a party to be held liable for induced infringement, some other *single entity* must be liable for direct infringement (the "single entity" rule). This latter holding was expressly overruled in the *Akamai* en banc decision in 2012, as discussed below.

BMC Resources involved a patent that claimed a computerized method for processing debit transactions between a merchant and a customer that necessarily involved the participation of several actors: the payee's agent, a debit network, and a financial institution. When BMC sued Paymentech for direct and induced infringement, both parties agreed that actors other than Paymentech (i.e., a debit network and a financial institution) performed at least three steps of the patented process that Paymentech was allegedly infringing.

The *BMC Resources* panel set forth the rule that a party is liable for joint infringement as a direct infringer if it "controlled or directed" the actions of others who performed the other steps of the claim. The panel noted that direct infringement requires performance of *all* steps or elements of the patent claim by a single entity, and that indirect liability exists only when direct liability is shown as a predicate. Although this would seem to create a loophole—a party could escape direct liability by simply leaving it to a third party to carry out one or more of the steps on its behalf and by escaping direct liability also cut off any potential claims of indirect liability—the court cautioned that the law avoids such a perverse result through application of traditional rules of vicarious liability. The court stated, "A party cannot avoid infringement . . . simply by contracting out steps of a patented process to another entity. In those cases, the party in control would be liable for direct infringement. It would be unfair indeed for the mastermind in such situations to escape liability" (*BMC Resources, Inc. v. Paymentech, L.P.*, 2007, p. 1381). The *BMC Resources* court thus seemed to reject the second category of joint infringement liability based upon cooperation or connection in favor of what appeared to more closely resemble an agency-based rule: direction or control. The *BMC* court did not explicitly invoke agency doctrine, however, leaving open the possibility that the Federal Circuit was contemplating a standard similar, but not identical, to agency theory.

The *BMC Resources* court acknowledged the limitations of the control or direction standard that it was articulating. For example, parties could enter into a contract under which neither controlled or directed the other, but nonetheless agreed to divvy up the steps of a patent in order to avoid infringement, acting as co-equals. The court dismissed this potential loophole, however, stating that the risk could be "offset by proper claim drafting" (*BMC Resources, Inc. v. Paymentech, L.P.*, 2007, p. 1381).

In *Muniauction, Inc. v. Thomson Corp.*, decided in 2008, the Federal Circuit fleshed out slightly the "control or direction" standard it had laid out in *BMC Resources* almost 10 months earlier. The patent at issue in

Muniauction involved electronic methods for conducting original issues of municipal bond auctions over the Internet. Both parties agreed that no single actor performed every step of the claims at issue. The *Muniauction* court expanded on the *BMC Resources* standard, stating that "a defendant cannot . . . avoid liability for direct infringement by having someone else carry out one or more of the claimed steps on its behalf." Rather, a "claim is directly infringed only if one party exercises 'control or direction' over the entire process such that every step is attributable to the controlling party, i.e., the 'mastermind.'" However, "mere 'arms-length cooperation' will not give rise to direct infringement by any party" (*Muniauction, Inc. v. Thomson Corp.*, 2008, p. 1318). The *Muniauction* court's language invokes the principles of agency law. In fact, the court emphasized the role that vicarious liability theory plays in evaluating joint infringement cases, stating that, under *BMC Resources*, "the control or direction standard is satisfied in situations where the law would traditionally hold the accused direct infringer vicariously liable for the acts committed by another party that are required to complete performance of a claimed method" (*Muniauction, Inc. v. Thomson Corp.*, 2008, p. 1330).

Lower courts did not find the *BMC Resources* / *Muniauction* standard easy to apply. As noted by one trial court, the *Muniauction* court set out a "spectrum" of possible relationships (*kSolo, Inc. v. Catona*, 2008). At one end is "mere arms-length cooperation," which does not support a finding of infringement; at the other end is "'control or direction over the entire process such that every step is attributable to the controlling part [sic], i.e., the mastermind,' which is sufficient to establish infringement" (*Emtel, Inc. v. LipidLabs, Inc.*, 2008, p. 829). Where along that spectrum behavior crosses from non-infringement to infringement, however, was uncertain. As a result of this uncertainty, subsequent lower courts felt that they were faced with a restrictive definition of joint infringement (*Global Patent Holdings, LLC v. Panthes, BRHC, LLC*, 2009). And indeed, the Federal Circuit itself found it difficult to apply this standard, leading to its August 2012 en banc decision in *Akamai Technologies, Inc. v. Limelight Networks, Inc.*

B.   The *Akamai* / *McKesson* en banc: Moving Joint Infringement from Direct Infringement to Inducement

Two Federal Circuit panel decisions, *Akamai Technologies, Inc. v. Limelight Networks, Inc.*, decided in 2010, and *McKesson Technologies, Inc. v. Epic Systems Corp.*, decided in 2011, led to a 2012 en banc hearing by the Federal Circuit on the issue of joint infringement. While commentators are sure to focus on the radical change that this en banc wrought in patent infringement liability, *Akamai* is equally worthy of scholarly attention for what it indicates about the Federal Circuit's understanding and application of traditional common law doctrines. Instead of turning to traditional tort and agency law doctrines to resolve the conundrum of joint infringement, the majority crafted a sui generis rule, based on a tortured reading of the patent statute, leading four of the dissenting judges to criticize the majority for "telling us that the term 'infringement' . . . can mean different things in different contexts" (*Akamai Technologies, Inc. v. Limelight Networks, Inc.*, 2012, p. *104).

1.   The panel decisions

In *Akamai*, the combined actions of the defendant and its customers were needed to complete the claimed method at issue, which involved improved methods for storing webpage content. In *McKesson*, the patent at issue involved a method of using personalized web pages to foster electronic communication between doctors and their patients. In both cases, the method involved necessarily contemplated the participation of multiple parties in completing the steps of the claim.

The *Akamai* panel set out to fill in the parameters of joint infringement set forth initially in *BMC Resources* and expanded upon in *Muniauction*. The *Akamai* panel ultimately set forth a rather tight test for joint infringement: joint infringement can arise "only" where: (1) there is "an agency relationship between the parties who perform the method steps" or (2) "one party is contractually obligated to the other to perform the steps." With regard to the first branch of this test, the court emphasized that "control or direction" alone is insufficient; the court looks to "not merely the exercise of control or the providing of instructions, but whether the relationship between the parties is such that acts of one may be attributed to the other." This requires a principal-agent relationship as defined within the law of agency set forth by the US Supreme Court (*Dixon v. U.S.*, 1984) and section 101 of the *Restatement (Third) of Agency*. The *Akamai* panel found no such agency or contractual relationship present between the accused infringer and its customers (*Akamai Technologies, Inc. v. Limelight Networks, Inc.*, 2010, p. 1320).

The April 2011 panel decision in *McKesson Technologies, Inc. v. Epic Systems Corp.* brought the issue of the Federal Circuit's doctrine on joint infringement to a head. McKesson alleged that the defendant, Epic, induced infringement by licensing its allegedly infringing software to healthcare providers who then offered it to their patients. As an indirect form of infringement, inducement must be supported by direct infringement. No single party had performed all of the claimed steps, but McKesson argued that the actions of the patients and the doctors could be combined to support a finding of direct joint infringement that would in turn support the inducement action against Epic.

In a short opinion, the *McKesson* panel (in a 2-1 decision) applied the *Akamai* two-part agency / contract test to find that there was no joint infringement because the patients were in no way the agents of the health-care providers who made the allegedly infringing software available to them, nor were the patients in any way contractually obligated to perform any of the claimed method steps. Because there was no direct infringement by the doctors and patients under the joint infringement theory, there could be no indirect infringement by Epic under the inducement theory.

The *McKesson* panel majority then went on to discuss the role of joint torts in resolving such disputes. Patent law, the majority noted, is a "creature of statute," and hence it would be inappropriate for the court to expand direct infringement in such a way as to undermine the indirect infringement statutory scheme. In the majority's view, the indirect infringement theories of contributory and induced infringement already adequately addressed the issue of joint tortfeasors; expansion of direct infringement rules to reach joint infringement behavior was thus both unnecessary and inappropriate.

The panel's decision was hardly unanimous. Judge Bryson concurred reluctantly, stating: "I agree that the decision in this case is correct in light of the court's decisions in *BMC Resources*, *Muniauction*, and *Akamai Technologies*. Whether those decisions are correct is another question, one that is close enough and important enough that it may warrant review by the en banc court in an appropriate case" (*McKesson Info. Solutions, LLC v. Epic Sys. Corp.*, 2011, p. *15). Judge Newman, on the other hand, wrote a vehement dissent in which she argued that precedent required only that "all of the claimed steps of the process must be performed" and that the panel majority had misread that precedent to require that all of the steps be performed by a single party (*McKesson Info. Solutions, LLC v. Epic Sys. Corp.*, 2011, p. *20). Recent panel holdings had reached similar incorrect results, "holding that neither collaboration nor joint action nor facilitation nor authorization nor invitation can overcome the immutable barrier to infringement when all of the participating entities are not under the 'control or direction' of a mastermind infringer" (*McKesson Info. Solutions, LLC v. Epic Sys. Corp.*, 2011, p. *16). This, Judge Newman argued, contravened earlier precedent which "applied the law of infringement as a straightforward matter of tortious responsibility" (*McKesson Info. Solutions, LLC v. Epic Sys. Corp.*, 2011, p. *35). Somewhere along the line, the Federal Circuit had morphed those straightforward rules into a crabbed interpretation of "patent" in a manner that "disserve[d] commerce, fairness, and the innovation incentive" (*McKesson Info. Solutions, LLC v. Epic Sys. Corp.*, 2011, p. *17).

2. The *Akamai / McKesson* en banc decision

Judge Bryson's call in *McKesson* for an en banc hearing on joint infringement doctrine soon bore fruit. On 18 November 2011, the Federal Circuit sat en banc to hear oral argument in both *Akamai* and *McKesson*. Its joint decision in the two cases, captioned *Akamai Technologies, Inc. v. Limelight Networks, Inc.*, was issued on 31 August 2012, in a 6-5 decision that generated two dissenting opinions. The court had asked the *Akamai* parties to brief a very specific question regarding direct infringement: "If separate entities each perform separate steps of a method claim, under what circumstances would that claim be directly infringed and to what extent would each of the parties be liable?" (*Akamai Technologies, Inc. v. Limelight Networks, Inc.*, 2011). Instead of addressing direct infringement, however, the majority shoehorned joint infringement into the indirect infringement category of induced infringement, overruling at least in part its decision in *BMC Resources*.[5] The *Akamai* en banc thus set joint infringement doctrine on a completely new and unanticipated course.

The majority opinion in *Akamai* was an unsigned per curium opinion joined by Chief Judge Rader and Judges Lourie, Bryson, Reyna, Moore, and Wallach. Not only did the majority immediately reframe the issue of joint infringement from one of direct infringement to one of indirect infringement, it jettisoned the single-entity rule laid out in *BMC Resources* as it applied to induced infringement. The majority saw this reframing as a way of mitigating the potentially harsh effects of direct infringement liability, which is a strict liability. The majority held that an actor may be liable under § 271(b) for inducement of infringement whether the infringement results from the actions of a single party or from the actions of multiple parties who have no agency or other relationship that would lead to vicarious liability for direct patent infringement. The majority expressly refrained from addressing the liability of multiple actors for direct infringement under § 271(a) (*Akamai Technologies, Inc. v. Limelight Networks, Inc.*, 2012).

The majority then went on to completely rewrite the predicate of direct infringement that had traditionally underpinned inducement liability. While the majority stated that there cannot be inducement without performance of "acts necessary to infringe," it also stated that "[r]equiring proof that there *has been* direct infringement as a predicate for induced infringement is not the same as requiring proof that a single party would be *liable* as a direct infringer" (*Akamai Technologies, Inc. v. Limelight Networks, Inc.*, 2012, p. *19). The majority thus explicitly overruled the single-entity rule of *BMC Resources*, stating that a "party who knowingly induces others to engage in acts that collectively practice the steps of the patented method—and those others perform those acts—has had precisely the same impact on the patentee as a party who induces the same infringement by a single direct infringer; there is no reason, either in the text of the statute or in the policy underlying it, to treat the two inducers differently" (*Akamai Technologies, Inc. v. Limelight Networks, Inc.*, 2012, p. *20). The court found this outcome was supported by the structure of the statute and its legislative history, as well as analogies provided by criminal law and the Restatement of Torts (*Akamai Technologies, Inc. v. Limelight Networks, Inc.*, 2012).

Judge Linn wrote a dissent, which was joined by Judges Dyk, Prost, and O'Malley, in which he argued that the Federal Circuit should have stood by its earlier decisions in *BMC Resources* and *Muniauction*, which held that: (1) inducement under § 271(b) required a predicate act of direct infringement under § 271(a); and (2) direct infringement required "that all steps of a claimed method be practiced, alone or vicariously, by a single entity or joint enterprise" (*Akamai Technologies, Inc. v. Limelight Networks, Inc.*, 2012, p. *106). Judge Linn took particular issue with the majority's attempt to distinguish the *act* of direct infringement from the *existence* of a direct infringer: "Divorcing liability under § 271(a) from liability under § 271(b) is unsupported by the statute, subverts the statutory scheme, and ignores binding Supreme Court precedent" and "is a sweeping change to the nation's patent policy that is not for this court to make" (*Akamai Technologies, Inc. v. Limelight Networks, Inc.*, 2012, pp. *107, *120). Finally, Judge Linn argued that the fact that Congress knew of *BMC Resources* and *Muniauction* when it reformed the 1952 Patent Act in 2011 in the Leahy-Smith America Invents Act "indicates that Congress did not intend to abrogate the single entity rule for direct infringement, or broaden indirect infringement liability beyond its intentionally limited scope" (*Akamai Technologies, Inc. v. Limelight Networks, Inc.*, 2012, p. *124).

Judge Newman, who had dissented in *McKesson*, wrote a vigorous dissent in the *Akamai* en banc as well. Judge Newman criticized the majority for "creat[ing] a new, ill defined, and open-ended theory of liability" of joint infringement and the Linn dissent for failing to recognize that the single-entity rule is "inadequate" for addressing the problem of joint infringement (*Akamai Technologies, Inc. v. Limelight Networks, Inc.*, 2012, p. *59). She argued that the "court should simply acknowledge that a broad, all-purpose single-entity requirement is flawed, and restore infringement to its status as occurring when all of the claimed steps are performed, whether by a single entity or more than one entity, whether by direction or control, or jointly, or in collaboration or interaction" (*Akamai Technologies, Inc. v. Limelight Networks, Inc.*, 2012, p. *71). In short, she called for a return to traditional joint tortfeasor doctrine.

C. Lessons from the *Akamai* en banc: Paths for Future Research

The *Akamai* en banc decision provides rich fodder for patent law scholars and commentators for extensive analyses of the issues relating to statutory interpretation and the scope of joint infringement liability. *Akamai* and earlier joint infringement cases also tell us about how the Federal Circuit understands and applies traditional common law doctrines in the context of its patent decisions and that in turn tells us much about the role of a specialized patent court within the legal system.

The specialized nature of the Federal Circuit enables it to be an expert in a complex and economically important area of the law; this expertise can, as discussed earlier in this chapter, lead to more uniform precedents, more predictable outcomes in disputes, and stronger patent rights overall. However, the narrow and specialized jurisdiction of the Federal Circuit can also hamper the court's ability to see connections with other areas of US law and can deter it from creating patent law doctrines that comport with the overall US legal system and its traditional norms and rules.

The development of joint infringement doctrine in the federal courts, from its early agency law origins to the very recent en banc in *Akamai*, provide some key lessons about the risks inherent in having a specialized patent court. Three of these lessons are summarized briefly below, but these (and other lessons) are worthy of more detailed analysis and scrutiny in future works.

1. Traditional common law doctrines, such as tort and agency, should apply in patent law just as they do in other contexts

US patent law has a statutory foundation (the Patent Act of 1952, as amended) and it has some characteristics not generally found in the US legal system (e.g., government-sanctioned monopolies are a fairly rare creature in US law). Patent law is not so unique that patent doctrine should be completely divorced from the mainstream of US law, however. Traditional doctrines of agency and tort, for example, should apply in the joint infringement arena in the same manner that they apply in other situations outside patent law that implicate vicarious liability issues.

The fact that early courts turned to these theories in addressing joint infringement disputes indicates that the theories are relevant in the patent law context, yet the increasingly refined joint infringement theories articulated by the Federal Circuit move joint infringement further and further from traditional doctrine. The *Akamai* en banc, interestingly, seemed to shift joint infringement doctrine back closer to the traditional tort and agency law fold, even as it switched joint infringement from direct to indirect liability, as the *Akamai* majority decision and both dissents discussed the role that joint tortfeasor doctrine can play in resolving joint infringement cases (even though they disagreed upon the extent to which and the settings in which the doctrine should apply).

The Federal Circuit's narrow subject matter jurisdiction may lead it to conclude that patent law is somehow more "unique" than it really is. Scholars should explore in more detail the application of traditional tort and agency law doctrine in patent law cases generally, and in joint infringement cases particularly, with an eye to fashioning a more consistent and coherent joint infringement doctrine that comports with the general framework of US tort and agency law.

2. The Federal Circuit should actively seek out analogous areas of law outside its subject matter jurisdiction

Because the Federal Circuit has narrow subject matter jurisdiction, it does not have the opportunity to see a broad range of cases, as do the regional appellate courts, whose jurisdiction is not so narrowly defined. In this sense, the specialized jurisdiction of the Federal Circuit is a double-edged sword. Although the Federal Circuit is able to be an expert in the complex field of patent law and to provide a degree of uniformity and depth previously lacking in the patent field, that same specialized jurisdiction can lead to inadvertent tunnel vision.

For example, the *Akamai* en banc majority and both dissents struggled with the notion of strict liability for direct patent infringement. One reason the majority turned to inducement, with its *scienter* requirement, rather than direct infringement, to address joint infringement was its discomfort with the strict liability nature of direct infringement:

> Because liability for inducement, unlike liability for direct infringement, requires specific intent to cause infringement, using inducement to reach joint infringement does not present the risk of extending liability to persons who may be unaware of the existence of a patent or even unaware that others are practicing some of the steps claimed in the patent (*Akamai Technologies, Inc. v. Limelight Networks, Inc.*, 2012).

The Linn dissent, by contrast, resolved its discomfort with the strict liability nature of direct infringement by pointing to the single-entity rule: "Because of the strict-liability nature of direct infringement, this court has limited direct infringement liability 'to those who practice each and every element of the claimed invention'" (*Akamai Technologies, Inc. v. Limelight*

Networks, Inc., 2012, p. *135). Judge Newman, in her dissent, went even further, arguing that direct patent infringement is not correctly termed a "strict liability." Rather, she argued, "[t]he tort principle of 'strict liability' applies when injury results from inherently hazardous or dangerous activity, not from patent infringement" (*Akamai Technologies, Inc. v. Limelight Networks, Inc.*, 2012, p. *86). This, she argued, misleads the rest of the court to incorrectly conclude that "every participant in an interactive or collaboration method is fully responsible for the entire harm caused by the infringement" (*Akamai Technologies, Inc. v. Limelight Networks, Inc.*, 2012, p. *86). Rather, she asserted, traditional tort law would apportion liability based on such factors "as the relative contribution to the injury to the patentee, the economic benefit received by the tortfeasor, and the knowledge and culpability of the actor" and this method would work in joint infringement cases as well as a method for appropriately limiting liability to relevant actors (*Akamai Technologies, Inc. v. Limelight Networks, Inc.*, 2012, p. *87).

The Federal Circuit is understandably made nervous about the possibility of strict liability being used in the joint infringement context to draw in parties whose relationship to the infringement is tenuous at best. However, statutory strict liability is not unheard of in US law. The Comprehensive Environmental Response, Compensation and Liability Act (CERCLA), for example, employs strict liability standards. Much has been learned about the fair application of strict liability to joint actors, the divisibility of injury, and the apportionment of damages in the context of this environmental statute over the past three decades (Oswald, 1995; Oswald, 1993). CERCLA claims fall outside the subject matter jurisdiction of the Federal Circuit, however, and while the Federal Circuit could of course access and examine that set of case law for guidance on application of strict liability in statutory settings, the Federal Circuit does not encounter such cases on a routine basis, as do the regional courts of appeals. The Federal Circuit simply has no regular occasion to look at CERCLA case law and so it appears to be missing a seemingly apt analogy.

3. The role of the court is to interpret statutes and apply the law, not create policy

Commentators have worried that the Federal Circuit, because of its specialized jurisdiction, could become too active in making patent law, as opposed to interpreting and applying it; i.e., that it could, in the words of Judge Posner, "become a booster of its speciality" (Thomas, 2003).

Both *Akamai* dissents echoed this concern. Judge Newman's dissent harshly criticized the majority for issuing a "new rule ... not in accordance with statute, precedent, and sound policy" (*Akamai Technologies,*

Inc. v. Limelight Networks, Inc., 2012, p. *51); the Linn dissent accused the majority of "assum[ing] the mantle of a policy maker" (*Akamai Technologies, Inc. v. Limelight Networks, Inc.*, 2012, p. *103). Both of these complaints flowed from the majority's decision to rewrite the predicate underlying indirect infringement and to house joint infringement under the indirect, rather than direct, liability umbrella (*Akamai Technologies, Inc. v. Limelight Networks, Inc.*, 2012).

Certainly, the role of the court is to interpret congressional intent and policy, not to rewrite it to fit the court's own notion of what is fair or just, or what it thinks Congress would have intended had it thought about the issue. Other scholars have examined this aspect of the Federal Circuit in considerable detail (e.g., Dreyfuss, 2004), and the *Akamai* en banc decision will provide additional opportunity for exploration of the Federal Circuit's view of its role as a court versus a policymaker.

One aspect of Judge Newman's dissent merits specific mention. The majority, by deciding the case on the grounds of indirect inducement infringement instead of direct infringement, deviated substantially from the question posed to the parties by the court and briefed by both the parties and the amici curiae. Judge Newman criticized the majority on this ground, stating: "Before the law is changed so that only an inducer can be liable for divided infringement, on loose criteria for inducement, this court should at least obtain the advice of those who understand the consequences of this change in infringement law" (*Akamai Technologies, Inc. v. Limelight Networks, Inc.*, 2012, p.*55). Judge Newman's statement is curious. If the court is merely interpreting and applying existing statute and precedent, the voice of amici in particular should not be so critical. Judge Newman seems to contemplate, however, that the court can indeed change law and policy in the manner undertaken by the majority, provided it gains the input of relevant constituencies. This, however, begins to sound like agency rulemaking or congressional statute-making activities that should be far afield from the court's ambit.

IV. CONCLUSION

Although joint infringement doctrine is scarcely an example of the "isolated and sterile jurisprudence" commentators initially feared might flow from a specialized Federal Circuit (Nard & Duffy, 2007), the case law on joint infringement does seem to suggest that at some level, the Federal Circuit is acting in an outcome-determinative manner, without giving sufficient thought to the theoretical underpinnings of the legal rules that it is creating and to the manner in which those rules fit into the larger picture of traditional common law principles and the US legal system. Returning explicitly and openly to the foundations of the tort and agency law doctrines that underlie joint infringement doctrine would enable the Federal Circuit to articulate liability rules that are more principled, more grounded in the traditional legal doctrine, and, indeed, more consistent with the overall patent liability scheme itself. The lessons that can be drawn from the joint infringement scenario thus give important insight into how a specialized patent court should structure its decision-making process to ensure that its patent law decisions are consistent with the underlying legal doctrine of the jurisdiction in which it operates and provide important insight into the larger picture of understanding the role of an appellate court with specialized jurisdiction.

NOTES

* Copyright 2013, Lynda J. Oswald.
1. Traditionally, the courts have the term "joint infringement" in discussing the liability of multiple actors for patent infringement. The first use of "divided infringement" in the federal courts appears in a 2008 case (*Pharmastem Therapeutics, Inc. v. Viacell, Inc.*, 2008). The wholesale use of "divided infringement" by the *Akamai* en banc has likely cemented this term as the preferred one in the patent lexicon. Although the courts and literature seem to treat the terms as interchangeable, it is worth exploring in future research whether the terms are in fact different in such a way that would lead to different analyses and outcomes. For the purposes of this chapter, however, the terms are assumed to be synonymous.
2. The CAFC's website states:

> Appeals to the court come from all federal district courts, the United States Court of Federal Claims, the United States Court of International Trade, and the United States Court of Appeals for Veteran's Claims. The court also takes appeals of certain administrative agencies' decisions, including the United States Merit Systems Protection Board, the Boards of Contract Appeals, the Board of Patent Appeals and Interferences, and the Trademark Trial and Appeals Board. Decisions of the United States International Trade Commission, the Office of Compliance, an independent agency in the legislative branch, and the Government Accountability Office Personnel Appeals Board, and the Department of Justice Bureau of Justice Assistance are also reviewed by the court.

www.cafc.uscourts.gov/the-court/court-jurisdiction.html
3. Federal senior judge status is defined by 28 U.S.C. § 371. Senior judges are technically retired but often continue to hear cases on a part-time basis. They do not participate in *en banc* decisions of the court. 28 U.S.C. § 46(c); Fed. R. App. P. 35(a). Senior judges typically handle 15 percent of the annual workload of the federal courts. http://www. uscourts.gov/Common/FAQS.aspx
4. However, the *On Demand* panel offered no analysis of joint infringement and instead focused on a claim construction issue that ultimately controlled the outcome of the case.
5. The Federal Circuit thus remanded both *Akamai* and *McKesson* for determination of whether there was induced infringement.

REFERENCES

Adams, C.W. (2006). Symposium Review: A Brief History of Indirect Liability for Patent Infringement. *Santa Clara Computer & High Technology Law* Review, **22**(3), 369–98.

Administrative Offices of the U.S. Courts (1981). Retrieved from http://hdl.handle.net/2027/uiug.30112079448095?urlappend=%3Bseq=51.

Akamai Technologies, Inc. v. Limelight Networks, Inc., 692 F.3d 1301 (Fed. Cir. 2012).

Akamai Technologies, Inc. v. Limelight Networks, Inc., 419 Fed. Appx. 989 (Fed Cir. 2011).

Akamai Technologies, Inc. v. Limelight Networks, Inc., 629 F.3d 1311 (Fed. Cir. 2010).

Bartholomew, M. (2009). Copyright, Trademark and Secondary Liability after *Grokster. Columbia Journal of Law & the Arts*, **32**(3), 445–70.

Bartholomew, M. & Tehranian, J. (2006). The Secret Life of Legal Doctrine: The Divergent Evolution of Secondary Liability in Trademark and Copyright Law. *Berkeley Technology Law Journal*, **21**(4), 1363–1419.

BMC Resources, Inc. v. Paymentech, L.P., 498 F.3d 1373 (Fed. Cir. 2007).

Carbice Corp. of Am. v. Am. Patents Dev. Corp., 283 U.S. 87 (1931).

Comprehensive Environmental, Response, Compensation and Liability Act, Pub. L. No. 96-510, 94 Stat. 2767 (1980), codified as amended at 42 U.S.C. §§ 9601 et seq.

Cotropria, C.A. (2010). Determining Uniformity within the Federal Circuit by Measuring Dissent and En Banc Review. *Loyola of L.A. Law Review*, **43**(3), 801–25.

Crowell v. Baker Oil Tools, 143 F.2d 1003 (9th Cir. 1944).

Dixon v. U.S., 465 U.S. 482, 505 (1984).

Dreyfuss, R.C. (2004). The Federal Circuit: A Continuing Experiment in Specialization. *Case Western Reserve Law Review*, **54**(3), 769–801.

DSU Medical Corp. v. JMS Co., 471 F.3d 1293 (Fed. Cir. 2006).

Emtel, Inc. v. LipidLabs, Inc., 583 F. Supp. 2d 811 (S.D. Tex. 2008).

Faroudja Laboratories, Inc. v. Dwin Electronics, 1999 U.S. Dist. LEXIS 22987 (N.D. Cal. Feb. 24, 1999).

Free Standing Stuffer, Inc. v. Holly Dev. Co., 187 U.S.P.Q. 323 (N.D. Ill. 1974).

Fromson v. Advance Offset Plate, Inc., 720 F.2d 1565 (Fed. Cir. 1983).

Gardner, J. (2007). Complicity and Causality. *Criminal Law and Philosophy*, **1**(2), 127–41.

Global Patent Holdings, L.L.C. v. Panthes, BRHC, L.L.C., 586 F. Supp. 2d 1331 (S.D. Fla. 2009).

Global-Tech Appliances, Inc. v. SEB, S.A., 131 S. Ct. 2060 (2011).

Gupta, D. (2012). Virtually Uninfringeable: Valid Patents Lacking Protection Under the Single Entity Rule. *Journal of Patent & Trademark Office Society*, **94**(1), 61–74.

Harmon, R.L. (1991). *Patents and the Federal Circuit*. Washington, DC: BNA.

Hewlett-Packard Co. v. Bausch & Lomb, Inc., 209 F.2d 1464 (Fed. Cir. 1990).

Hill v. Amazon, 2006 U.S. Dist. LEXIS 3389 (E.D. Tex. Jan. 19, 2006).

Koenig, G.K. (1980). *Patent Invalidity: A Statistical and Substantive Analysis*. New York: Clark Boardman.

kSolo, Inc. v. Catona, 2008 U.S. Dist. LEXIS 9571-7 (C.D. Cal. Nov. 10, 2008).

Lemley, M.A. (2005). Inducing Patent Infringement. *University of California-Davis Law Review*, **39**(1), 225–47.

Lemley, M.A., O'Brien, D.W., Kent, R.M., Ramani, A. & Van Nest, R. (2005). Divided Infringement Claims. *AIPLA Quarterly Journal*, **33**(3), 255–84.

Lowrie, M., Littman, K.M. & Silva, L. (2011). The Changing Landscape of Joint, Divided and Indirect Infringement—The State of the Law and How to Address It. *Journal of High Technology Law*, **12**(1), 65–106.

Marley Mouldings Ltd. v. Mikron Indus., Inc., 2003 U.S. Dist. LEXIS 7211 (N.D. Ill. Apr. 29, 2003).

McKesson Info. Solutions, LLC v. Epic Sys. Corp., 2011 U.S. App. LEXIS 7531 (Fed. Cir. Apr. 12, 2011).

McKesson Info. Solutions, LLC v. Epic Sys. Corp., 2009 U.S. Dist. LEXIS 88158 (N.D. Ga. Sept. 6, 2009).

Merges, R.P. (1992). *Patent Law and Policy*. Charlottesville: Michie Co.

Metabolite Labs., Inc. v. Lab. Corp. of Am. Holdings, 370 F.3d 1354 (Fed. Cir. 2004).

Mobil Oil Co. v. W.R. Grace & Co., 367 F. Supp. 207 (D. Conn. 1973).

Muniauction, Inc. v. Thomson Corp., 532 F.3d 1318 (Fed. Cir. 2008).

Nard, C. & Duffy, J. (2007). Rethinking Patent Law's Uniformity Principle. *Northwestern University Law Review*, **101**(4), 1619–76.

On Demand Machine Corp. v. Ingram Industries, Inc., 442 F.3d 1331 (Fed. Cir. 2006).

Oswald, L.J. (2006). The Intent Element of "Inducement to Infringe" Under Patent Law: Reflections on *Grokster*. *Michigan Telecommunications and Technology Law Review*, **13**(1), 225–46.

Oswald, L.J. (2003). The Personal Liability of Corporate Officers for Patent Infringement. *IDEA*, **44**(1), 115–46.

Oswald, L.J. (1995). New Directions in Joint and Several Liability under CERCLA? *Univ. of California Davis Law Review*, **28**(2), 299–365.

Oswald, L.J. (1993). Strict Liability of Individuals under CERCLA: A Normative Analysis. *Boston College Environmental Affairs Law Review*, **20**(4), 579–637.

Patent Act of 1790, ch. 7, 1 Stat. 109-112.

Patent Act of 1952, as amended, 35 U.S.C. § 100 et seq.

Petherbridge, L. (2009). Patent Law Uniformity? *Harvard Journal of Law and Technology*, **22**(2), 421–73.

Pharmastem Therapeutics, Inc. v. Viacell, Inc., 491 F.3d 1342 (Fed. Cir. 2008).

Prosser, W.L., Keeton, W.P., Dobbs, D.B., Keeton, R.E. & Owen, D.G. (1984). *Prosser and Keeton on the Law of Torts*. St Paul, MN: West Group.

Rader, R.R. (2001). The United States Courts of Appeals for the Federal Circuit: The Promise and Perils of a Court of Limited Jurisdiction. *Marquette Intellectual Property Law Review*, **5**(1), 1–11.

Restatement (Second) of Agency (1958).

Restatement (Third) of Agency (2006).

Saxe v. Hammond, 1 Holmes (U.S.) 456 (1875).

S. Rep. No. 82-1979 (1952), reprinted in 1952 USCCAN 2394.

S. Rep. No. 97-275 (1981), reprinted in 1982 USCCAN 11.

Thomas, J.R. (2003). *Patent Law and Innovation: The Creation, Operation, and a Twenty-Year Assessment of the U.S. Court of Appeals for the Federal Circuit*. Washington, DC: Congressional Research Service: Penny Hill Press.

US Court of Appeals for the Federal Circuit (2011). Retrieved from http://www.cafc. uscourts.gov/images/stories/the-court/statistics/Caseload_by_category_2011.pdf

US Courts (2011). *Federal Judicial Caseload Statistics 2011*. Retrieved from http:// www.uscourts.gov/Statistics/FederalJudicialCaseloadStatistics.aspx

US Patent and Trademark Office, Dec. 2011. Extended Year Set-Patents by Country, State, and Year: Utility Patents. Retrieved from http://www.uspto. gov/web/offices/ac/ido/oeip/taf/cst_utlh.htm.

Vacca, R. (2011). Acting Like an Administrative Agency: The Federal Circuit En Banc. *Missouri Law Review*, **76**(3), 733–62.

Wagner, R.P. & Petherbridge, L. (2004). Is the Federal Circuit Succeeding? An Empirical Assessment of Judicial Performance. *University of Pennsylvania Law Review*, **152**, 1105–82.

7. The transformation of patents into information containment tools

Daniel R. Cahoy, Joel Gehman and Zhen Lei*

A patent system's role in disseminating information is as important as the incentive it provides to invent and innovate. Rapid information disclosure is viewed as part of the bargain with the patentee. However, patents achieve their incentive ends through a broad power to exclude. It is now becoming apparent that the use of that power may in some cases interfere with the system's disclosure mission. In particular, when reproduction or use of the patented invention is necessary to evaluate its potential impacts on the rest of the world, patent rights can actually serve as an information barrier. The lack of an effective information production exception in the law and the failure to preserve current disclosure incentives in recent legislative reform has compromised the ability to achieve a complete understanding of an invention. Overall, the US may be experiencing the unexpected emergence of patents as an information containment tool at the same time that their disclosure function has been weakened.

This chapter considers the emergence of patents as information containment tools and highlights the significance of this development by overlaying the theory onto one of the most controversial technological practices of our time: hydraulic fracturing in natural gas extraction. Hydraulic fracturing has generated a classic information problem. There is growing concern over the use of dangerous chemicals in hydraulic fracturing and disclosure to date has been deemed to be inadequate. Companies may soon be required to produce public lists of chemicals used, even when trade secrets are involved (Reser & Ritter, 2011). But a complete understanding of the impact of hydraulic fracturing chemicals cannot be gained from a mere list of the compounds used. It is just as important to understand how they interact with each other and consider how they act in the real world. Field and laboratory experimentation is necessary to fully capture how the exploitation of shale gasses impacts the environment. Simply knowing the structure of the chemicals or the steps in a method of use is not sufficient. Normally, third parties such as NGOs and universities would be able to fill this information gap by conducting their own experiments. However, it appears that patents may play a new and surprising role in limiting this important source of information production.

The use of patents to contain information is an important new chapter in the business legal environment. As evidenced by the case of hydraulic fracturing, the consequences of unchecked patent power can be severe. Some attenuation of broad rights may be in order, but for the time being, current flexibilities in the law can be exploited for some relief.

I. THE EVOLVING RELATIONSHIP BETWEEN PATENTS AND INFORMATION

Patents are often referred to as monopolies. There is a negative connotation with that characterization that is largely undeserved. Rather than a naked government grant of market exclusivity, patents actually represent a societal bargain. In exchange for limited monopoly over an invention, a patent applicant agrees to disclose the invention to the world. The likely outcome of a world without patents would be more secrecy, as inventors would work to foil free riders by cloaking their ideas for as long as possible. Patent exclusivity eliminates the need for secrecy, and forced disclosure prevents opportunists from trying to have it both ways.

However, the disclosure framework only operates to provide access to information related to the nature of the actual invention. Follow-on information regarding patented products is not necessarily so free flowing. In fact, through the use of restrictions in patent licensing, it may be possible to use the putative disclosure device to inhibit information creation and dissemination. The nature of patents as information inhibitors has been historically overlooked, but it may be one of the most important issues on the new technology horizon.

A. Patents Promote Information Disclosure

At the very core of the modern patent right is the concept that an invention will be revealed to the world, and eventually will be available for others to exploit (Fromer, 2009). The term "patent" is derived from open communications ("letters patent" or "literae patentes") issued from a monarch to his or her subjects (Goodman, 2006). The declarations, which eventually encompassed exclusive rights to inventions in addition to land patents, were meant to be public and accessible. In a sense, the dissemination of information is more historically attached to patents than the demonstration of new inventions.

Functionally, modern patents are designed to continue the tradition of information disclosure. Although initially pursued in secret, patent applications become open documents unless abandonment occurs early on in the process. In part, this is due to the fact that issued patents are published, and always have been (Walterscheid, 1997). Additionally, communications between the US Patent and Trademark Office (PTO) and the applicant are publicly available. Indeed, these documents, known as the file wrapper, are considered to be a part of the patent and may play a role in interpreting the claimed invention or characterizing the integrity of the prosecution. More recently, information from non-issued patents has been made available. As a result of 1999 revisions to the law requiring applications to be published after 18 months (except in a relatively narrow range of cases), patent applications and file wrappers are open to the public (Patent Act of 1952, § 122(b)). And, not surprisingly, all of these materials are available online through the PTO and various third-party providers.

Importantly, the public nature of modern patents extends beyond information accessibility; it also relates to information quality. A patent applicant is required to disclose a sufficient amount of information to enable others to practice the invention (Patent Act of 1952, § 112). No secret step or ingredients can exist that will foil copiers. Until recently, that enablement requirement included the need to disclose a "best mode" of practicing an invention, if one is known to the applicant. However, the 2011 Leahy-Smith America Invents Act (AIA) eliminated failure to disclose the best mode as a means for invalidating a patent (AIA, § 15). Still, patent disclosures must be detailed and accurate, commensurate with the claims.

Against the pro-disclosure rules of the patent system, it is possible that some aspects of the recent AIA reforms will result in an increased preference for secrecy in some cases. On its face, the new law seems to compel earlier disclosure by transitioning the United States into what is often referred to as a "first inventor to file" system (AIA, § 3). Part of this mechanism is the law's recognition of an inventor's pre-application disclosure as invalidating later filers, but not their own. In other words, there is a built-in incentive to disclose one's invention early to knock out competing applicants. However, tempering the early disclosure benefits is the AIA's newly expanded protection for prior users (AIA, § 5). This rule permits one to avoid infringement liability if one used the invention internally and commercially more than one year before the patent was filed or the invention was disclosed. As a result of this rule, one can keep an invention secret without worrying that another will patent it and preclude its use. On balance, at least some inventions will now likely remain secrets instead of entering the patent system. Of course, even though recent AIA reforms may weaken the incentives to patent in order to preserve use of the invention, one might expect inventors to use patenting to their advantage in other respects.

Philosophically, information disclosure is considered to be an important part of an efficient patent system. To minimize the deadweight losses inherent in a limited monopoly grant, the public disclosure of inventive information permits others to fully utilize the invention as soon as the patent expires (Strandburg, 2004). In addition, the disclosure of the invention while the patent is in force should allow others to design around and create new ways of accomplishing the same ends (Fromer, 2009). The hope is that patents enrich the innovation environment by bringing forward those ideas that benefit from the limited monopoly protection.

Despite the powerful disclosure incentives inherent in patents, the scope of information involved is in practice still limited. Functional details related to the invention are covered, but additional aspects of a product embodying the invention, including its safety profile and other applied know-how, may not be evident from the compelled disclosure. This is why, for example, patented pharmaceutical compounds must undergo years of testing to obtain FDA approval; the patent process may not address safety and effectiveness. There may be other means of obtaining this information, but such efforts may be thwarted if the power of a patent is utilized to control information production.

B.   Patents Can Block Information Produced through Follow-on Discovery

Although a limited property right, a patent permits a great deal of control over an invention during the term of enforceability. The right allows its owner to exclude another from making, using, selling or importing the invention for essentially any reason (Patent Act of 1952, § 271). The purpose is to forestall competition and enable monopoly profit-taking for a period sufficient to induce innovative behavior (Nordhaus, 1969). Given the information disclosure requirements described above, that right is not a direct barrier to information dissemination, as long as it only relates to the nature of an invention itself. But when there is a need for information on products or processes related to the invention (i.e., information that can be generated only by impacting one of the patent owner's restrictive rights), a patent can severely impact the availability of information.

One of the most obvious ways in which patents can restrict information is when they limit follow-on research that can lead to further discovery and extension of a field. Innovation is a cumulative process (Garud, Gehman & Kumaraswamy, 2011), and the absence of foundational or enabling technology can mean that some amount of third-party basic research does not occur. Information production is depressed as the research field fails to grow to its full potential. Murray and Stern (2007) demonstrated the depression effect empirically by looking at citation rates for papers associated with patented inventions. They found that there was a significant decrease in citations to initial papers after the associated patents were granted, suggesting that third-party researchers may be avoiding the technology.

A recent and controversial application of this form of blocking was asserted in *Association for Molecular Pathology v. U.S. Patent and Trademark Office* (2010), a case concerning patents for DNA segments that are useful in the detection of breast cancer. Most of the debate has related to whether such compounds should be patentable at all or be in the public domain. However, underlying this litigation is a basic question of information control (Simon, 2011). In *AMP*, Myriad Genetics and others were sued for a declaratory judgment that Myriad's patents covering the BRCA1 and BRCA2 genes were invalid. Motivating the litigation were allegations that Myriad had used its patents to stop cancer research by those who had not purchased the right to use the genes from Myriad. According to the plaintiffs, the issuance of patents that could convey such power was wrong for at least two reasons. The primary reason, and eventual core of the case, was that unmodified DNA does not qualify as patentable subject matter. An additional argument was that the patents constitute an unconstitutional limitation on speech.

The district court dismissed the speech argument early on, but ruled for the plaintiffs on the subject matter case (*Association for Molecular Pathology v. U.S. Patent and Trademark Office*, 2010). On appeal to the Federal Circuit, this too was reversed and the patents were determined to be not invalid (*Association for Molecular Pathology v. U.S. Patent and Trademark Office*, 2011). Although the Supreme Court's subsequent decision in *Mayo Collaborative Services v. Prometheus Laboratories, Inc.* (2012) vacated the Federal Circuit's initial decision, it was later affirmed under essentially the same reasoning (*Association for Molecular Pathology v. U.S. Patent and Trademark Office*, 2012). To date, the judicial system essentially conceded that Myriad's enforcement behavior is within its patent grant, despite the impact it may have on the creation of medical knowledge. However, the US Supreme Court granted certiorari in the Myriad case in December 2012 and the landscape may change yet again.

In the end, the negative impact of patents on knowledge creation in follow-on discovery could be viewed as a necessary consequence of intellectual property rights. If society grants temporary ownership over a fundamental invention, one would expect to see less exploitation by others, particularly competitors. More of a concern is the impact of patent rights on understanding the invention itself. This is a less studied and likely less acceptable information reduction.

C. Patents Can Restrict a Full Understanding of the Invention Itself

In essence, by giving owners broad powers of exclusion, patents can be used to lock down just about any third-party use, even if unrelated to competition in the marketplace. That includes testing or other analysis (Simon, 2011). The reason for this is that, outside of medical products, experimental use of patents is limited only by a common law exception in the United States (Holbrook, 2006).

The concept of free space for experimental use has been part of American patent law for some time. The exception was originally articulated in an 1813 case, *Whittemore v. Cutter*, in which Justice Story stated that the law should not punish one's use for "philosophical experiments" or "the sufficiency of a machine to produce its described effects." It remains as a limitation on the rights of a patent owner, justified in part by the requirement to disclose, but also the small impact on the economic power of patents. Such a limitation could play a very significant role in setting patent boundaries—similar to fair use in copyright law—but it has not to date been utilized to a great degree. Since its initial articulation, the exception has appeared in only a few cases, always in a non-commercial context (Boyle, 2010).

While there has always been some ambiguity about the extent of the experimental use exception—with the general notion that it is limited to uses for "amusement, idle curiosity . . . or philosophical inquiry"—recent case law has rendered it nearly irrelevant. This is primarily a result of the US Court of Appeals for the Federal Circuit decision in *Madey v. Duke* (2002), which found that a university's unauthorized use of a patented laser constituted infringement. The court determined that even experimentation within the confines of a university is commercial because research is an institution's business. After *Madey*, patent scholars question what, if any, use would be non-commercial (Strandburg, 2004). Indeed, there have been apparently no successful applications of the common law experimental use exception since the *Madey* decision at the Federal Circuit.

The effect of *Madey* and subsequent cases is that patent owners have the ability to exclude uses of an invention that might generate harmful information or negative publicity. This can be achieved in one of two ways, depending on how the invention is made available to the public. If the patent rights relate to an article or process that is held closely by the owner, simply suing for infringement can prevent third-party use. Although there can be a question of whether a third party is actually using the invention, enforcement is facilitated when a good faith belief of infringement is coupled with the rather broad discovery process in the United States.

Somewhat more complicated is the case wherein a patent owner sells an article embodying an invention to the public. The doctrine of exhaustion operates to limit a patentee's control over a sold product (*Quanta Computer Inc. v. LG Electronics, Inc.*, 2008). Theoretically, a purchaser could then use the invention in any manner desired, so long as the invention was not remade or copied in the process. However, it has been generally accepted that patent owners can limit subsequent use through contracts. In essence, a sale can be transformed into a license that may prevent experimentation or other data creation outside of limited parameters.

As restricted as the patent environment is in the US, it is possible that there may be more international flexibility. Although not required by international agreements such as the Trade-Related Aspects of Intellectual Property Agreement (TRIPS, 1994), many countries have an explicit— statutory or common-law—experimental use exception (Australian Government, 2005). Although the boundaries may be wider, it is not entirely clear that the exceptions in other nations extend to safety testing. And while the exception for pharmaceutical experimentation is relatively established globally, it is extremely limited in context and cannot provide the flexibility necessary to address safety concerns.

Through a combination of litigation and tight licensing, patent owners can control a great deal of information. With no relief valve available, it then becomes more important to assess patent accumulation in fields of great public concern.

II. PATENTS AND SHALE DRILLING: A CASE STUDY IN INFORMATION CONTAINMENT

The world's growing appetite for oil and gas has pushed exploration and production companies to expand the scale and scope of their operations in ways scarcely imaginable several decades ago. As the quest for hydrocarbons has intensified, the use of hydraulic fracturing has become nearly ubiquitous, especially in unconventional oil and gas fields (Montgomery & Smith, 2010). According to the American Petroleum Industry (2010), "Recent innovations combining [hydraulic fracturing] technology with horizontal drilling in shale formations has [sic] unlocked vast new supplies of natural gas, allowing the nation to get to the energy it needs today, and transforming our energy future." As the industry has honed its techniques, hydraulic fracturing operations have become more complex, requiring the use of more water and chemicals—millions of gallons per well, rather than tens of thousands of gallons used in the past.

While remarkable technical achievements, hydraulic fracturing innovations have sparked heated controversy over tradeoffs between meeting our increasing energy demands and the potential environmental, health and safety hazards associated with these techniques and practices. Practices taken for granted in communities that are dependent on the oil and gas industry have been translated into areas not familiar with oil and gas development, raising new questions and concerns, including air quality, wastewater disposal and wildlife encroachment. In the case of the Marcellus region, there is "no history of activity like this in the modern age" (Huls, 2010).

The growing concern over the use of dangerous chemicals in hydraulic fracturing has led to a call for greater disclosure. Companies may soon be required to produce public lists of chemicals used, even when trade secrets are involved. But this may not solve the information problem. A complete understanding of the impact of hydraulic fracturing chemicals cannot be gained from a mere list of the compounds used. It is just as important to understand how they interact with each other and consider how they act in the real world. Field and laboratory experimentation is necessary to fully capture how the exploitation of shale gasses impacts the environment. Similar to agricultural technologies like genetically modified crops, simply knowing the structure of the chemicals or the steps in a method of use is not sufficient. Normally, third parties like NGOs and universities would be able to fill this information gap by conducting their own experiments. However, it appears that patents may play a new and surprising role in limiting this important source of information production.

A. Hydraulic Fracturing Information Has Raised Concerns

A wide variety of chemical products are required during well drilling, completion and workover operations (Sanders, Tuck & Sherman, 2010). The oilfield products and services required for the exploitation of shale and other unconventional gas reservoirs bring with them a spectrum of distinct and significant environmental and health hazards. "From the first day the drill bit is inserted into the ground until the well is completed, toxic materials are introduced into the borehole and returned to the surface along with produced water and other extraction liquids" (Colborn, Kwiatkowski, Schultz & Bachran, 2011, p. 1053). Along the way, each well produces hundreds of tons of drill cuttings and thousands of gallons of slops, much of it highly toxic. For instance, "many of the fracking additives are toxic, carcinogenic or mutagenic" (Howarth & Ingraffea, 2011,

p. 477). There are also considerable land use changes such as drilling pads, pipelines and compressor stations, along with numerous other potential community impacts such as drilling and fracking truck traffic, temporary workers and related stresses. Given the breadth and complexity of these issues, stakeholders have raised numerous questions about potential environmental, safety and health hazards.

First, environmental hazards include issues such as acute and chronic aquatic toxicity, bioaccumulation, biodegradation, endocrine disruption, ozone depletion, volatile organic compounds (VOCs), and the use of chemicals considered "priority pollutants" by the US Environmental Protection Agency (EPA) (Protection of Environment, 2011). Despite the fact that many of these chemicals are toxic, such additives are important in hydraulic fracturing. In particular, hydraulic fracturing typically involves a complex cocktail of chemicals from different functional categories, including acids, biocides, breakers, clay stabilizers, corrosion inhibitors, crosslinkers, defoamers, friction reducers, gellants, pH buffers, proppants, scale inhibitors and surfactants (Colborn et al., 2011).

Second, in addition to their possible environmental hazards, hydraulic fracturing activities can endanger human health. These include safety hazards related to explosives, flammability, oxidizers and corrosives. For instance, "spills of chemical additives during transport or well site operations could pose far greater risks because the concentrations of as received additives are two to three orders of magnitude greater than they are after blending with water to formulate the fracturing fluid" (Brannon et al., 2011, p. 2). The chemicals involved in hydraulic fracturing may contain hydrochloric or muriatic acid, hydroxyethyl cellulose, glutaraldehyde, petroleum distillate, ammonium bisulfate, 2-hydroxy-1, 2,3-propanetricaboxylic acid, N,N-dimethylformamide, ethylene glycol or 2-butoxyethanol, fluorocarbons, naphthalene, butanol, and formaldehyde (Kargbo, Wilhelm & Campbell, 2010). Following hydraulic fracturing, some of these chemicals are returned to the surface, potentially contaminating soil, air and water, whereas other chemicals are left underground, potentially contaminating subsurface aquifers. Other potential causes of health hazards include improper handling of drilling sludge and produced water, chemical and waste spills, and fugitive gas emissions.

As oil and gas exploration and production activities move closer to human populations, these associated hazards "are more likely to have a direct effect on the health of those living, working and going to school in proximity" (Witter et al., 2008, p. 5). Indeed, the few existing studies available show that exposure to air pollutants, toxic chemicals, metals, radiation, noise and light pollution causes a range of diseases, illnesses, and health problems. As a result, those living in close proximity to oil and gas activities may be at increased risk for a variety of health problems affecting the skin, eye and sensory organs; brain and nervous system; gastrointestinal tract, liver and kidneys; and the immune system. Negative health outcomes such as cancer, cardiovascular disease and blood disorders, endocrine disruption, respiratory problems and asthma, and genetic, reproductive and developmental toxicity also have been linked to oil and gas activities, among others (Brannon et al., 2011).

B. Information Necessary for Assessment Is Limited

Despite the many questions stakeholders have posed about hydraulic fracturing and related oilfield products and services, those who have attempted to assess these issues have reported that necessary information is often not available. For instance, the types and quantities of chemicals involved are often not readily disclosed (Colborn et al., 2011). The exact reasons for these information shortages are not entirely clear. For instance, some have noted that even though the chemical formulations of hydraulic fracturing fluids are "highly researched," they are also "closely guarded" (Kargbo et al., 2010, pp. 5679, 5681). Others maintain that "because shale-gas development is so new, scientific information on the environmental costs is scarce" (Howarth & Ingraffea, 2011, pp. 271–2). Another possible difficulty is that drilling companies are not legally required to list the chemicals used in hydraulic fracturing, making it difficult to know the contents of fracking fluids (Finkel & Law, 2011). A lack of standards may also be a culprit. Finally, "ever-present concerns of compromising supplier proprietary information" make obtaining the necessary information difficult, even for industry insiders willing to sign confidentiality agreements and utilize third-party intermediaries (Brannon et al., 2011, p. 3).

The quantification of potential environmental, safety and health hazards is further complicated by the fact that "evaluating and communicating the hazards of chemicals is done in a highly variable manner across the world" (Jordan, Daulton, Cobb & Grumbles, 2010, p. 4). Simply gathering data on oilfield products is challenging. For instance, it is not uncommon for a given Material Safety Data Sheet (MSDS) to have gaps in information (Colborn et al., 2011). The problems stem in part from the fact that the US Occupational Safety and Health Administration (OSHA) provides only general guidance. It is not uncommon for an MSDS to omit the chemical composition of a product, to report on only a fraction of the total composition (sometimes less than 0.1 percent), or to provide only a general description of a product (such as "plasticizer") (Colborn et al., 2011). Even in cases where information is provided, Chemical Abstract Service (CAS) numbers are often not provided. Reflecting on these problems, the US

General Accounting Office concluded bluntly that "many MSDSs contain inaccurate or incomplete information" and OSHA "lacks an effective process for detecting inaccuracies" (US General Accounting Office, 1991, pp. 28, 31).

Even "a fully compliant OSHA-mandated [MSDS] in the US is likely to have significant gaps in the data needed to assess its environmental, safety and health hazards" (Jordan et al., 2010, p. 4). For one thing, an OSHA MSDS requires no environmental information. Additionally, in cases where OSHA classifies all the components of a particular product as non-hazardous, manufacturers are not required to identify any of the product's specific substances. However, OSHA's "non-hazardous" classification "does not account for potential environmental hazards" and if a substance is not identified on an MSDS "no database searching can be accomplished for environmental data" (Jordan et al., 2010, p. 4). In other cases, oilfield products were mixed together before use, but little data was available for most of the mixtures, requiring interested stakeholders to make their own judgments by combining the profiles of individual components based on their weighted contribution to the overall mixture. Finally, "much of the necessary but missing data (including the names of specific constituent chemicals) was considered proprietary or trade secret by the chemical supplier" (Jordan et al., 2010, p. 4).

To the extent these basic information challenges can be overcome, interpreting the results can still be complicated. For instance, even if the inherent environmental, safety and health hazards of particular chemicals can be determined, these individual product hazards do not account for use conditions or exposure scenarios (Jordan et al., 2010). For instance, hydraulically fracturing a horizontal shale well requires three to seven million gallons of water per well; however, it is only by making basin-wide evaluations that the cumulative impacts of such withdrawals and their concomitant disposals can be evaluated (Arthur & Coughlin, 2011). But without better information on the quantities, timing and locations of such water withdrawals and disposals it is difficult to assess their overall impacts. The applicability of isolated product assessments can be misleading in other ways too. For instance, on their own, silica-based proppants are considered inorganic substances, and appear to have low environmental, safety and health hazards, but such an assessment "is totally unrelated to the product's ultimate and long-term use underground in a hydraulic fracture" (Jordan et al., 2010, p. 5).

Although interested stakeholders have identified numerous potential health hazards associated with hydraulic fracturing and related oilfield products and services, further assessment of these hazards depends on access to sufficient information. However, the "data necessary to completely assess the health and social impacts of the oil and gas industry are missing in all areas, including population demographics, health status, psychological status, social measures, worker health, and environmental exposure" (Witter et al., 2008, p. 2). Yet, timely and unbiased environmental monitoring is not readily available to the public. In other cases, the studies that have been submitted to the US Environmental Protection Agency (EPA) are not publicly available because they are considered proprietary to the industry (Colborn et al., 2011).

Separate from the many third-party assessment efforts described above, there is growing realization that federal and state regulators are faced with similar limitations. For one thing, "the speed at which the resource is being developed often forces regulatory agencies to make policy decisions based on little data" (Soeder, 2010, pp. 277–8). Complicating matters is the fact that oil and gas exploration and service companies have traditionally been secretive about additives in the fluids used for hydraulic fracturing and the volumes of water recovered after each treatment. According to some, "even the EPA does not know what proprietary chemicals are contained in fracking fluids" (Schnoor, 2010, p. 6524).

As evidence of these limitations has accumulated, a growing number of stakeholders have concluded that part of the information problem may be the result of inadequate regulatory oversight of oil and gas production. For instance, the oil and gas industry is exempt from several major federal regulations that would otherwise require important disclosures, or restrict some of the industry's most controversial practices, including exemptions from the Comprehensive Environmental Response, Compensation and Liability Act; Resource Conservation and Recovery Act; Safe Drinking Water Act; Clean Water Act; Clean Air Act; National Environmental Policy Act; and Emergency Planning and Community Right-to-Know Act (Kosnik, 2007).

Faced with growing demands for increased disclosure and transparency, the oil and gas industry has recently attempted to demonstrate that it is capable of regulating itself. The industry's most prominent effort to date is FracFocus.org, a hydraulic fracturing chemical registry website that was launched on April 11, 2011, as a joint effort between the Ground Water Protection Council (GWPC) and the Interstate Oil and Gas Compact Commission (IOGCC). In just over two months of operation, forty-two companies pledged to participate, and disclosures related to more than 1,000 wells were provided. Even before FracFocus.org had been launched, efforts at great disclosure had begun in several states.

But perhaps more important is what is not disclosed. Rather than providing the complete recipe—each ingredient and its precise amount—oil and gas operators are allowed to withhold chemical components deemed trade secrets. For instance, a review of the 25 most recent disclosures, totaling almost 1,300 ingredients, found that trade secrets were claimed for about 15 percent of the chemical components reported to FracFocus (Wilder, 2012). The reports are also posted as individual PDF documents, making it impossible to easily search and download the entire database for further analysis. Finally, and perhaps most importantly, FracFocus has been criticized for diverting attention from the environmental and health hazards to disclosure. "Just focusing on disclosure allows the real issue of requiring prevention of contamination or harm to slip through the cracks and be ignored" (Fugleberg, 2011). In short, whatever else it might accomplish, FracFocus is unlikely to adequately address the numerous information limitations detailed above.

C.   Access to Fluid Information Is Not Enough; Use Is Required

In view of the need for more information on fracturing materials, parties unrelated to the extraction process will likely play a greater role. University scientists may need to generate data from independent experiments. Public interest groups may contract with universities or private labs to learn more about the impact of fracturing. And government agencies likely will be called upon to engage in more extensive reviews. Each of these activities will require more than knowledge about the chemical make-up of compounds and basic fracturing techniques; it will require use.

The need to use hydraulic fracturing products in order to assess their properties and performance is well established in the oil and gas industry, with a long history of going back and forth between laboratory and field experiments, from *in vitro* to *in vivo* experiments (Howard & Fast, 1970). For instance, since the early days of fracturing, laboratory testing has been used to help provide measurements of certain parameters known to be critical to the outcome of the treatments. Along the way, service company research laboratories have spent millions of dollars researching and developing fracturing fluids (Jennings, 1996). At the same time, what works in the laboratory has to be constantly adjusted to conditions in the field, and what works in one field needs to be adjusted to conditions in another. In the same way, it is only through using hydraulic fracturing products that their direct environmental and health effects can be assessed.

In addition to assessing the potential for hydraulic fracturing to cause direct environmental and health hazards, it is important to consider how the practice might interact with host materials. There are numerous "chemical and physical reactions that can occur in the open wellbore, induced fractures, natural fractures, and the surrounding matrix ... as a result of interactions between fracture fluids and the geologic target formations during the hydraulic fracturing process" (US Environmental Protection Agency, 2011, p. 40). For instance, formation waters are variable within and between formations, including concentration levels of the most common VOCs and semi-VOCs. Likewise, drilling and hydraulic fracturing "causes fluid-rock interactions that have the potential to mobilize heavy metals" such as barium, uranium, chromium, and zinc that are naturally enriched in the shale formation (US Environmental Protection Agency, 2011, p. 39). However, the only way to determine the extent to which these heavy metals are mobilized during fluid-rock reactions is to perform extraction studies "using a measured mass of ground and sieved shale and a known volume of chemical extractant" (US Environmental Protection Agency, 2011, p. 39).

Although many reactions in wells are subject to normal catalytic and restriction influences, others are subject to "a set of specific limiters that are found in few other places in [the] chemical industry" (US Environmental Protection Agency, 2011, p. 40). For instance, the influences of temperature and pressure are reasonably predictable, but "other reaction controls such as reaction rate are strongly influenced by the area and mixing constraints described by the location of the reaction, the area-to-volume ratio and the behavior and stability of the byproducts," all of which can only be assessed by putting the products in question to use in real-world settings (US Environmental Protection Agency, 2011, p. 40). Similarly, degradation reactions related to well construction and pipe and cement stability cannot be easily assessed, even with formation access. Re-precipitation compounds must also be considered. Again, given the many complexities and uncertainties involved, such interaction hazards can only be assessed in the field during actual hydraulic fracturing processes; mere knowledge of the hydraulic fracturing products and procedures would not be sufficient.

Another challenge to assessing any potential environmental and health hazards is obtaining representative samples. For instance, the only way to determine whether some materials are present or not (e.g., endocrine disruptors and carcinogens) is through analytical tests conducted directly on flowback waters (US Environmental Protection Agency, 2011). Additionally, "because fluids will undergo physical, chemical, and/or biological changes as they are moved from a geologic reservoir to the surface, sampling and preservation techniques affect the results" (US Environmental Protection Agency, 2011, p. 85). To further complicate matters, the composition of fluid varies non-linearly with flowback progress, necessitating time-series sampling. Other analyses can only be carried out through "sub-sampling at the wellhead based on analyte" (US Environmental Protection Agency, 2011, p. 86). Additionally, in the case of volatiles and reactive species, speed is important, and some samples may need to be processed within 48 hours. Other samples may need to be preserved under well conditions.

But even such unfettered access may not be sufficient: "Many standard analytical methods apply to the analysis of [hydraulic fracturing] fluids and flowback water samples. However, they will perform poorly in some cases involving high levels of interferents" (US Environmental Protection Agency, 2011, p. 97). Again, all of these requirements suggest that hydraulic fracturing fluid disclosure is not sufficient to assess the concerns that have been raised about the practice. Rather hydraulic fracturing products may need to be assessed in action (Latour, 1987). Given an absence of rigorous data on the migration of hydraulic fracturing fluids, the Department of Energy has recently proposed conducting a field experiment in which tracers would be used to assess whether the fluids migrate from the target production formation into drinking water aquifers (US Environmental Protection Agency, 2011).

As the level of IP related to hydraulic fracturing increases, more than simple disclosure is needed. Not only must the processes and products used be disclosed, third-party access to these processes and products—for non-commercial purposes—must also be made available. Without the ability to analyze the consequences of specific products and processes, the disclosure of their use is largely inconsequential.

Strong state enforcement programs are essential to ensure that drinking water supplies are protected as more natural gas is produced from tight shale formations, witnesses told a hearing of the US Senate Environment and Public Works Committee and its Water and Wildlife Subcommittee. Some lawmakers suggested that a bigger federal role might be necessary if states fall short (Snow, 2011).

D. The Prominence of Patents Has Increased in Hydraulic Fracturing

Strategically, there has been a shift in the perceived importance of patents. The emphasis on obtaining such rights related to hydraulic fracturing has increased over the last 20 years. Companies have become more aware of the utility of protecting intellectual property, and among businesses in general, there is a greater effort to capture rights as part of overall research and development investments. According to one commentator, from 1981 to 2003, the PTO issued about 50 hydraulic fracturing patents per year; the trend was remarkably steady over those 23 years, with a high of 73 in 1993 and a low of 25 in 1982 (Rutt, 2011). Then suddenly, from 2004 to 2010, the PTO issued an average of more than 150 patents a year—more than tripling the patenting output of the preceding two decades. In 2010 and 2011, the PTO issued 257 and 224 hydraulic fracturing-related patents respectively; never before had more than 200 hydraulic fracturing-related patents been issued in a single year (Rutt, 2012). Moreover, the increase in hydraulic fracturing patents occurred in contrast to other technologies employed in gas extraction with broader applications. Patents related to well completion have increased only moderately, and patents related to horizontal drilling have remained nearly flat, with few issuing per year.

E.   Patents Emerge as the Paradoxical Information Constraint

With the increased ownership of patents and consequential ability of companies to assert them as a downstream information control mechanism, patents can become the very antithesis of their statutory intent. Rather than disclosing important aspects of hydraulic fracturing materials, patents become functionally more important as a constraint. This is true even if information control was not a primary motivator in obtaining the patents in the first place. A company that reflexively patents or even seeks patents as a market exclusion device may find itself with tremendous power to protect sensitive information. One would expect that such a company would be more likely to employ restrictive licensing terms in order to preserve the option of exploiting the value of downstream information.

The need for active experimentation to obtain information is a critical issue if the material in question is under patent. As stated above, the use of patented compounds impacts two of the patent owner's fundamental rights of exclusivity: making and using the invention. A third party interested in investigating the impact of fracturing fluids on the environment or evaluating issues beyond discrete chemical composition (such as interactions between different chemicals) will need to make use of the patented materials. Without a license, it is unlikely that any exception in patent law would excuse such activity from infringement. A patentee can assert its rights to control testing and experimentation, and thereby shape the information environment.

If patents can pose such an important barrier, one might ask why they have not been identified as an issue to date? It appears that the application of patents as a significant information barrier is a relatively new phenomenon in gas extraction. In the past, conflicts between patent rights and information generation were relatively unlikely to occur because the number of patents related to fracturing compounds and methods was small, and entities that would be inclined to make infringing use of the materials existed primarily in industry. The primary concern on the part of patent owners would be restricting competition rather than controlling the public exposure of information. However, patent factors have changed, placing the focus more squarely on property rights as a potential barrier.

Perhaps even more interesting is the fact that patents can be expected to play a greater role in information constraint in the future. As noted above, the pressure to disclose more about fracturing chemicals is increasing. Searchable databases will likely become available and the nature of the extraction materials used will become more public. And, the more that basic information disclosure is required, the more that patents will likely be used to lock up secondary information production.

This seeming paradox of increased information disclosure rules resulting in more contracts is a consequence of opposing levers. As one method of protecting information—trade secrecy—becomes less viable, fracturing innovators will be more likely to pursue downstream protection over uses through patents. Such disclosure will essentially eliminate much of the protection that is now provided by trade secret law. The loss is not likely to be stemmed by the argument that forced disclosure is a taking of property, as it has been recognized that voluntary disclosure of information to government agencies does not implicate constitutional protections (*Ruckelshaus v. Monsanto Co.*, 1984). As we craft additional rules to compel disclosure, companies will be expected to employ patents more frequently as a means to lock up information. And the increasing population of patents suggests that this means for restricting information dissemination already exists.

III. BROADER IMPLICATIONS OF INFORMATION CONTAINMENT FOR BUSINESS STRATEGY

The use of patents as information containment tools extends beyond the case of natural gas extraction. There are many other contexts in which patents can impede safety information or knowledge of performance-related issues, and the implications of the emerging understanding of this power are significant. Clearly, the information containment properties of patents are more general legal issues that should impact industrial and innovation policy within the firm as well as government and society.

A. Information Containment in Other Industries

To gain an appreciation of the breadth of the new patent-information relationship one may look to other examples of containment that recently emerged. One of the most important contexts is in the field of genetically modified (GM) seed inventions. GM seeds have become dominant in several crops in the United States, particularly corn and soybeans. In general, multiple utility patents protect these modifications (Barton & Berger, 2001). Farmers obtain seeds subject to a license rather than an outright sale, and the license contains restrictive terms related to seed saving and other planting restrictions, as well as to distributing the seeds to others. Researchers may also obtain seeds, but such purchases are often on significantly different terms from the typical farming license. This restrictive environment has the potential to significantly impact information flow.

The problem with seed licensing practices is that contract terms can prevent basic research on issues such as plant safety profiles, drift between fields, mutations, resistance, etc. Researchers must negotiate for the use of seeds in particular contexts, and there is always the possibility that confidentiality conditions may apply to the results. The restrictions make sense for the seed producers; negative information can damage sales by raising safety and comparative efficacy issues that would otherwise be unknown. And, widely publicized risks could bring additional regulatory scrutiny. Coupled with the already fragile reputation of genetically modified crops, this additional negative information could be devastating for producers.

The legal legitimacy of restrictive seed licenses has been upheld. Most prominently, in *Monsanto v. McFarling* (2004), the Court of Appeals for the Federal Circuit upheld Monsanto's breach of contract claim and rejected McFarling's claims of patent misuse. According to the court, Monsanto was within its rights as a patentee in restricting the saving and replanting of seeds through its license, as the terms read on the same invention articulated in the claims. This case followed on the court's earlier decision in *Mallinckrodt, Inc. v. Medipart, Inc.* (1992), in which the court upheld a label license's restriction on the reuse of a medical device. Although the Supreme Court had an opportunity to rein in the power of licenses to prevent exhaustion of patent claims, it passed, implying that the practice is legitimate (*Quanta Computer, Inc. v. LG Electronics, Inc.*, 2008). The Court may consider the issue again when it determines whether seed sales exhaust patent rights for subsequent generations of seeds in a case granted certiorari in October 2012 (*Bowman v. Monsanto Co.*, 2012).

The result of various seed-licensing systems is that at least some basic safety research on the patented products is not being carried out. Additionally, the research that is being performed may be subject to disclosure limitations. To the extent that genetically modified seeds pose hidden dangers, patent rights may prevent this information from seeing the light of day.

In a recent article, Simon highlights the containment problem in radio-frequency identification technology and genetic testing. She particularly describes the power of patents to limit investigation into the "quality" of a patented invention (Simon, 2011). Simon notes that quality assessments are not clearly exempted under current law, and implies that the use of the invention by a putative tester would result in infringement.

It is likely that other examples exist and the issue will continue to arise in new fields. The fact that the issue is not industry specific but rather tied to the modern nature of patents suggests that it should be addressed generally. A government-imposed or self-regulatory approach that focuses on a specific type of information misses the true scope of patent-oriented information containment.

B. Information Containment as Mechanism for Competitive Advantage

The possibility that patents can be used as a means of information limitation presents opportunities for business. Although it is true that patent impacts can be socially negative—as appears to be the case in natural gas extraction—this does not necessarily mean that information containment cannot also have a positive economic effect, particularly at a firm level. It is reasonable for businesses to explore the competitive advantages in using patents to protect proprietary information. Such uses may coexist with regulatory efforts to ameliorate problems related to safety and product effectiveness, though conflicts may exist.

The most prominent use of information containment will be to prevent use and experimentation in research and development. As noted above, the enforcement limitation for pharmaceuticals is quite narrow, and will not prevent patent enforcement in other settings. The development of competing products that perform better or have more desirable safety profiles may be delayed during the term of the patent. Patents could theoretically restrict even comparison testing that aids consumer decision-making.

To be sure, the advantages in information containment may be slight, and generally difficult to enforce. Against the backdrop of high prosecution costs, businesses may be disinclined to pursue patents solely for this purpose. But for a firm that has a generally aggressive practice of pursuing patents as a broad strategy, the advantages of information containment may add fuel to the prosecution fire.

One can certainly argue that the use of information containment for competitive advantage often flies in the face of the goals of the patent system. From one perspective, this use is merely an exploitation of the full extent of the patent grant. But one can also view it as an unfair reneging on the patent owner's bargain with society to fully disclose all aspects of the invention. Regardless, businesses are likely to make use of what legal advantages patents provide, and information containment can be a valuable tool derived from the corporate IP portfolio.

C. Policy Reform to Confront the Negative Effects of Information Containment

Regardless of business interest in information containment, when such patent enforcement impacts safety or security, legal reformers may be compelled to act. As with any other federally created property system, the law can be changed on a national scale to curtail rights and increase openness. Two obvious routes for reform would be creating a legislative exception for experimental use related to safety or broadening the boundaries of the judicially created doctrine through the courts. However, courts and the legislature face substantial obstacles. Both will have difficulty in articulating a new rule that is properly positioned to increase information flow while preserving innovation.

One option favored by Simon is the recognition of a quality assessment defense in litigation (Simon, 2011). This defense would act like an expanded fair use. However, given the existence of safety issues that may in some cases even trump performance questions, prescriptions related to quality may not go far enough to address the full extent of information needs. When use of the invention is necessary to understand its impact in a real-world environment, greater relief is necessary. The use of an invention in the real world may present dangers that are impossible to understand in the lab—spillovers and externalities—that exist even if the invention is functioning exactly as intended. This need to understand safety through testing is the rationale behind government pharmaceutical approval systems, and the potential for patents to interfere is the reason behind the specific statutory infringement exemption (Patent Act of 1952, § 271(e)).

Congress has the power to create an exception for experimental uses that would cover safety investigations, quality assurance or even competitor research and development. Such an exception would not need to be justified as "non-commercial" to be enforceable, but could serve any purpose related to promoting the progress of the useful arts. This is essentially what occurred in 1984 with the passage of the Hatch-Waxman Act (Drug Price Competition and Patent Term Restoration Act of 1984 (HWA)), creating rules for pharmaceutical regulation that included a research exception for submissions to the FDA. This limitation on rights is known as the *Bolar* exemption in reference to its overruling of a Federal Circuit case, *Roche Products, Inc. v. Bolar Pharmaceutical Co.* (1984), which found no infringement limitation for clinical testing in preparation for generic drug applications. The rule is facially commercial in furtherance of its public mission. Essentially, Congress created an exception to permit generic pharmaceutical companies to have an approved drug ready to market as soon as the patent expired (Mossinghoff, 1999). This reduces patent owner profitability and creates a more favorable environment for competitors, but it does so for an important social goal. The *Bolar* exception does not affect patentability; rather, it simply carves out part of the patent owner's enforcement rights.

Similarly, in 1996 an exception was enacted that limited the enforcement of patents on surgical procedures (Patent Act of 1952, § 287(c)). The exception was specifically directed to physicians and their places of practice to address the concern that the threat of litigation would compromise medical care. As with pharmaceutical patents, the basic enforceability of the right was left in place.

The major limitation with any legislative reform is that an enactment that reduces or eliminates existing property rights may run afoul of the US Constitution's Fifth Amendment unless compensation is provided. Congress generally avoids the constitutional issue by ensuring that any reduction of rights applies prospectively. A second limitation with any legislative reform is that it is broad enough to permit necessary testing while limited enough to maintain innovation incentives. Moreover, legislative initiatives related to patent property rights must generally act prospectively to avoid constitutional takings issues.

If there is a ray of hope, it is the fact that patent exclusion is not automatic. The nature of the litigation process as well as the likely defendants involved provides some flexibility for retaining information flow. Before overreacting to patent obstacles, it is important to appreciate current options and identify the actors with flexibility. In the end, spreading awareness of the problem of patent restriction will likely be the most effective means of ensuring that the threat of strong patents does not encumber necessary research.

NOTES

* Copyright 2013, Daniel R. Cahoy, Joel Gehman and Zhen Lei. Portions of this chapter are excerpted from an earlier published article appearing in the *Michigan Telecommunications and Technology Law Review* (Cahoy, Gehman, & Lei, 2013). Thanks to John Bagby, Tony Briggs, Arvind Karunakaran, Lynda Oswald and the participants of the colloquium, "The Changing Face of American Patent Law and Its Impact on Business Strategy," sponsored by the Stephen M. Ross School of Business at the University of Michigan and the Smeal College of Business at Penn State University. Each author contributed equally to this chapter and the author order is alphabetical only.

REFERENCES

Agreement on Trade-Related Aspects of Intellectual Property Rights (TRIPS), Apr. 15, 1994, Marrakesh Agreement Establishing the World Trade Organization, Annex 1C, 1869 U.N.T.S. 299, 33 I.L.M. 1197 (1994).

American Petroleum Industry (2010, Jul. 19). *Freeing Up Energy: Hydraulic Fracturing: Unlocking America's Natural Gas Resources.* Retrieved from http://www.api.org/policy/exploration/hydraulicfracturing/upload/hydraulic_fracturing_primer.pdf.

Arthur, J.D. & Coughlin, B.U. (2011, Mar. 21–23). *Cumulative Impacts of Shale-Gas Water Management: Considerations and Challenges.* Society of Petroleum Engineers Americas E&P Health, Safety, Security, and Environmental Conference.

Ass'n for Molecular Pathology v. U.S. Patent and Trademark Office, 702 F.Supp.2d 181 (S.D.N.Y. 2010).

Ass'n for Molecular Pathology v. U.S. Patent and Trademark Office, 653 F.3d 1329 (Fed. Cir. 2011).

Ass'n for Molecular Pathology v. U.S. Patent and Trademark Office, __ 689 F.3d 1303 (Fed. Cir. 2012).

Australian Government, Advisory Committee on Intellectual Property (2005). *Patents and Experimental Use.* Retrieved from http://www.acip.gov.au/library/acip%20patents%20&%20experimental%20use%20final%20report%20final.pdf.

Barton, J.H. & Berger P. (2001). Patenting Agriculture. *Issues in Science and Technology*, **17**(4), 43–50.

Bowman v. Monsanto, __ U.S.__,133 S. Ct. 420.

Boyle, M.E. (2010). Leaving Room for Research: The Historical Treatment of the Common Law Research Exemption in Congress and the Courts, and Its Relationship to Biotech Law and Policy. *Yale Journal of Law & Technology*, **12**(2), 269–310.

Brannon, H.D., Daulton, D.J., Hudson, H.G. & Jordan, A.K. (2011, Oct. 30–Nov. 1). *Progression Toward Implementation of Environmentally Responsible Fracturing Processes.* Society of Petroleum Engineers Annual Technical Conference and Exhibition.

Cahoy, D., Gehman, J. & Lei, Z. (2013). Fracking Patents: The Emergence of Patents as Information Containment Tools in Shale Drilling. *Michigan Telecommunications & Technology Law Review*, **19**(2).

Colborn, T., Kwiatkowski, C., Schultz, K. & Bachran, M. (2011). Natural Gas Operations from a Public Health Perspective. *Human & Ecological Risk Assessment*, **17**(5), 1039–56.

Drug Price Competition and Patent Term Restoration Act of 1984 (HWA), Pub. L. No. 98-417, 98 Stat. 1585 (as amended).

Finkel, M.L. & Law, L. (2011). The Rush to Drill for Natural Gas: A Public Health Cautionary Tale. *American Journal of Public Health*, **101**(5), 784–5.

FracFocus.org, Chemical Disclosure Registry. Retrieved from http://fracfocus.org/node/31.

Fromer, J.C. (2009). Patent Disclosure. *Iowa Law Review*, **94**(2), 539–606.

Fugleberg J. (2011, Apr. 11). National "Fracking" Fluid Database Unveiled. *Billings Gazette.* Retrieved from http://billingsgazette.com/news/state-and-regional/wyoming/article_6088c631-669b-537e-bb39-c0a0b48799eb.html

Garud, R., Gehman, J. & Kumaraswamy, A. (2011). Complexity Arrangements for Sustained Innovation: Lessons from 3M Corporation. *Organization Studies*, **32**(6), 737–67.

Goodman, A. (2006). The Origins of the Modern Patent in the Doctrine of Restraint of Trade. *Intellectual Property Journal*, **19**(2), 297–332.

Holbrook, T.R. (2006). Possession in Patent Law. *Southern Methodist University Law Review*, **59**(1), 123–76.

Howard, G.C. & Fast, C.R. (1970). *Hydraulic Fracturing*. New York: Society of Petroleum Engineers.

Howarth, R.W. & Ingraffea, A. (2011). Natural Gas: Should Fracking Stop? *Nature*, **477**(7364), 271–5.

Huls, B. (2010, Oct. 19–21) *Maximizing the Marcellus Gold Rush while Minimizing Negative Impacts*. Canadian Unconventional Resources and International Petroleum Conference.

Jennings, A.R. (1996). Fracturing Fluids – Then and Now. *Journal of Petroleum Technology*, **48**(7), 604–10.

Jordan, A.K., Daulton, D.J., Cobb, J.A. & Grumbles, T. (2010, Sept. 19–22). *Quantitative Ranking Measures Oil Field Chemicals Environmental Impact*. SPE Annual Technical Conference and Exhibition. Florence, Italy: Society of Petroleum Engineers.

Kargbo, D.M., Wilhelm, R.G. & Campbell, D.J. (2010). Natural Gas Plays in the Marcellus Shale: Challenges and Potential Opportunities. *Environmental Science & Technology*, **44**(15), 5679–84.

Kosnik, R.L. (2007). *The Oil and Gas Industry's Exclusions and Exemptions to Major Environmental Statutes*. Washington, DC: Earthworks.

Latour, B. (1987). *Science in Action*. Cambridge, MA: Harvard University Press.

Leahy-Smith America Invents Act (AIA). Pub. L. No. 112-29, 125 Stat. 284 (2011).

Madey v. Duke, 307 F.3d 1351 (Fed. Cir. 2002).

Mallinckrodt, Inc. v. Medipart, Inc., 976 F.2d 700 (Fed. Cir. 1992).

Mayo Collaborative Services v. Prometheus Laboratories, Inc., __U.S. __ 132 S. Ct. 1289 (2012).

Monsanto v. McFarling, 363. F.3d 1336 (Fed. Cir. 2004).

Montgomery, C.T. & Smith, M.B. (2010, Dec.). Hydraulic Fracturing: History of an Enduring Technology. *Journal of Petroleum Technology*, pp. 26–40.

Mossinghoff, G. (1999). Overview of the Hatch-Waxman Act and Its Impact on the Drug Development Process. *Food & Drug Law Journal*, **54**(2), 187–94.

Murray, F. & Stern, S. (2007). Do Formal Intellectual Property Rights Hinder the Free Flow of Scientific Knowledge? An Empirical Test of the Anti-Commons Hypothesis. *Journal of Economic Behavior & Organization*, **63**(4), 648–87.

Nordhaus, W.D. (1969). *Invention, Growth, and Welfare: A Theoretical Treatment of Technological Change*. Cambridge, MA: M.I.T. Press.

Patent Act of 1952, 35 U.S.C. §§ 1-376 (1952) (as amended).

Protection of Environment, 40 C.F.R. § 423 Appx. A (2011).

Quanta Computer Inc. v. LG Electronics, Inc., 553 U.S. 617 (2008).

Reser, R.J. & Ritter, D.T. (2011). State and Federal Regulation of Hydraulic Fracturing. *The Advocate*, pp. 32–3.

Roche Products, Inc. v. Bolar Pharmaceutical Co., 733 F.2d 858 (Fed. Cir. 1984).

Ruckelshaus v. Monsanto Co., 467 U.S. 986 (1984).

Rutt, J.S. (2011, Mar. 20). U.S. Patent Explosion for Hydraulic Fracturing Technology: Impact on Marcellus Shale. *Foley & Lardner Cleantech & Nano Blog*. Retrieved from http://www.nanocleantechblog.com/2011/03/20/

u-s-patent-explosion-for-hydraulic-fracturing-technology-impact-on-marcellus-shale/.

Rutt, J.S. (2012, Feb. 26). Recent Hydraulic Fracturing Patenting Shows Connections with Cleantech and Nanotech. *Foley & Lardner Cleantech & Nano Blog.* Retrieved from http://www.nanocleantechblog.com/2012/02/26/recent-hydraulic-fracturing-patenting-shows-connections-with-cleantech-and-nanotech/.

Sanders, J., Tuck, D.A. & Sherman, R.J. (2010, Apr. 12–14). *Are your Chemical Products Green? A Chemical Hazard Scoring System.* Society of Petroleum Engineers International Conference on Health, Safety and Environment in Oil and Gas Exploration and Production.

Schnoor, J.L. (2010). Regulate, Baby, Regulate. *Environmental Science & Technology,* **44**(17), 6524–5.

Simon, B.M. (2011). Patent Cover-Up. *Houston Law Review,* **47**(5), 1299–1355.

Snow, N. (2011, Apr. 18). Strong State Programs Key to Safe Shale Gas Activity, Senators Told. *Oil & Gas Journal.* Retrieved from http://www.ogj.com/articles/2011/04/strong-state-programs.html.

Soeder, D.J. (2010). The Marcellus Shale: Resources and Reservations. *Eos, Transactions,* **92**(32), 277.

Strandburg, K.J. (2004). What Does the Public Get? Experimental Use and the Patent Bargain. *Wisconsin Law Review,* **2004**(1), 81–156.

US Environmental Protection Agency (2011, Nov.). *Plan to Study the Potential Impacts of Hydraulic Fracturing on Drinking Water Resources.* EPA Publication 600/R-11/122. Washington, DC.

US General Accounting Office (1991). OSHA *Action Needed to Improve Compliance with Hazard Communication Standard.* GAO Publication HRD-92-8. Washington, DC.

Walterscheid, E.C. (1997). Charting a Novel Course: the Creation of the Patent Act of 1790. *AIPLA Quarterly Journal,* **25**(4), 445–529.

Whittemore v. Cutter, 29 F. Cas. 1120, 1121 (C.C.D. Mass. 1813).

Wilder, F. (2012, Mar. 13). Fracking Disclosure Law Falls Short, Critics Say. *Texas Observer.* Retrieved from http://www.texasobserver.org/forrestforthetrees/texas-fracking-disclosure-law-falls-short-critics-say.

Witter, R., Stinson, K., Sackett, H., Putter, S., Kinney, G., Teitelbaum, D. & Newman, L. (2008). Potential Exposure-Related Human Health Effects of Oil and Gas Development: A White Paper. *University of Colorado Denver Working Paper.*

8. Will the America Invents Act post-grant review improve the quality of patents? A comparison with the European Patent Office opposition

Susan J. Marsnik*

After years of attempts to reform its 60-year-old patent law, in September 2011 the United States enacted the Leahy-Smith America Invents Act (AIA). The law ushers in substantial changes in US patent law and practice. Significant among the changes are a number of new trial proceedings through which third parties may challenge patents at the US Patent and Trademark Office (PTO) once the patent has issued. The AIA law introduced three new or revised post-issuance *inter partes* proceedings: post-grant review, *inter partes* review, and a specialized post-grant review for certain business methods. These proceedings address rising concerns over a perceived proliferation of poor quality patents due to substantial increases in the number of patent applications in the US. The primary avenue for testing the validity of patents in the US has been litigation, which is both costly and time-consuming. A primary justification for the new post-issuance proceedings was to provide a faster and less expensive alternative to litigation.

Providing an opportunity for third parties to intervene post-issuance is not new in the US system. Since 1981, third parties or the patent owner have been able to request an examination of an already issued patent through an *ex parte* reexamination. In 1999, the American Inventors Protection Act introduced an administrative *inter partes* reexamination, which was not been widely used. The AIA replaces *inter partes* reexamination with the *inter partes* review. This chapter focuses primarily on post-grant review, the most powerful and broadest of the new post-issuance proceedings.

Post-issuance review systems have long been debated in US academic, legal and business circles as a way to reduce the incidence of invalid or poor quality patents in a more cost-efficient manner. It was natural to turn to the European system as part of the discussion. For almost four decades, the European Patent Office (EPO) has heard and decided post-grant oppositions under the European Patent Convention (Convention on the Grant of European Patents [EPC], 2010). Empirical studies demonstrate that the more valuable or technologically important a patent, the more likely it will trigger an opposition in the EPO, just as it is more likely to be litigated in the US. The opposition system has been successful in correcting EPO examination errors through invalidating or narrowing patents. The success of the European opposition system has served as a justification for post-grant review in the US. Proponents have argued that allowing a patentee's competitors to intervene post-issuance at the PTO will improve the quality of patents granted since competitors often have access to critical art not available to the examiners. Society as a whole will also benefit from reducing the number of invalid patents earlier and without the costs and delays of patent litigation.

The AIA incorporates certain features of the European opposition into the post-grant review. However, substantial differences exist that make post-grant review in the US a less effective tool for improving the quality of patents. This chapter begins with Part I discussing the rationale for the new post-grant review and shortcomings under the pre-AIA system, including utilizing the litigation system as the primary vehicle for invalidating patents after grant. Part II considers the post-grant opposition system operating in Europe followed by a description of the new AIA post-grant review system in Part III. Part IV analyzes whether the new American system will fulfill the rationale of a more cost-efficient, faster means of ensuring patent quality in the United States. The author concludes that the costs associated with post-grant review and its potent estoppel rules make it an unlikely tool for improving the quality of patents or stemming the tide of patent litigation in the US.

I.   RATIONALE FOR POST-ISSUANCE REVIEW

The traditional utilitarian justification for patents is that providing incentives to invent benefits both society and inventors. In the US the *quid pro quo* of the patent system requires complete disclosure of the invention in exchange for powerful rights granted to the patentee to exclude others from making, using, and selling the patented invention. The public benefits. Full disclosure facilitates further innovation and invention based on the patent and the patented invention enters the public domain in 20 years. The patent owner benefits from the ability to exploit the patent. Patents that are invalid or too broad place an unwarranted burden on innovation

and society. Uncertainty about the validity of a patent can deter investment and impact the direction of innovation (Farrell & Merges, 2004).
Bad quality patents can encourage infringement lawsuits and settlements,
which raise transaction costs that are passed on to consumers (Merrill,
Levin & Myers, 2004). Therefore, invalid patents can have a powerful
negative impact and society benefits by eliminating them.

Concerns over declining patent quality have been linked to a dramatic
increase in the number of patent applications filed with and granted by the
PTO. In 1980, 104,329 utility patent applications were filed. The number
almost quintupled to 503,582 in 2011. During the same period, the number
of utility patents granted increased from 61,819 to 224,505 (PTO Patent
Statistics Report, 2012). A number of factors contribute to the dramatic
expansion in applications. In part, it results from an increased interest in
acquiring, using and enforcing patents domestically as well as by foreign
applicants who wish to exploit their inventions in the US. Courts in the
US have also expanded patentable subject matter to include those related
to biotechnology, computer software and business methods. Patents have
grown increasingly complex in terms of the number of claims and references to prior art, making examination a more arduous task. All of these
factors contribute to an examination backlog. The PTO reported more
than 1.2 million pending utility patent applications in its most recent
Performance and Accountability Report (PTO, 2011a). The sheer number
of patent applications, the substantial backlog, and increased productivity
pressures at the PTO pose serious threats to the quality of patents issued
(Thambisetty, 2007; Hall & Harhoff, 2004). Improving the quality of
examination so that fewer questionable patents are granted could provide
a solution to the patent quality conundrum. However, this would not be
desirable as most patents are not valuable. It makes more sense to focus
resources on patents likely to have the greatest societal impact in terms of
both innovation and competitors.

In the US, litigation provides the primary avenue for contesting 'bad'
patents. Not all questionable patents are challenged in court. Litigation
focuses on the most important technologically and commercially viable
patents (Allison, Lemley & Walker, 2009; Allison, Lemley, Moore &
Trunkey, 2004; Graham & Harhoff, 2006). Litigation is a costly vehicle
to test patents. The American Intellectual Property Law Association
Law Practice Management Committee reported the median costs of
patent litigation with between $1 million and $25 million at risk at $1.5
million through the end of discovery and $2.5 million inclusive of all
costs (AIPLA, 2011). Not only is it costly, but asymmetries existing in
the litigation system impact results. Farrell and Merges explain that
patentees have much greater incentives to pursue infringement lawsuits

or defend vigorously on the issue of patent validity than putative infringers have to bring an action (2004). The press and academic literature are filled with reports of non-practicing entities, often characterized as trolls, filing infringement lawsuits against numerous small competitors and then settling for a licensing fee. The alleged infringers have little economic incentive to challenge the validity of a patent in court. Litigating and losing may be far worse than paying the patent owner's demand for a license, even though the alleged infringer may not believe the patent is valid. Challenging validity in court could bankrupt a small company or lead to an injunction that could shut down its business. Furthermore, if the court upholds the patent, the patentee may refuse to license essential technology the infringer needs to operate. A better business alternative for a competitor might be to avoid the lawsuit completely or settle the lawsuit by accepting a license from an owner of a questionable patent. The costs can be passed on to the consumer. The pass-through of costs related to questionable patents illustrates the public's stake in lawsuits challenging patents in a way that does not exist in other economic lawsuits (Farrell & Merges, 2004). The ability to settle litigation runs counter to society's interest in ensuring that patents are valid. When a lawsuit related to a questionable patent is settled, society may never know whether that patent really was valid. This can hamper innovation and investment.

For years, scholars, practitioners and government bodies have advocated instituting post-issuance administrative trial proceedings at the PTO to determine validity more efficiently than litigation (Matal, 2012; Carrier, 2011; Carlson & Migliorina, 2006; Farrell & Merges, 2004; Merrill et al., 2004; Federal Trade Commission, 2003; McKie & Edward, 1974). Because of the European Patent Office's history with post-grant oppositions, a procedure imbedded in the EPC in 1973, many have turned to that model as a rationale for instituting post-grant review in the US. Empirical studies demonstrated the efficiencies of oppositions, particularly since the most valuable patents granted by the EPO are opposed (Caviggioli, Scellato & Ughetto, 2012; Hall & Harhoff, 2004; Graham, Hall, Harhoff & Mowery, 2002). The value of patents determines whether those patents are opposed in the EPO, just as the most valuable patents are litigated in the US. A number of factors indicate whether a patent will be opposed. Patents will be attacked more frequently if they contain a higher number of backward citations to previous patents. Scellato et al. (2011) posit that the positive correlation between a higher incidence of oppositions and a larger number of previous patent citations may indicate a more questionable inventive step: that the patent doesn't meet non-obviousness criteria. The owners of the cited patent may more readily become aware of the newly granted patent and so can make a decision about filing an opposition more quickly than another third party. Forward citations in subsequent patents are also relevant to value. Greater numbers of citations in subsequent inventions indicate the patent contributes to the state of the art (Scellato et al., 2011). The number of claims, which can indicate the relative complexity of the patent, is also positively and significantly correlated with the likelihood of opposition (Caviggioli et al., 2012).

Currently, approximately 5 percent of all granted European patents are opposed (Boff, 2011; Caviggioli et al., 2012). This indicates a downward trend from a norm of 9.25 percent between 1980 and 2000. Scellato et al. (2011) suggest the decrease might have resulted from improvements in EPO examination or greater number of marginal patents not opposed. However, given the significant increase in patent applications to the EPO during the same period the PTO has experienced increases, it is probable the more valuable patents opposed may represent a smaller percentage of the total number of patents granted by the EPO. There may also exist a free rider problem. If a patent of questionable quality negatively impacts multiple competitors, individual firms may wait for someone else to bear the cost of opposition (Scellato et al., 2011).

Oppositions correct a significant number of examination mistakes. Roughly one-third of oppositions are rejected with the patents remaining intact as granted. Approximately one-third are revoked in their entirety and one-third are maintained in amended form that narrows their breadth (Boff, 2011; Hall & Harhoff, 2004). Oppositions serve a positive screening function of weeding out a substantial number of bad patents and narrowing a substantial number that are too broad. This positive screening function led to advocacy on this side of the Atlantic to include a strong post-grant review mechanism in the US patent system. Indeed, the stated purpose of the post-grant review procedure in the AIA is to "establish a more efficient and streamlined patent system that will improve patent quality and limit unnecessary litigation costs" (PTO, Rules of Practice, 2012).

II. EUROPEAN PATENT SYSTEM

The EPO houses the largest and most successful system of post-issuance *inter partes* review. The contours of the European opposition provide a good background against which to measure the new procedures in the AIA. The legal landscape for protecting patents within Europe is substantially different from that in the US. Rather than a unitary patent application and enforcement system that covers the entire territory, Europe has a dual system of multinational and national patent law. What we call a

"European" patent is not a single patent covering all of Europe.[1] It is a set of independent national patents created under the EPC using a single application through the EPO where it is examined. A person wishing to patent an invention in an EPC contracting state may either file a national application in the patent office in each country in which protection is sought, or file one application with the EPO in Munich designating all of the contracting states in which she desires protection. Because all contracting states have transposed the EPC into national law, the law should be harmonized such that if a person takes the national route, a patent that is granted in Germany should also be granted in France and the UK. However, this is not always the case as European nations do not all approach patenting in the same manner. It is possible for one national office to grant a patent and another to deny it. National offices subject patent applications to different examination procedures, interpretations of the law and requirements and formats for claims. Even if the patent is granted by more than one national office, a patent for the same invention may differ in both form and scope from one country to another (Hoyng, 2006). The resulting lack of consistency makes the single EPO application process a more attractive avenue. If the EPO grants the European patent, it begins its life with the same form and scope in each European country.

The European patent does not immediately become a German or Italian patent. The owner must validate or "nationalize" the patent in each of the countries it has designated. The European patent becomes a bundle of national patents governed by national patent law and enforced in that country (EPC Art. 64(1); Rudge, 2012). Once validated in a contracting state, the patent is entirely independent of the validated patent in every other contracting state. Enforcement and revocation become entirely matters of national law. Because of differences in national law and differing legal traditions, it is possible for a patent granted by the EPO to be revoked in one contracting state, but not another (Marsnik & Thomas, 2011). The primary exception to national sovereignty over a European patent once it has been granted and validated is the post-grant opposition procedure within the EPO.[2] A number of factors make a third-party challenge to validity through an opposition more attractive than bringing a revocation proceeding in each country. A primary advantage is consistency. If the EPO determines a patent should not have been granted or narrows the scope of the claims, that decision has immediate application in all of the EPC contracting states in which the patent had been validated. If a party is seeking patent protection in a number of European nations, the EPO application and opposition system is more efficient than the national route, both in terms of cost and uniformity.

A.   The EPO Opposition and Appeal

Any third party, except the proprietor of the patent, who believes that the patent should not have been granted may file an opposition (EPC, 2010, Art. 99). The third party need not have an interest. It is possible for a third party to keep his identity secret from the patent owner by using a "straw man" to file the opposition on his behalf (Case G 9/93, 1994). The opposition must be filed within nine months of the grant of the patent (EPC, 2010, Art. 99). If a challenger misses the nine-month window, the only way to challenge the validity of the patent is through a patent revocation procedure under the national laws of the countries in which the patent is validated. Article 100 lists the broad grounds upon which oppositions may be based, including the "invention" does not meet patentability criteria, was not sufficiently disclosed or the subject matter extends beyond the original application (EPC, 2010). The EPO's Opposition Division examines the notice to ensure that the opposition is admissible, that it meets the formal requirements for opposition (EPO 2012, Part D). If so, it proceeds to a panel of three experienced technical examiners, one of whom may have been involved in the original examination. If particular legal expertise is required, a legally qualified examiner may be added. The opposition is not a reexamination. It is an *inter partes* proceeding in which the Opposition Division acts in a quasi-judicial role. However, unlike a court, the Opposition Division is not required to limit its determination to the grounds invoked by the parties. On its own motion, the Opposition Division may consider other grounds for opposition (EPC, 2010, Rule 8).

There are four possible outcomes to an opposition: (1) the opposition may be rejected; (2) the patent may be fully revoked as invalid; (3) the patent may be maintained, but in an amended form that narrows the patent by modifying its claims; or (4) the opposition may be closed without an outcome, typically because the opposition is withdrawn or the patent has lapsed for failure to pay maintenance fees in all EPC member states in which it has been filed. Narrowing the scope of the patent often takes the form of a negotiation between the parties with the Oppositions Division panel serving as mediator (Graham & Harhoff, 2006). Although settlement is possible, once an opposition has been filed, parties' opportunities are restricted. Rule 84(2) of the Implementing Regulations allow the EPO to proceed with the opposition on its own motion after the parties have withdrawn (EPC, 2010). If the Opposition Division has reasonable grounds to believe that a limitation or revocation is likely, it will proceed despite the absence of the parties. This serves as a powerful deterrent against settlement, since the EPO may modify or invalidate the patent without regard to the parties' settlement agreement and without their input. It also discourages using the opposition strategically to harass a patent holder (Graham & Harhoff, 2006). Only a small number of opposition cases close without reaching an outcome. Hall and Harhoff (2004) reported the number closing without outcome to be 5.3 percent and most likely capture incidences in which the parties have settled.

Either party or both may appeal the decision of the Opposition Division to the EPO Technical Boards of Appeal (the Board). There are 27 Boards, each highly specialized in a particular subject matter expertise. The particular Board hearing an opposition appeal interprets and applies the EPC and case law. One-third of oppositions are appealed (Hall & Harhoff, 2004). Filing the appeal prevents the Opposition Division's decision from entering into force until the appeal is resolved (EPC, 2010, Art 109; Veronese, 2009). This means that a patent revoked in opposition remains valid pending the outcome of the appeal. The Board may uphold the decision, modify the decision, or remand the case to the Opposition Division for further action. In most cases, the Board's decision is final since further appeal of an opposition to the Enlarged Board of Appeal is only possible in very limited circumstances, such as fundamental procedural violations or criminal acts (Veronese, 2009). Appeal to a court is impossible. No multinational court exists for that purpose and a direct appeal is not within the jurisdiction of national courts.

Oppositions can take an excessively long time to complete. According to the EPO, the grant procedure takes about three to five years from the application date. The average opposition takes 2.2 years if the patent is revoked and four years if the patent is amended. Appeals can add another two years (Scellato et al., 2011). The entire process can average between seven and eleven years, although it can last much longer. The European patent application for the famous genetically modified OncoMouse, filed in June 1985, was initially denied as unpatentable by the EPO. The process of moving through opposition and appeal culminated 19 years later when the Board remitted the matter to the Opposition Division in July 2004 with directions to enter a modified patent (*Harvard/Transgenic animal*, 2005). Ultimately, the patent was revoked because the owner didn't pay the fees. Although the average case is not as time-consuming, the OncoMouse example illustrates the impact the process can have on the inventor and on society. The longer an opposition takes to reach a conclusion on patentability, the more detrimental the impact on the patent holder and competitors. Uncertainty about the scope of the patent impacts the patent owner's exploitation of the invention. Competitors may not invest if the possibility of their infringing is not clear (Caviggioli et al., 2012).

B. The Relationship between EPO Oppositions and National Courts

Once the opposition and appeal have concluded finding a patent invalid, the matter has ended. It will be revoked retroactively in each contracting state in which it was validated. If the process finds the patent is valid entirely or in amended form, validity may only be challenged in each country individually under that country's law. The EPC has harmonized grounds for revocation in contracting states in Article 139 (EPC, 2010). The broad grounds for revocation track those for invalidity in oppositions, including: the subject matter is not patentable, the invention is not sufficiently disclosed, or the subject matter extends beyond the application. National court challenges to patent validity may arise as defenses to infringement suits or in separate actions to declare the patent invalid (Jacobs, 2012). Differences in procedural and substantive law and the time it takes to resolve a case can lead to very different validity outcomes in different countries. And, how a nation deals with revocation proceedings can impact the use of EPO opposition proceedings by its nationals. The majority of European countries handle issues of infringement and validity in the same court (Moss & Jones, 2008; Judge, 2002). A minority, including Germany, bifurcate issues of infringement and validity. German law mandates that only the Bunderpatentgericht, the Federal German Patent Court, may determine validity. If validity is raised as a defense in a German infringement suit before the Bundegerchitshof (BGH), the Federal Court of Justice, the party raising the defense must file a separate action for invalidity with the Bunderpatentgericht. The BGH has no jurisdiction to declare the patent invalid. The Bunderpatentgericht has no jurisdiction to decide infringement. Only 25 percent of parties sued for infringement in BGH cases file separate invalidity actions (Jacobs, 2012). The BGH may stay the infringement action pending the outcome of the invalidity proceeding, but it is unlikely to do so unless it is obvious that the patent is invalid (Marsnik & Thomas, 2011). This means that if the BGH decides infringement before the Bunderpatentgericht determines validity, which is often the case, a defendant is put at a commercial disadvantage. Since he has been found to be infringing, he may not be able to sell his products pending the outcome of the invalidation suit (Jacobs, 2012). This bifurcation feature of the German system may positively impact the number of oppositions filed by Germans: 61.2 percent of all European patents opposed have at least one German opponent, a rate nearly six times as high as the next highest opposing country. Furthermore, 72 percent of European oppositions in which a German is a party are against other Germans. No other country has such a high fraternal opposition rate (Boff, 2012). The bifurcated German system has an impact.

Parties may not have to wait until the conclusion of an existing EPO opposition to challenge the validity of a European patent in a national court. In many countries, a national revocation proceeding or trial may run parallel with an EPO opposition. In countries in which parallel proceedings are possible, national courts determine whether their cases will be stayed during the pendency of the opposition. UK courts typically will not stay court proceedings unless the opposition is close to a decision (Boff, 2011). Under German law, a validity action cannot be filed with the Bunderpatentgericht as long as an opposition may still be filed or while opposition proceedings are pending (Patentgesetz, 2009, §81(2)).

A determination on an issue by the Opposition Division or Board does not preclude a party from raising and arguing the same issues in a national revocation case. The EPC contains no estoppel provision (Gupta & Feerst, 2012; Boff, 2011). The probability of winning a suit in a national forum having lost before the Opposition Division and the Board is low. Graham and Harhoff (2006) conducted a study of patents surviving European opposition that were later challenged before the German Bunderpatentgericht. They found that opposition hardened the patent rights. National courts defer to EPO decisions since judges endeavor to interpret their national laws in a manner that doesn't contradict the EPC and the decisions of the EPO (Scellato et al., 2011). Despite this deference, it is possible for a party to successfully convince a national court that a patent granted by the EPO should be revoked, even after it has been validated in opposition. However, the revocation decision of the national court applies only in that country.

C.   Costs of EPO Oppositions and National Revocations

It costs less to oppose patents in the EPO than individually challenging the patent in each European country in which it has been validated. The filing fees for oppositions and appeals are €705 ($915) and €1180 ($1532) respectively. Total average costs of European oppositions range from $15,000 to $50,000 through decision, but can be more if the case is complex or there are multiple parties opposing the patent. The costs of appeal can approach or surpass the cost of the opposition (Boff, 2011). Although each party typically bears the cost of the opposition, unlike the loser pays rule in typical European national litigation, the Opposition Division may order a party to pay all costs for "reasons of equity" (EPC, 2010, Art. 104). The equity provisions apply when "the costs are culpably incurred as a result of irresponsible or even malicious actions" (EPO, 2012, Part D, IX, 1.4). This rule has been characterized as an anti-troll provision that protects against abuse of the opposition proceeding (Graham & Harhoff, 2006).

The cost for nullifying or invalidating a patent at the national level varies. No published source exists with this information across jurisdictions. In most European jurisdictions, an infringement and revocation action costs between €100,000 ($130,000) and €200,000 ($260,000) (Moss & Jones, 2008). The amount can vary greatly by jurisdiction, particularly since some jurisdictions have more liberal discovery and others may regulate lawyers' fees. Even a relatively straightforward suit in England will cost £500,000 ($812,000), with more complex cases costing in excess of £1 million ($1.6 million). Similar amounts can be spent on an appeal (Moss & Jones, 2008).

In most instances the European opposition is a more attractive option than national litigation for reasons of cost, national judicial procedure and for purposes of initially securing a uniform patent across European countries.

III. POST-GRANT REVIEW UNDER THE AMERICA INVENTS ACT

The AIA added multiple options within the PTO that allow third parties to challenge the validity of patents post-issuance in trial-like proceedings. This chapter focuses on post-grant review, the proceeding that most closely resembles European opposition. The new *inter partes* review, a reworking of the previous *inter partes* reexamination, has no EPC equivalent. It is a narrower proceeding limited to third-party challenges available only after post-grant review and only on novelty and non-obviousness grounds. It is primarily designed to address issues of prior art in patents and printed publications after the post-grant review window has closed. There is also a post-grant review for certain business method patents that also has no equivalent under the EPC. Because of its special nature, it is beyond the scope of this chapter.

Congress added the post-grant review mechanism to the American patent system to provide competitors with a faster and less expensive route to testing the validity of newly granted patents of dubious validity (Matal, 2012). The new post-issuance proceedings under the AIA are not America's first experiment with third-party intervention at the PTO. More than a decade ago, the American Inventors Protection Act of 1999 introduced *inter partes* reexamination, allowing third parties to initiate an administrative alternative to litigation on grounds of novelty and non-obviousness based on prior art consisting of patent or printed publications (Patent Act of 1952, §303(a)). The *inter partes* reexamination was rarely used and is no longer available. According to the most current published data, only 1,659 *inter partes* reexaminations have been filed in total (PTO, *Inter Partes* Reexamination Filing Data, 2012). It did not fulfill its potential of providing an effective, low-cost alternative to litigation. In large part, its estoppel provisions prevented wide use. In a civil action following the *inter partes* reexamination, the person requesting the reexamination was estopped from asserting the invalidity of any claim found to be valid on any grounds it "raised or could have raised" during the reexamination (Patent Act of 1952, § 315(c)). The broad consensus among patent experts indicated the estoppel risk to a challenger was too great (Farrell & Merges, 2004). Similar, although less restrictive, estoppel provisions in both *inter partes* review, which replaces *inter partes* reexamination, and post-grant review could have a similar impact.

A.   Post-grant Review

The AIA post-grant review resembles European opposition in a number of key features and differs in significant ways. Post-grant review and oppositions are similar in terms of who may file, the time frame for filing, and the relationship of validity grounds in the administrative trial to those used in civil cases. Under § 321 of the AIA, any person who is not the owner of the patent may file a petition to institute a post-grant review no later than nine months after the date of the patent grant or issuance of a reissue patent (Leahy-Smith America Invents Act, 2011, § 321). Similar to the European opposition, patentability may be challenged on broad grounds. Under the AIA, these include novelty, non-obviousness, abandonment, and failure to comply with requirements for the specification (Leahy-Smith America Invents Act, 2011, § 321). The Director reviews the petition and may not authorize the review unless the petition presents information, which if not rebutted, demonstrates "that it is more likely than not at least 1 of the claims challenged in the petition is unpatentable" or that is raises a "novel or unsettled legal question" important to other patents or applications (Leahy-Smith America Invents Act, 2011, § 324). This threshold essentially requires the petitioner to present a *prima facie* case. Its practical effect requires petitioners to closely tie its challenges to particular arguments against particular claims (Matal, 2012). Thus, the AIA incorporates a higher initial threshold showing than is required in the EPO. The grounds for determining a European opposition inadmissible are primarily based on technical non-compliance with filing rules, not a threshold showing of invalidity. The post-grant review will be heard by a newly created Patent Trial and Appeal Board (PTAB) sitting in panels of three administrative judges having both legal and technical competence. The composition of the PTAB differs from the typical panel of three technical experts on the

Opposition Division panels. Their functions differ, as well. Opposition Division panels function in a quasi-judicial capacity while the PTAB's function is judicial. A critical difference between the European opposition and the post-grant review is the duration of the proceeding. The AIA mandates that the PTAB must issue its final determination one year from the PTO's notice of proceeding, although the decision may be delayed for up to six months for good cause (Leahy-Smith America Invents Act, 2011, § 326). The EPC has no such time limit.

As with European oppositions, there are four possible outcomes of the post-grant review. The PTAB must issue a written decision and: (1) publish a new certificate cancelling any claim determined to be unpatentable; (2) publish a certificate confirming any claim determined to be patentable; (3) publish a certificate incorporating new or amended claims determined to be patentable; or (4) terminate the post-grant review (Leahy-Smith America Invents Act, 2011, § 328(b)). Section 327 mandates that the post-grant review be terminated with respect to any petitioner upon a joint request by the petitioner and patent owner upon submission of a settlement agreement, unless the post-grant review has been decided prior to the filing of the termination (Leahy-Smith America Invents Act, 2011). However, the PTAB retains discretion to terminate the review or continue reviewing a challenged patent even if no petitioner remains in the post-grant review (Leahy-Smith America Invents Act, 2011, §327(a); PTO, Rules of Practice, 2012, § 42.74(a)). The PTO takes the view that the issue of patentability is not subject to settlement and will consider the facts of each case in determining whether to proceed to written decision. The final rules provide that the PTAB may independently determine any question of patentability (PTO, Rules of Practice, 2012, §42.74(a)). This discretion to continue deciding patentability without the parties may prove to be as powerful a deterrent against settlement as Rule 84(2) of the EPO's Implementing Regulations. However, post-grant review petitioners have incentives to settle under Section 327 that do not exist in the European opposition. If a petitioner settles under Section 327 and the post-grant review is terminated and no estoppel attaches to the petitioner, its real party in interest or privy. Because estoppel is not an issue in EPO oppositions, the same incentive to settle does not exist. For this reason, a petitioner under the AIA may prefer to settle a post-grant review rather than proceed to a final written determination. Either party may appeal the PTAB judgment directly to the Court of Appeals for the Federal Circuit (CAFC) (Leahy-Smith America Invents Act, 2011, § 141).

B.   Relationship of Post-grant Review and Other Proceedings

The AIA includes rules governing the relationship between post-grant review and other proceedings. The estoppel provisions are among the more controversial due to their broad scope and how early they attach.

Parties who have a final written decision from the PTAB may not assert in a subsequent PTO proceeding, such as an *inter partes* review, or in a civil action, whether it be federal court or an action before the International Trade Commission, any grounds for invalidity that the petitioner "raised or reasonably could have raised during that post-grant review" (Leahy-Smith America Invents Act, 2011, § 325(e)). The "reasonably could have raised" estoppel provision is troublesome. The language was meant to soften the estoppel provisions of *inter partes* reexamination, which precluded a party raising an issue it "could have raised" in reexamination in subsequent litigation. Matal, in his legislative history of the AIA, quotes Senator Kyle's explanation that adding the modifier "reasonably" was meant to "ensure that the could-have-raised estoppel extends only to that prior art which a skilled searcher conducting a diligent search reasonably could have been expected to discover" (Matal, 2012). The "reasonably could have raised" standard was added to the new *inter partes* review, replacing *inter partes* reexamination (Leahy-Smith America Invents Act, 2011, § 314(e)). It was meant to prevent duplicative administrative and judicial proceedings. The standard was never meant to apply across the board to all proceedings subsequent to post-grant review. Earlier versions of patent reform bills limited post-grant review estoppel in subsequent civil cases only to issues actually raised and decided. Business and patent law professional associations supported the limitation in subsequent litigation, fearing that if the estoppel effects of post-grant review were too harsh, it would not be used. In all versions of the bill, except the final version, the "reasonably could have raised standard" for post-grant review only applied to subsequent administrative proceedings such as *inter partes* review. However, in the final version of the bill the "reasonably could have raised" standard applied to civil litigation as well. Since nothing in the record acknowledged this change, it appears to be an error made in the final version (Matal, 2012).

Post-grant review estoppel relating to civil actions attaches early. Section 325(e)(2) provides that a post-grant review that results in a final written decision precludes a petitioner, real party in interest or privy from raising invalidity grounds it raised or reasonably could have raised. This language indicates estoppel attaches upon the written decision, not after the appeals have been exhausted. Given that post-grant review determinations must be made within 12 or 18 months, estoppel may have a fairly imminent impact. It is unclear how the CAFC will interpret the estoppel language. In a recent case, the CAFC held that the estoppel effect of an *inter partes* reexamination required all appeals be exhausted before estoppel attached (*Bettcher v. Bunzl*, 2011), which could take six years (McKeown, 2011). It is possible the CAFC could interpret the post-grant review language in a similar manner.

The AIA contains rules governing the relationship between post-grant reviews and civil actions. A post-grant review may not be instituted if a petitioner has previously filed a declaratory judgment for invalidity. However, that party may file a petition for a post-grant review challenging the validity of one or more claims any time after filing a declaratory judgment action. Filing the post-grant review triggers an automatic stay of the court action. The stay may not be lifted until the patent owner moves the court to lift the stay, the patent owner files an action or counterclaim for infringement, or the post-grant review petitioner moves the court to dismiss the claim (Leahy-Smith America Invents Act, 2011, § 325(a)). Given the post-grant review estoppel provisions, the PTAB will make the final determination on patentability of a particular claim. Post-grant review proceedings may only coexist with litigation if the patent owner has filed a claim or counterclaim for infringement. If the patent owner files a preliminary injunction action alleging infringement within three months of the patent grant, the court may not stay the action on the grounds that the petitioner has filed a post-grant review (Leahy-Smith America Invents Act, 2011, § 325(b)). Therefore, if a post-grant review is progressing parallel to a court action under circumstances allowed by the AIA, a ruling by the PTAB on patentability will estop the court from determining validity. A ruling by the trial court does not have the same effect on proceedings before the PTAB.

C.   Costs of Post-grant Review and Other Procedural Issues

A key reason for incorporating third-party post-grant proceedings in the America Invents Act was to provide a more cost-effective alternative to litigation. On 14 August 2012, the PTO published its final rules, including fees, and estimated the costs of a post-grant review. The filing fee, which must be submitted with the post-grant review petition, depends upon the number of claims (PTO, Changes to Implement, 2012, § 42.203). The basic fee of $35,800 applies to petitions challenging up to 20 claims with $800 added for each additional claim (PTO, Rules of Practice, 2012, § 42.15(b)). Therefore, if 60 claims are contested, the filing fee totals $67,800. Although these fees are lower than the escalating fees originally proposed in February 2012, they are exponentially higher than the €705 ($915) fixed filing fee for an EPO opposition. Several comments made during rulemaking suggested setting a low filing fee with no additional fees for additional claims (PTO, Rules of Practice, 2012). The fees remain substantial because AIA does not provide for setting post-grant review fees at below the cost to the PTO (Leahy-Smith America Invents Act, 2011, § 321(a)).

Attorney fees for a post-grant review dwarf the filing fee. The PTO estimated the cost of a post-grant review based on the AIPLA mean private firm attorney fee of $371 per hour and the number of hours to prepare for various stages in the proceedings (PTO, Rules of Practice). Based on these figures, the PTO calculates the attorney fees to prepare a petition at $61,333. The patent holder is allowed to make a preliminary response prior to the PTO threshold determination, estimated to cost $34,000. Once the PTO has made a determination that the petition meets the statutory requirements, the patent owner may reply and a third party may make a statement, estimated at $29,000 each. The PTO projects the average post-grant review will include eight motions, oppositions and replies at an average cost of $44,200 each, including the cost of experts and preparing briefs (PTO, Rules of Practice, 2012). Until 2017, an information technology fee of $1,750 for up to 20 claims and $75 for each additional claim will also be assessed. Based on these estimates, a petitioner will spend nearly half a million dollars for a petition contesting 20 or fewer claims. The patent owner faces similar expenditures, less the filing fee, but may have to face a subsequent *inter partes* review or potential litigation by a person not the petitioner or one of its real parties in interest or privies.

The proposed rules set a maximum of 80 pages for post-grant review petitions in 14-point type or larger and double-spaced regardless of the number of claims challenged or the complexity of issues presented. The petition must identify all real parties in interest and certify that the petitioner is not estopped from proceeding. It must identify all claims challenged, the grounds upon which the challenge to each claim is based, provide claim construction and show how the construed claim is unpatentable based on the grounds alleged. The petition may include a statement of material facts. The table of contents, table of authorities, and certificate of service and appendix of exhibits are not included in the page count. The page limit may be waived by motion, but the petitioner must show that doing so would be in the interests of justice and must append a copy of the proposed petition exceeding the page limit (PTO, Rules of Practice, 2012 § 42.24). Given the growth in the number of patent claims and the complexities of technology, the page limits may not be sufficient to fully address the post-grant review threshold requirement of "more likely than not at least 1 of the claims challenged in the petition is unpatentable." In order to meet the page limit restrictions, it may be necessary for petitioners to file multiple petitions focusing on different claims, and pay the minimum filing fee each time. This will increase costs to petitioners and decrease efficiency.

IV.   POST-GRANT REVIEW WILL NOT IMPROVE THE QUALITY OF PATENTS

It is unlikely the AIA post-grant review system will accomplish the social welfare benefits of improving patent quality and providing an efficient alternative to litigation. This section delimits some of the flaws in post-grant review that will hamper its effectiveness. No post-grant system for opposing patents will be successful unless it is used. Factors such as cost, page limits of the petitions and the harsh estoppel provisions may make it an unattractive alternative to third parties who might otherwise benefit from a finding of invalidity.

A.   Factors Limiting the Effectiveness of Post-grant Review

Only patents issued under the new AIA first-inventor-to-file (FITF) system are eligible for post-grant review. Given that the FITF does not go into effect until 16 March 2013 and petitioners will likely take the nine months allowed to prepare their petitions, it will be some time until the effectiveness of post-grant review is known. However, it is not likely to be effective. The United States does not have a history and tradition of trial-like *inter partes* post-issuance review. Given proper incentives, US-based third parties would use the systems, but the AIA does not include the proper incentives. Americans are the second most likely nationality to oppose European patents after the Germans, accounting for approximately 11.5 percent of European oppositions (Boff, 2012). Many of the incentives for utilizing European oppositions are the same for Americans as for others using the system. European oppositions are relatively inexpensive and preferable to national revocation proceedings, particularly in Germany. Despite the efficiencies of the European system, only about 5 percent of all patents are opposed. Based on statistics for granted utility patents in 2011, if the PTO were faced with post-grant review filings at the EPO rate, it would be flooded with over 25,000 filings. The AIA empowers the PTO to limit the number of *inter partes* reviews and post-grant reviews during the AIA's first four years. The PTO does not expect to limit the number of petitions granted. However, if the PTO rejects a substantial number of *inter partes* review petitions on these grounds, after the petitioner has incurred the expense of filing, whether a third party chooses the non-litigation route may be impacted. Too many rejections may undermine confidence during the early years of the system when a tradition of using post-issuance reviews should be built.

When post-issuance administrative review is too expensive, the incentives for potential challengers to use it diminish. Graham and Harhoff (2006) calculate that when the cost of a post-grant review reaches $500,000, the welfare benefits are eroded. As demonstrated, the cost of pursuing a post-grant review can approach that amount, even when 20 or fewer claims are contested. The costs escalate when there are a large number of claims involved or when multiple post-grant reviews must be filed to cover a substantial number of challenges within the administrative page limit requirements. Fewer competitors will likely use a very expensive system, which will negatively impact the usefulness of the system to catch and correct weak or invalid patents.

The cost may particularly deter individuals and small to medium-sized companies. Just paying the filing fee and filing the petition for the post-grant review is projected to cost more than the average cost of the entire European opposition. The difference between a €705 filing fee (approximately $915) and one that begins at $35,800 and escalates in increments of $800 per claim is immense. The EPO's lower fee encourages use of the system and shields independent inventors and small and medium-sized enterprises from strategic abuse of the system (Hall & Harhoff, 2004). The AIA contains no such protection for small to medium-sized entities. Moreover, it is unlikely to be used by smaller entities subject to infringement litigation. Under litigation threat by non-practicing entities, often described as trolls, most companies settle to avoid expensive litigation and the potential of a permanent injunction that could destroy their business (Thomas, 2006). Trolling activities are unlikely to decrease even though post-grant opposition in the US has been touted as a way to limit them (Mayergoyz, 2009). If a non-practicing patentee sues, post-grant review is a viable alternative only if the lawsuit is filed early in a patent's life. If sued after the nine-month post-grant review window, the small entity may resort to an *inter partes* review on narrower grounds and based only on published prior art. The *inter partes* review is subject to some of the same negative features as the post-grant review, including estoppel and high and escalating fees, although set 33 percent lower than those for post-grant review due to more limited grounds. McKeown (2012) has pointed out that the economics of the "troll game" make the proposed AIA fee structure an unworkable alternative. Non-practicing entities will typically dismiss a party from a lawsuit for a licensing fee of $100,000 to $300,000 (McKeown, 2012). Given the cost of a post-grant review, it may be more economically feasible and less risky for a small entity to settle the lawsuit without resorting to post-grant or *inter partes* review.

The estoppel provisions may serve as the most effective barrier to the success of American post-grant review. These provisions are likely to plague post-grant review in the same way estoppel precluded *inter partes* reexamination. The broad consensus among patent experts and the PTO recognized that estoppel was the most frequently identified issue for deterring third parties from filing requests for *inter partes* reexamination (Carlson & Migliorina, 2006; Farrell & Merges, 2004). A third party could file a request for *inter partes* reexamination at any time (Patent Act of 1952, § 311(a)). This provided ample time for those willing to brave the estoppel provisions to determine which novelty or non-obviousness attacks had the most merit and to brief them without page limit restrictions. In contrast, a petitioner for post-grant review has only nine months to determine whether a post-grant review is feasible and present all the grounds it wishes to preserve against particular claims in a petition limited to 80 pages. The nine-month post-grant review window may prove particularly burdensome in industries such as pharmaceuticals or medical devices requiring clinical trials and for those selling products with thousands of component parts containing patents, such as the computer or cell phone industry (Carrier, 2011). It may not be possible to discover a potentially invalid patent and to file a review on all possible grounds within nine months. Given the time frame, it may not be desirable. Estoppel in a post-grant review attaches upon a written decision of the PTAB, 12 to 18 months from the date the proceeding was initiated because of the statutory requirement it must be completed during that time period. The 12 months mandated under the AIA to reach a decision is about one-third the average 36.1-month pendency of an *inter partes* reexamination (PTO, *Inter Partes* Reexamination Filing Data, 2012). Challengers may not trust the PTAB to correctly rule in a post-grant review given how quickly the determination must be made. Even though the outcome of the post-grant review may be appealed to the CAFC, it is as yet unclear whether estoppel will attach upon a PTAB judgment or after the appeal. Furthermore, the challenger forever loses its opportunity to have the issue fully adjudicated on different later discovered grounds or evidence, if those grounds were raised or reasonably could have been raised during the post-grant review.

Post-grant review's broad "reasonably could have raised" standard was never meant to apply to civil litigation. Given the broadness of the estoppel provision, how quickly a party must determine whether to oppose a granted patent and the speed at which the PTAB must reach its final conclusion, a third party is unlikely to risk a post-grant review. It must be remembered that the EPC contains no estoppel provisions preventing further litigation on the same issues decided by the EPO. Although national courts may defer to EPO decisions, the lack of estoppel provides a check on the accuracy of the European opposition system by national courts. No evidence exists that this practice has exposed patentees to multiple challenges. More importantly, it has allowed the national courts to serve the interests of the public by subjecting patents to an additional level of scrutiny. Limiting estoppel in litigation circumstances in the United States to grounds actually raised in a post-grant review would make the procedure more palatable to potential users. It would also better serve society in offering additional avenues to test patents.

A post-grant review system allowing for easy settlement erodes the very purpose of a system designed to improve patents. Prior to joining the EPC, the UK patent law included both pre-grant and post-grant opposition procedures with no barriers to settlement. Seventy-five percent of all UK oppositions ended in settlement, which did not preclude UK courts from later revoking the opposed patents (McKie & Edward, 1974). As McKie observed 40 years ago, competitors oppose patents to protect their interests, not the public's interest. If a third party can reach the result he wishes through a negotiated license, that will be the likely path, rather than an expensive opposition (McKie & Edward, 1974). The AIA mandates terminating the proceeding as to any petitioner upon joint request of the petitioner and the patent owner unless the PTAB has decided on the merits. Such a termination means that no estoppel attaches to that petitioner, its real party in interest or its privy. Although the AIA grants the PTAB discretionary power to terminate the review or proceed to a final written decision, the contours of that discretion are yet to be tested. The PTO has indicated its decision to terminate the review or to proceed to a final written decision depends on the particular facts (PTO, Rules of Practice, 2012). How the PTAB approaches those facts and makes its determination will determine whether the AIA settlement provisions open the system to misuse. If too lenient in continuing to a final written decision without the petitioners, a competitor could file a post-grant review to force a patentee into negotiating a license, or risk invalidation or narrowing of claims. Settling the post-grant review in exchange for the license may make it a more commercially viable option. Liberally allowing for settlement without the threat of a final PTO determination on patentability would mean neither the parties nor society at large would ever know whether the challenged patent truly was valid. An opposition system discouraging settlement more effectively supports the goal of improving the quality of patents. The EPO's procedures allowing the Opposition Division to continue after the parties have withdrawn have acted as a "powerful deterrent" to settlement (Hall & Harhoff, 2004). Unless the AIA systemic barriers to hinder settlements are enforced it is unlikely the public will benefit from a post-grant review. Therefore, the PTAB should exercise its discretion to determine patentability whenever possible.

B.   Post-grant Review in National Systems

Administrative post-grant review may be more appropriate and effective in multinational patent systems. Few countries maintain post-grant time-limited administrative review systems. Only 30 percent of EPC contracting states have post-grant oppositions as part of their national systems (European Patent Academy, 2010). It is not surprising that Germany, whose nationals file the majority of European oppositions, includes an opposition for patents filed nationally. German law requires filing national oppositions within three months of the grant, making its general usefulness questionable. Before acceding to the EPC, the UK had two oppositions systems, one that allowed third-party intervention prior to issuance and the other allowing for opposition within one year of the grant. The system was used in only about 1 percent of cases and was often used for delaying tactics or to harass patentees (McKie & Edward, 1974). Neither form of national opposition made it into the UK Patents Act 1977, enacted to transpose the EPC requirements into UK law.

More recently, Japan abolished its time-limited post-grant opposition system in favor of a single, non-time-limited patent invalidation trial within the Japanese Patent Office (Carlson & Migliorina, 2006). In 1996, Japan implemented a post-grant opposition system to replace a pre-grant opposition system, which had been misused and delayed the grant of patents. In 2003, only seven years after introducing the system, Japan abolished its post-grant oppositions. It found a dual system of opposition and a separate trial system for invalidation burdened patentees who were subjected to repeated attacks against the same patent (Sun, 2004; Tessensohn & Yamamoto, 2003). The current system provides for an invalidation trial within the Japanese Patent Office as the sole mechanism to invalidate patents issued or filed after 2004. The parties may appeal through the court system. Nothing in the law estops a challenger from filing subsequent requests for a new invalidity trial based on different grounds (Carlson & Migliorina, 2006).

Evidence from these examples indicates that when post-grant oppositions coexist with other avenues for invalidation on a national level, opportunities to misuse the system occur. The America Invents Act provides what has been characterized as an "arsenal" of proceedings to weed out low-quality patents (Tran, 2012). Besides litigation and post-grant review, procedures include supplemental examination, *ex parte* reexamination, *inter partes* review, and a separate post-grant review for business methods relating to financial services and products. These routes to reexamination and reconsideration overlap, making the US system much more complex than other national or multinational systems by the sheer number of avenues available for challenging patents in addition to litigation. These multiple avenues for invalidation raise the potential of undue harassment of patentees and duplicate patent office resources in administration of parallel systems (Carlson & Migliorina, 2006). Some of the abuses experienced in other nations' systems may be ameliorated in the US system by the high cost of the procedure and the post-grant review estoppel provisions. However, those are two of the very provisions that may ensure the procedure is not used.

The landscape is different in the multinational European system. Without a post-grant oppositions and appeals procedure in the EPO, invalidation of patents in Europe would be piecemeal and lead to differing results in different nations. A central procedure for oppositions at the EPO lowers costs and enhances predictability, since the invalidation or narrowing of the patent has immediate effect in all EPC national jurisdictions. The structure of national infringement and invalidation proceedings makes the European opposition more appealing to some nationals than others. Germans have a long history of using their national opposition system prior to joining the EPC (McKie & Edward, 1974). Oppositions are often used as a way to narrow patents. Structural reasons exist for a German propensity to use oppositions as a primary route to challenging the validity of patents. Within a national system in which infringement and invalidation are bifurcated into two separate courts—courts that can and do reach decisions on infringement and validity at different times—European opposition proves to be a less risky route to invalidation.

V. CONCLUSION

Post-grant review under the America Invents Act will not improve the quality of patents in the US. Although it has been characterized as the most powerful tool in an arsenal of new post-grant administrative proceedings (Tran, 2012), it is unlikely to be a useful tool without substantial changes to the law. Following the example of the European opposition, the fee structure must be modified to make the cost of filing and perusing post-grant review a feasible option. This is particularly important in order to shield independent inventors and small and medium-sized enterprises from strategic misuse of the system. This cannot be accomplished without modification of § 321(a) requiring the PTO to consider the aggregate costs of the post-grant review in setting fees. Estoppel is not a feature of European opposition law. No evidence suggests that a lack of estoppel has led to strategic abuse by parties between the multinational and national systems. Furthermore, it serves the public interest of assuring patents administered at the national level are valid. Estoppel poses similar and different issues in the US national system in which a party may bring other administrative proceedings or civil actions. Patentees should be protected from harassment by third parties misusing the system. However, the public's interest in valid patents should outweigh that interest given the purpose of the patent system to advance the useful arts. Preventing the rehearing of issues actually decided by the PTAB in post-grant reviews could more equitably accomplish this goal. Legislative history indicates that Congress never intended "reasonably could have raised" estoppel to prevent subsequent litigation on patent validity. As predicted, this provision will serve as a significant obstacle to post-grant review's usefulness. At a minimum, it is imperative Congress act to correct this mistake.

Uncertainty in the AIA settlement and termination provisions has the potential to undermine the purpose of post-grant review to ensure the quality of patents. Given the PTO's discretion to continue to a final written decision without petitioners indicates the AIA may contain the same powerful deterrent to settlement that exists in the EPC. Without this safeguard, if a substantial number of post-grant reviews terminate in settlement without a PTO decision on patentability, the public's interest in the quality of patents would be compromised.

NOTES

* The author wishes to thank Daniel Cahoy and Lynda Oswald for organizing the May 2012 colloquium, "The Changing Face of American Patent Law and Its Impact on Business Strategy," sponsored by the Stephen M. Ross School of Business at the University of Michigan and the Smeal College of Business at Penn State University, and for their efforts in editing this book. The author is grateful to all of the participants for their rigorous reading, comments and thoughtful suggestions. Very special thanks to Ryan F. Brackin, University of St. Thomas Law School class of 2013, for his indefatigable research assistance on this and other projects. Copyright 2013, Susan J. Marsnik.
1. The EPC is not a convention of the European Union (EU). Despite efforts to join the EPC, the EU is not a party, although each of the 27 EU Member States are among the 40 European nations that are Contracting States to the EPC.
2. A second exception exists. EPC 2000 introduced a new proceeding allowing patent owners to limit claims in a granted patent under Article 105(a). Under this procedure, a patent can be narrowed or revoked and the result will apply retroactively in each of the countries in which the patent has been validated (Rudge, 2012).

REFERENCES

Allison, J.R., Lemley, M.A. & Walker, J. (2009). Extreme Value or Trolls on Top? The Characteristics of the Most-litigated Patents. *University of Pennsylvania Law Review*, **158**(1), 1–U37.

Allison, J.R., Lemley, M.A., Moore, K.A. & Trunkey, R.D. (2004). Valuable Patents. *Georgetown Law Journal*, **92**(3), 435–79.

American Intellectual Property Law Association (AIPLA) (2011). *AIPLA Report of the Economic Survey 2011*. Arlington, VA.

Bettcher v. Bunzl, 661 F. 3d 629 (2011).

Boff, J. (2011). *Challenging European Patents and Applications, AIPLA 2011 Spring Meeting, AIPLA IP Practice in Europe Committee*. Retrieved from http://www.docstoc.com/docs/98459516/Challenging-European-Patents-and-Applications-in-the-EPO.

Boff, J. (2012). Bifurcation – Good for Patent Attorneys, Bad for Industry? *CIPA Journal*, **41**(7), 386–8.

Carlson, D.L. & Migliorina, R.A. (2006). Patent Reform at the Crossroads: Experience in the Far East with Oppositions Suggests an Alternative Approach for the United States. *North Carolina Journal of Law & Technology*, **7**(2), 261–319.

Carrier, M.A. (2011). Post-grant Opposition: A Proposal and a Comparison to the America Invents Act. *University of California Davis Law Review*, **45**(1), 103–36.

Case G 9/93. (1994). *Official Journal of the European Patent Office, 12*, 891. (Enlarged Board of Appeal, July 6, 1994).

Caviggioli, F., Scellato, G. & Ughetto, E. (2012). *Understanding Patent Quality: Evidence from Patent Opposition Cases at the European Patent Office*. Working paper presented at the 6th Annual Conference of the European Policy for Intellectual Property Association. Brussels, BE.

Convention on the Grant of European Patents (EPC), Oct. 5, 1973, as revised Nov. 29, 2000. (2010). *The European Patent Convention* (14th ed.), Munich, Germany: European Patent Office.

European Patent Academy (2010). *Patent Litigation in Europe: An Overview of the National Patent Litigation Systems in Europe* (2nd ed.). Munich: European Patent Office.

European Patent Office (EPO) (2010, October 23). Implementing Regulations to the Convention on the Grant of European Patents, Oct. 5, 1973. Retrieved from http://www.epo.org/law-practice/legal-texts/html/epc/2010/e/ma2.html.

European Patent Office (EPO) (2012, June 12). *Guidelines for Examination in the European Patent Office*. Available at http://www.epo.org/law-practice/legal-texts/guidelines.html.

Farrell, J. & Merges, R.P. (2004). Incentives to Challenge and Defend Patents: Why Litigation Won't Reliably Fix Patent Office Errors and why Administrative Patent Review Might Help. *Berkeley Technology Law Journal*, **19**(3), 943–70.

Federal Trade Commission. (2003). *To Promote Innovation: The Proper Balance of Competition and Patent Law and Policy*. Washington, D.C.: The Federal Trade Commission.

Graham, S., Hall, B.H., Harhoff, D. & Mowery, D.C. (2002). *Post-Issue Patent "Quality Control:" A Comparative Study of U.S. Patent Re-examinations and European Patent Oppositions*. (Working Paper No. 8807). Cambridge,

MA: National Bureau of Economic Research & Competition Policy Center, University of California, Berkeley.

Graham, S. & Harhoff, D. (2006). *Can Post-Grant Review Improve Patent System Design? A Twin Study of U.S. and European Patents.* (Discussion Paper No. 5680). Washington, D.C.: Center for Economic Policy Research.

Gupta, P.R. & Feerst, A. (2012). The U.S. Patent System After the Leahy-Smith America Invents Act. *European Intellectual Property Review*, **34**(1), 60–64.

Hall, B.H. & Harhoff, D. (2004). Post-Grant Reviews in the U.S. Patent System-Design Choices and Expected Impact. *Berkeley Technology Law Journal*, **19**(3), 989.

Harhoff, D. & Reitzig, M. (2004). Determinants of Opposition Against EPO Patent Grants—the Case of Biotechnology and Pharmaceuticals. *International Journal of Industrial Organization*, **22**(4), 443–80.

Harvard/Transgenic animal (T315/03) (2005) European Patent Office Reports, **31** (Technical Board of Appeal, Jul. 6, 2004).

Hoyng, W.A. (2006). The European Patent Convention. In W.A. Hoyng & F.W.E. Eijsvogels (eds) *Global Patent Litigation: Strategy and practice.* (EPC 1 – EPC 38) London: Kluwer Law International.

Jacobs, R. (2012). To Bifurcate or Not To Bifurcate: That Is the Question. *CIPA Journal*, **41**(6), 328–31.

Judge, I. (2002). Developments in the Harmonisation of European Patent Law and Litigation. In H. Hansen (ed.) *International Intellectual Property Law and Policy*, **7** (28-1 – 28-5). Huntington, NY: Juris Publishing, Inc.

Leahy-Smith America Invents Act. (2011). Pub. L. No. 112-29, 125 Stat. 284.

Marsnik, S.J. & Thomas, R.E. (2011). Drawing a Line in the Patent Subject-Matter Sands: Does Europe Prove a Solution to the Software and Business Method Patent Problem? *Boston College International and Comparative Law Review*, **34**(2), 227–327.

Matal, J. (2012). A Guide to the Legislative History of the America Invents Act: Part II of II. *The Federal Circuit Bar Journal*, **21**(4), 539–653.

Mayergoyz, A. (2009). Lessons from Europe on how to Tame U.S. Patent Trolls. *Cornell International Law Journal*, **42**(2), 241–70.

McKeown, S.A. (2011, Sept. 29). New *Inter Partes* Review Grounds to Stay Most Patent Litigation? *Patents Post Grant Blog.* Retrieved from http://www.patents postgrant.com/lang/en/2011/09/new-inter-partes-review.

McKeown, S.A. (2012, Feb. 22). Post Grant Fee Structure a Boon for Patent Trolls? Modern Patent Troll Business Model Insulated from New Post Grant Challenges. *Patents Post Grant Blog.* Retrieved from http://www.patentspostgrant. com/lang/en/2012/02/proposed-PTO-post-grant-fee-structure-a-boon-for-patent-trolls.

McKie, J. & Edward F., (1974). Proposal for an American Patent Opposition System in the Light of the History of Foreign Systems. *Journal of the Patent Office Society*, **56**, 94–102.

Merrill, S.A., Levin, R.C. & Myers, M.B. (eds). (2004). *A Patent System for the 21st Century.* Washington, D.C.: The National Academies Press.

Moss, G. & Jones, M. (2008, June 1). Litigating Patents in Europe: Navigating the Minefield. *BNA World Intellectual Property Report*, **22**(6), 28–32.

Patent Act of 1952. (1952). 35 U.S.C. §§ 1-376 (as amended).

Patents Act 1977. (1977). U.K.

Patentgesetz (zuletzt geändert durch Gasetz vom 31. Juli 2009) (2009); Germany,

Patent Law (as amended by the Law of July 31, 2009). English translation at http://www.wipo.int/wipolex/en/details.jsp?id=6128.

Revised European Patent Convention and Implementing Regulation, Nov. 29, 2000. (2003). *Official Journal of the European Patent Office*, **1**.

Rudge, A. (2012). *Guide to European Patents*. Eagan, MN: Thompson Reuters.

Scellato, G., Calderini, M., Caviggioli, F., Franzoni, C., Ughetto, E., Kica, E. & Rodriguez, V. (2011). *Study on the Quality of the Patent System in Europe, DG MARKT, tender MARKT/2009/11/D*. Retrieved from http://ec.europa.eu/internal_market/indprop/docs/patent/patqual02032011_en.pdf.

Sun, H. (2004). Post-Grant Patent Invalidation in China and the United States, Europe, and Japan: A Comparative Study. *Fordham Intellectual Property, Media & Entertainment Law Journal*, **15**(1), 273–331.

Tessensohn, J. & Yamamoto, S. (2003). Japan: Patents – New Invalidity Appeal System. *European Intellectual Property Review*, **10**, 154–5.

Thambisetty, S. (2007). Patents as Credence Goods. *Oxford Journal of Legal Studies*, **27**(4), 707–40.

Thomas, R.E. (2006). Vanquishing Copyright Pirates and Patent Trolls: The Divergent Evolution of Copyright and Patent Laws. *American Business Law Journal*, **43**(4), 689–739.

Tran, S. (2012). Patent Powers. *Harvard Journal of Law & Technology*, **25**(2), 1–67.

United States Patent and Trademark Office (PTO) (2011a). *FY 2011 PTO Performance and Accountability Report*. Retrieved from http://www.PTO.gov/about/stratplan/ar/2011/index.jsp.

United States Patent and Trademark Office (PTO) (2011b). *Summary of Total Pending Patent Applications*. Retrieved from http://www.PTO.gov/web/offices/ac/ido/oeip/taf/us_stat.pdf.

United States Patent and Trademark Office (PTO) (2012). *U.S. Patent Statistics Report*. Retrieved from http://www.PTO.gov/web/offices/ac/ido/oeip/taf/us_stat.pdf.

United States Patent and Trademark Office (PTO) (June 30, 2012). *Inter Partes Reexamination Filing Data*. Retrieved from http://www.PTO.gov/patents/stats//IP_quarterly_report_June_30_2012.pdf.

United States Patent and Trademark Office (PTO) (2012, August 14). Rules of Practice for Trials before the Patent Trial and Appeal Board and Judicial Review of Patent Trial and Appeal Board Decisions; Final rule. *Federal Register*, **77**(157), 48611–48678.

United States Patent and Trademark Office (PTO) (2012, August 14). Changes to Implement Inter Partes Review Proceedings, Post-Grant Review Proceedings, and Transitional Program for Covered Business Method Patents, Final rule, *Federal Register* **77**(157), 48680–48732.

Veronese, A. (2009). Appeal Procedure before the European Patent Office. In T. Takenaka (ed.) *Patent Law and Theory: A Handbook of Contemporary Research* (pp. 224–45). Northampton, MA: Edward Elgar.

PART IV

Emergence of exclusion systems beyond patents

9. Biopharmaceuticals under the Patient Protection and Affordable Care Act: determining the appropriate market and data exclusivity periods

Donna M. Gitter*

With the enactment of the Biologics Price Competition and Innovation Act of 2009 (BPCIA) in March 2010 as part of the Patient Protection and Affordable Care Act (Patient Protection and Affordable Care Act, 2010), manufacturers of follow-on protein products, meaning biopharmaceuticals that are similar to branded biologic products,[1] will be able to file abbreviated applications for US Food and Drug Administration (FDA) approval for their products.[2] This abbreviated approval process will allow manufacturers of follow-on protein products, also known as biosimilars, to avoid at least some, though not necessarily all, of the costly pre-clinical and clinical testing necessary for regulatory approval by relying on data generated by branded products.

Even after enactment of the BPCIA, however, confusion remains regarding two of its most debated provisions, those relating to the periods of market and data exclusivity to which innovator pharmaceutical firms are entitled under the statute. Data exclusivity is defined as the period of time that an innovator pharmaceutical firm's pre-clinical and clinical data cannot be relied upon by a follow-on competitor in its application for FDA approval. During the data exclusivity period, however, a follow-on company is permitted to engage in the costly process of generating all of its data from scratch to obtain marketing approval for a follow-on version of the drug. Market exclusivity is defined as "a period of time during which the FDA affords an approved drug protection from competing applications for marketing approval" (Schacht & Thomas, 2009, p. 13). The follow-on company may have access to the innovator firm's data but may not receive FDA approval. Both data and market exclusivity differ from patent protection, which provides the patent holder with a limited monopoly during which the patent holder can prevent others from making, using, offering for sale, selling, or importing the patented article (Patent Act of 1952, § 271(a)). Unlike patent protection, data exclusivity does not prevent the introduction of generic versions of the innovator drug during the exclusivity period, as long as the approval of the generic version does not rely upon the innovator's pre-clinical and clinical data. Also unlike patents, data exclusivity is not challengeable in court and therefore harbors no uncertainty.

The branded biologic industry contends that patent protection is often of limited use with respect to biological products, thereby rendering data exclusivity all the more essential. According to the Biotechnology Industry Organization (BIO), the biotechnology industry trade group, because biologics are highly variable molecules, a manufacturer of follow-on products will be required only to demonstrate that the product is "similar" or "highly similar" to the corresponding innovator product, not that it is identical. As a result, a follow-on biologic might be sufficiently similar to the innovator biologic to rely on the FDA's finding of safety and effectiveness for the innovator product, but at the same time prove different enough from the innovator product to avoid a patent infringement claim. The follow-on product could thus achieve market entry before the innovator's patent expiry, which discourages investment in innovation. Second, because of characteristics specific to biologic products, which are large molecules produced by living organisms, patent protection is often narrower and easier to "design around" than for small molecule drugs.

Thus, manufacturers of innovator products and some members of Congress interpret the BPCIA to provide innovator products both market and data exclusivity in the first four years after FDA approval, followed by eight years of data exclusivity but not market exclusivity. However, manufacturers of biosimilar products, other members of Congress, consumer groups and payers contend that Congress intended to provide four years of both market exclusivity and data exclusivity, followed by eight years of market exclusivity but not data exclusivity.

Complicating matters further is the fact that President Barack Obama has urged Congress to reduce the period of exclusivity to only seven years, in order to promote economic growth in the biosimilar industry. What is more, some of the US's trading partners contend that a 12-year exclusivity provision violates international trade agreements.

Consideration of the appropriate data and market exclusivity periods for biosimilars pursuant to the Biologics Price Competition and Innovation Act of 2009 is particularly timely in light of the United States Supreme Court's constitutional review of the Patient Protection and Affordable

Care Act, of which the BPCIA forms a part. Now that the Court has upheld this legislation, Congress and/or the FDA must further clarify the legislation's meaning in the future.

Part I of this chapter will discuss the importance of biologic pharmaceuticals, also know as biologics, in the health care market. Part II will examine congressional intent when enacting the BPCIA, with respect to the establishment of market and data exclusivity periods for biosimilar pharmaceuticals, analyzing the plain language and legislative history of the legislation. Part III will then consider, apart from the legislative intent at the time the BPCIA was enacted, what the appropriate data exclusivity period ought to be. This part will examine the academic literature relating to market and data exclusivity for biosimilar pharmaceuticals. In addition, this part will consider the effect that the negotiation of international trade agreements has upon questions of data and market exclusivity.

I. THE IMPORTANCE AND HIGH COST OF BIOLOGICS

Biologics, which derive from living organisms, represent the fastest-growing segment of pharmaceuticals and are used to treat a variety of diseases. The majority of spending today on these drugs is for the treatment of cancer, rheumatoid arthritis and other autoimmune conditions, multiple sclerosis and anemia. As of early 2012, the FDA had approved 750 biologics, and 25 percent of the drugs in the development pipeline are biopharmaceuticals (Vogenberg, Larson, Rehayem, & Boress, 2012).

Although early biologics were solely physician-administered injectables or infusions, advances in medical technology led to the development of oral formulations that patients can self-administer. The fact that these pharmaceuticals are self-administered leads to complexity in terms of benefit coverage for these treatments, which can be considered either medical or pharmaceutical expenditures (Vogenberg et al., 2012).

Exacerbating the challenges in determining the appropriate means of benefit coverage for these treatments is their high cost, which accounts for a 17.4 percent change in prescription spending and the fastest growth of any drug category since 2004. The current price of the average biologic is more than 20 times that of a traditional, chemically synthesized small-molecule drug (Vogenberg et al., 2012).

In recent years, spending on biologics by pharmacy benefit plans rose by more than 15 percent, several times higher than the overall drug trend. Although biologics accounted for only 1 percent of the total prescription claims volume in 2010, 70 percent of drug cost trend in pharmacy benefit plans could be attributed to the rising cost of these drugs. Biologics are expected to represent 21 percent of all plan drug spending by 2013, and as much as 40 percent of plan drug spending by the end of 2020 (Vogenberg et al., 2012).

In light of the high cost and growing market share of biologics, the fact that patents on many blockbuster biopharmaceuticals are due to expire is of great significance. One recent report estimates that biologics responsible for $20 billion in annual sales will go off patent by 2015 (Evans, 2010). But unlike generic chemical drugs, there are high barriers to entry because of the technical challenges of manufacturing and storing biologics and the difficulty of proving biosimilarity. The estimated cost to bring a biosimilar to market is $150 million to $200 million, compared with between $1 million and $2 million to launch a generic drug (Fidler, 2012). In order to foster investment in the follow-on biologic market, Congress enacted the BPCIA in 2010.

II. WHAT WAS CONGRESS'S INTENT WITH RESPECT TO MARKET AND DATA EXCLUSIVITY PERIODS FOR BIOSIMILAR PHARMACEUTICALS UNDER THE BIOLOGICS PRICE COMPETITION AND INNOVATION ACT OF 2009?

Typically, the manufacturer of a new biologic applies for FDA approval by filing a biologic license application (BLA) (Biologics Price Competition and Innovation Act of 2009, § 262(a), 2010). For a follow-on biologic, however, the BPCIA provides that an application for a follow-on biologic "may not be submitted to the [FDA] until the date that is four years after the date on which the reference product was first licensed" (BPCIA, 2010, §262(k)(7)(B)). The law also specifies that the FDA "approval of an application under this subsection may not be made effective by the Secretary until the date that is 12 years after the date on which the reference product was first licensed" (BPCIA, 2010, §262(k)(7)(B)). This language gives rise to the question of what sort of exclusivity is provided during the balance of the 12-year period, after the first four years have elapsed.

The confusion regarding the exclusivity periods provided for under the BPCIA were apparent in the news media and scholarly literature just after the legislation's enactment. One article in a medical trade journal stated that "[m]anufacturers of original biologic drugs will have at least 12 years before others will be able to use their data to produce and sell similar versions of the drugs" (Trapp, 2010). Likewise, a scholar who had participated in congressional hearings concerning an abbreviated approval pathway for biologics wrote that "the legislation grants a new innovative biologic . . . 12 years of data exclusivity" (Grabowski, Long & Mortimer, 2011, p. 15). On the other hand, a legal commentator indicated that the BPCIA "establishes a 12-year period of market exclusivity," and the "first four years . . . is a period of data exclusivity" (Beaver, Maebius & Rosen, 2010). These differences in interpretation illustrate the conflicting positions of the branded and generic pharmaceutical industries.

Innovator drug companies and some members of Congress, from both chambers, interpret the BPCIA to provide four years of data exclusivity coupled with market exclusivity, succeeded by eight more years of data exclusivity. According to this view, the BPCIA precludes access by follow-on biologic drug manufacturers to an innovator's biologic drug data until the 12-year term has expired. In support of this view, a bipartisan group of members of Congress, Rep. Anna G. Eshoo (D-CA), Rep. Jan Inslee (D-WA) and Rep. Joe Barton (R-TX), who authored and sponsored the follow-on biologics portion of the health care reform bill, wrote a letter dated 21 December 2010 to the FDA. The impetus for the letter was language in the federal register requesting public input regarding what factors the FDA should consider in determining whether a modification to the structure of a licensed reference biological results in such a significant change that a subsequent biologic license application may be eligible for a "second 12-year period of marketing exclusivity." These representatives expressed that they felt compelled to address what appeared to them to be an error in the FDA's question. In their view, the BPCIA "does not provide 'market exclusivity' for innovator products" but rather "data exclusivity for 12 years from the date of FDA approval" (Letter from Representatives Anna G. Eshoo, Jan Inslee and Joe Barton, to the U.S. Food and Drug Administration, 2010). Two weeks later, a bipartisan group of senators, Kay Hagan (D-NC), Orrin Hatch (R-UT), Michael Enzi (R-WY) and John Kerry (D-MA), wrote a letter to the FDA dated 7 January 2011 affirming that their intent in enacting the legislation was to provide a 12-year period of data exclusivity (Letter from Senators Kay Hagan, Orrin Hatch, Michael Enzi and John Kerry to Dr. Margaret Hamburg, Commissioner, Food and Drug Administration, 2011).

The generic pharmaceutical industry, along with a group of senators, consumer groups and payers, interpret the BPCIA differently. They believe that the law provides four years of both market exclusivity and data exclusivity, followed by eight years of market exclusivity alone without data exclusivity. In support of this view, a bipartisan group of senators wrote a letter dated 24 January 2011 to FDA Commissioner Margaret Hamburg expressing their belief that "the statute is clear that the FDA can begin reviewing biogeneric applications during the 12 year exclusivity period" (Letter from Senators Sherrod Brown, John McCain, Charles Schumer and Tom Harkin, to Dr. Margaret Hamburg, Commissioner, Food and Drug Administration, 2011). This group, who during legislative debate opposed the 12-year exclusivity period, contends that the period between the end of the fourth and twelfth years after the innovator biologic is approved is a period of market exclusivity rather than data exclusivity. They warn that a 12-year data exclusivity period "could further delay the availability of generic biologic drugs, restricting access for many Americans and driving up costs for the Federal government" (Letter from Senators Sherrod Brown, John McCain, Charles Schumer and Tom Harkin, to Dr. Margaret Hamburg, Commissioner, Food and Drug Administration, 2011). Around this same time, a group of generic drug manufacturers, healthcare providers and industry and patient groups expressed the same view, warning that "[i]f the legislation is interpreted to prevent biosimilar filings for 12 years, consumers will have to endure an unknown period of delay of FDA review and approval that could stretch far beyond the 12-year total that was set in the legislation" (Letter from AARP, Aetna, CVS Caremark et al., to Dr. Margaret Hamburg, Commissioner, Food and Drug Administration, 2011).

It should be noted that the FDA ultimately indicated its agreement with the interpretation offered by Senators Harkin, McCain, Schumer and Brown in their 24 January letter to FDA Commissioner Hamburg. When the FDA published a 10 May 2011 User Fee Notice in the Federal Register relating to the BPCIA, the FDA stated that follow-on biologics applications submitted ten years or more after the date of first licensure "would be eligible for approval in two years or less, depending on the relevant filing dates" (Duane Morris, 2011).

As legislators debated the BPCIA's exclusivity period, President Obama sought to reduce the exclusivity period to seven years. Before signing the bill into law in March 2010, Obama urged unsuccessfully for a reduction of the 12-year period. Then, when the President presented his February 2012 budget, he called once again for the exclusivity period to be shortened to seven years rather than twelve in order to promote economic growth and deficit reduction.

It is a dubious business to deduce the intent of the legislators from their letters after the fact. Rather, analysis ought to center upon the plain language of the statute, the recorded legislative history, and a consideration of the underlying intent of the statute.

A.   The Plain Language of the BPCIA Seems to Support the Views of the Biosimilar Industry

As noted above, the BPCIA provides that an application for a follow-on biologic "may not be submitted to the [FDA] until the date that is four years after the date on which the reference product was first licensed." The law also specifies that the FDA "approval of an application under this subsection may not be made effective by the Secretary until the date that is 12 years after the date on which the reference product was first licensed" (BPCIA, 2010, §262(k)(7)(B)).

The language of the BPCIA closely tracks that of the Hatch-Waxman Act (HWA), congressional legislation that in 1984 implemented an abbreviated approval pathway for traditional chemical pharmaceuticals. The HWA provides that "no application may be submitted under this subsection ... before the expiration of five years from the date of the approval of the [innovator drug]" (Drug Price Competition and Patent Term Restoration Act of 1984 (HWA), 1984, § 355(j)(5)(F)(ii)). The HWA language is understood to refer to data exclusivity, meaning that manufacturers of chemical pharmaceuticals may not rely on an innovator firm's data until five years after approval of the branded product. This suggests that the "may not be submitted" language in both statutes refers to data exclusivity.

What then does one make of the BPCIA language further stating that no "approval" of an application for a follow-on biologic "may be made effective" for 12 years? This language does not track any in the HWA. Thus, one would infer that it means something different from the data exclusivity language, and therefore refers to market exclusivity. This interpretation suggests that a follow-on biologic manufacturer may use an innovator firm's pre-clinical and clinical data in the development of a follow-on biologic only after four years have elapsed since the approval of the branded product. However, the FDA cannot approve the follow-on biologic for an additional eight-year period. As noted by one commentator, the language stating that no approval of a follow-on biologic may be made for a 12-year period must logically refer to market exclusivity, as it would not even be possible to submit such an application without being able to rely on the innovator's data (Noonan, 2011).

B.   The Legislative History of the BPCIA Remains Ambiguous as a Result of the Politics Surrounding Its Passage

While the letters written by legislators after the BPCIA's enactment are a questionable way to discern legislative intent regarding the appropriate interpretation of the market and data exclusivity periods, the fact that these same legislators did take very strong positions during congressional debate could theoretically shed light on the meaning of the BPCIA. Senators Hagan, Hatch and Enzi, who later wrote to the FDA affirming that their intent in enacting the legislation was to provide a 12-year period of data exclusivity, had indeed advanced a version of the bill that included a four-year filing moratorium for filing biosimilar applications, representing both market and data exclusivity, as well as an additional eight years of data exclusivity. Representatives Eshoo, Inslee and Barton, who also wrote to the FDA advancing the same view as the aforementioned senators, had in fact originally proposed a bill offering the branded industry up to 14.5 years of data exclusivity. Representative Eshoo in particular was instrumental in arranging for the inclusion of the 12-year exclusivity period in the BPCIA. Conversely, Senator Waxman backed a competing bill that offered five years of data exclusivity and did not garner as much support as the bill proposed by Representatives Eshoo, Inslee and Barton. Likewise, an alternative measure proposed by Senator Sherrod Brown that offered a seven-year data exclusivity period met with rejection (Rimmington, 2009). Thus, one might conclude that the final legislation as enacted represents the views advanced by those legislators advocating for a longer data exclusivity period.

Nonetheless, it remains difficult to discern the legislative intent of Congress from the legislators' various legislative proposals relating to the BPCIA, given the amount of debate and compromise involved in the legislation's enactment. This is all the more true of the legislator's final votes, since the BPCIA formed but one part of the historic and controversial Patient Protection and Affordable Care Act, which greatly expanded health care in the United States. The legislators' voting records on this legislation divide neatly along party lines, with Republicans voting against the legislation and Democrats voting in favor, regardless of their position on relatively ancillary details such as the data exclusivity period for biologics.

C.   The Underlying Purpose of the BPCIA Requires a Difficult Balance between Providing Incentives for Innovation and Making Biologics More Affordable

Close reading of the plain language of the BPCIA and analysis of its legislative history must of course be informed by an understanding of the ultimate purpose of the statute. Modeled on the Hatch-Waxman Act, the BPCIA aims to establish an abbreviated approval pathway for follow-on biologics so as to foster a robust follow-on biopharmaceutical industry, thereby lowering prices for consumers, while maintaining incentives for innovation. Ultimately, the length of the exclusivity period comes down to a policy choice, and requires a careful balancing of incentives for innovator pharmaceutical firms versus the health care needs of consumers.

The difficulty of this policy choice is evident in the letter from the senators opposing a 12-year data exclusivity period. In it, they express concern that misinterpretation of the BPCIA "could further delay the availability of generic biologic drugs, restricting access for many Americans and driving up costs for the Federal government" (Letter from Senators Sherrod Brown, John McCain, Charles Schumer and Tom Harkin, to Dr. Margaret Hamburg, Commissioner, Food and Drug Administration, 2011). Indeed, because a follow-on manufacturer seeking to rely on the abbreviated approval pathway for biologics requires FDA access to the innovator's data prior to FDA approval, the denial of access to such data for the entire 12-year exclusivity period would be tantamount to a de facto extension of that period.

Some commentators, however, point out that the HWA offers manufacturers of branded traditional pharmaceuticals certain benefits in exchange for the access to their data to be used in the abbreviated approval process and that these safeguards are not included in the BPCIA. Pursuant to the HWA, manufacturers of innovator drugs are entitled to apply for patent term restoration for a portion of the time spent obtaining regulatory approval (HWA, § 156). Because the patent term runs from the time a patent application is filed, innovators lose some patent time while waiting for the FDA to complete its regulatory review of the patent and grant marketing approval. This patent term extension provision of the HWA aims to stimulate innovation by making up for some of this lost time and is viewed as a quid pro quo for the abbreviated approval pathway under the HWA.

In terms of the quid pro quo argument, however, the patent term extension provisions of the HWA already apply not only to new drug applications (NDAs) for approval of new conventional pharmaceuticals, but also to new biologics for which BLAs are filed (HWA, § 156). Thus, manufacturers of branded biologics have enjoyed patent term restoration without being required to allow manufacturers of follow-on biologics to rely on their data when seeking FDA approval. As noted by one commentator, "BLA filers have been benefiting from the quo without the quid, and the market exclusivity interpretation of the [BPCIA] finally gives the quid to biosimilar companies" (Noonan, 2011).

In light of what can arguably be considered a lack of clarity in the plain language and legislative intent of the BPCIA, it is wise to reconsider what *should* be the data and market exclusivity periods for biologics. The answer to this question is informed by the work of academics who have studied the subject and the experience of other nations that have enacted abbreviated approval pathways for biologics, along with a consideration of the United States' obligations pursuant to international treaties.

III.   AN ANALYSIS OF THE OPTIMAL DATA AND MARKETING EXCLUSIVITY PERIODS FOR BIOLOGIC PHARMACEUTICALS

A.   The Academic Literature Regarding Optimal Exclusivity Periods for Biologic Pharmaceuticals Is Inconclusive

One of the most influential scholars advocating for a data exclusivity period of 12 years or even more is Duke University economist Professor Henry Grabowski. In his 2008 article published in *Nature Reviews Drug Discovery*, Professor Grabowski analyzed a portfolio of biologic drugs based on clinical success probabilities, historical research and development costs, average historical sales data, and an expected rate of return to investors in order to estimate the average number of years before all the development costs are recouped and profit is earned. Economists term this analysis a "break-even analysis." Grabowski estimated the break-even time period to be between 12.9 and 16.2 years, depending upon the assumptions made about the costs of capital. He emphasized that a substantial exclusivity period is particularly essential for new biologics, which "rely on relatively narrow patents that are vulnerable to challenges by follow-on competitors" (Grabowski, 2008). As noted above, unlike patents, data exclusivity is not challengeable in court and therefore harbors no uncertainty.

A 2009 report by the Federal Trade Commission opposed Professor Grabowski's recommendation for a 12-year exclusivity period, arguing against any "special legislative incentives." The FTC contends that an "early mover" competitive advantage should be sufficient to maintain innovation incentives, basing this conclusion on its findings that, unlike for chemical pharmaceuticals, follow-on biologics face high costs of entry, lack of interchangeability with the reference product, concerns regarding their safety and efficacy, and barriers regarding insurance reimbursement. Indeed, the FTC estimates that biologic drugs are likely to retain 70 to 90 percent of their market share years after entry of follow-on biologics (Federal Trade Commission, 2009).

In response to the FTC's report, Professor Grabowski conducted a follow-up study in 2011 designed to take into account the impact on break-even time for manufacturers of pioneer biologics assuming that such pharmaceuticals would retain market share even after the market entry of follow-on products. He concluded that a 12- to 14-year exclusivity period is necessary for innovator firms to break even, and that 7- and 10-year exclusivity periods are inadequate (Grabowski, Long & Mortimer, 2011).

Former House Ways and Means Committee Chief Economist and American Enterprise Institute Research Fellow Alex Brill, however, takes issue with some of the assumptions upon which Professor Grabowski's work is based. In a November 2008 report funded by Teva Pharmaceuticals, the largest US manufacturer of generic pharmaceuticals, Brill concluded that seven to nine years of data exclusivity would provide sufficient incentive to innovate while fostering a competitive marketplace. Brill's work relies on Professor Grabowski's data but alters two key variables: the cost of capital and the contribution margin. Based on these assumptions, Brill estimates the "break-even" point at just less than nine years (Brill, 2008).

More importantly, Brill posits that the break-even point should be interpreted as an upper limit for the data exclusivity period, and not as an estimate of the optimal duration of data exclusivity. Because innovator firms can expect to earn profits even after the break-even point has been reached, the optimal data exclusivity period must necessarily be a shorter time period than the amount of time necessary to break even. As explained by Brill, in all analyses by researchers studying the impact of biosimilars on prices and market share, prices for innovator products "will not fall to a point where no profits are earned, and in all cases, the innovator drug will maintain a significant market share. Thus, even post-data exclusivity, the innovator will continue to earn rents" (Brill, 2008, p. 10). Brill states that investors can still expect to receive double-digit rates of return on investment with seven years of data exclusivity, with the break-even point increasing from nine to ten years, and considerable profits still expected after that time. Thus, he posits that a seven-year period of data exclusivity will preserve incentives for investment (Brill, 2008).

Professors Golec and Vernon disagree with Brill's analysis, however, offering a stinging critique of his work. Golec and Vernon claim that Brill greatly understates the true cost of capital for biotech research and development. In their paper published in *Applied Health Economics and Health Policy*, they assert that the biotech industry is by far the most research-intensive industry in the US, averaging a 38 percent ratio of R&D spending to total firm assets over the past 25 years, compared with an average of 25 percent for the pharmaceutical industry and 3 percent for all other industries. They conclude that biotech firms' financial risks increase their costs of capital and make them more sensitive to government regulation (Golec & Vernon, 2009).

Economists thus disagree sharply on the appropriate exclusivity period for follow-on biologics, based on their differing assumptions and models. For this reason, the FDA should consider, as an administrative matter, using the rulemaking process to establish the break-even period necessary for innovator firms to recoup the costs of research and development. In doing so, it is helpful to consider the example set by the European Union, which in 2004 became the first region to implement an abbreviated approval pathway for biologics, along with other nations that have implemented an abbreviated approval pathway.

B.   Data Exclusivity Periods for Biologics in Other Developed Nations Typically Range from Five to Eight Years

When considering the optimal data and market exclusivity periods for biopharmaceuticals in the United States, it is also instructive to consider the schemes established in other developed nations. Research revealed that data exclusivity periods for biologics range from five to eight years in such nations, with none approaching the 12 years advocated by the branded pharmaceutical industry in the United States. In 2004, the European Union became the first region to implement an abbreviated approval pathway for follow-on biologics. Throughout the EU, all branded medicinal products, including traditional chemical pharmaceuticals and biologics, are governed by the 8+2+1 rule. The innovator may receive up to eight years of data exclusivity, which means that a follow-on firm may not submit a biosimilar application that relies on an innovator firm's data until eight years after the EMA's authorization of the reference product. Moreover, the branded firm receives an additional two years of purely market exclusivity, meaning that the follow-on firm may not market the biosimilar product until ten years (i.e., 8+2) have elapsed from the EMA's authorization of the reference product. In addition, the period of exclusivity can be extended to a maximum of 11 years (8+2+1) if, during the first eight years of data exclusivity, the holder of the reference product "obtains an authorisation for new therapeutic indication(s) which bring(s) significant clinical benefits in comparison with existing therapies" (Follow-On Biologics, 2007). Professor Grabowski notes that the European Union's harmonization of data and market exclusivity periods for chemical and biologic pharmaceuticals avoids tilting incentives for innovation toward one industry at the expense of the other (Grabowski, Long & Mortimer, 2011).

The experience of follow-on firms in the EU market supports the implementation of a data exclusivity period of less than 12 years. According to a 2009 article in the *New England Journal of Medicine*, in the EU biosimilars have won a relatively small initial market share and only modest price reductions, in the range of 20 to 30 percent, as compared with up to 80 percent for other generic drugs (Engelberg et al., 2009). Consumers have not found these cost savings attractive enough to induce them to switch to the biosimilar products, thereby preserving incentives for innovator firms. Some industry participants predict, however, that as competition increases, discounts are also likely to increase. Significant discounts are unlikely in the short term, however, in light of the costs to research, develop and market a biosimilar.

Like the EU, Canada has implemented an abbreviated approval pathway for pharmaceuticals it terms of subsequent-entry biologics (SEBs). Moreover, like the EU, Canada has instituted the same data and market exclusivity periods for SEBs as for chemical pharmaceuticals. Canada provides for a six-year period of data exclusivity, providing that a manufacturer "may not a file . . . an abbreviated new drug submission . . . before the end of a period of six years" after approval of an innovative drug, and has also established an eight-year market exclusivity period, providing that "the Minister shall not approve that submission . . . in respect of the new drug before the end of a period of eight years" (International Federation of Pharmaceutical Manufacturers and Associations, 2011, p. 14). It should be noted that the language of Canada's statute tracks very closely that of the BPCIA, including language precluding "filing" of an application, as well as language precluding "approval" of an application. Since in Canada the former language is interpreted to refer to data exclusivity and the latter interpreted as market exclusivity, this suggests that the reading of the BPCIA advocated by the generic pharmaceutical industry is indeed valid.

Nations in the Asia-Pacific region, including Australia, New Zealand, Japan and South Korea, have implemented abbreviated approval pathways for biologics. These nations also provide the same level of data and market exclusivity to traditional chemical pharmaceuticals as to biologics. Australia and New Zealand have imposed five years of data and market exclusivity to run concurrently. Japan and South Korea have implemented six years of data and market exclusivity to run concurrently (International Standards Group. 2007).

Abbreviated approval pathways for biologics are relatively new in the markets in which they exist, and it is therefore too early to conclude what the optimal data and market exclusivity periods would be. Nevertheless, it is pertinent to note that nations typically accord the same data and market exclusivity periods to biologics as to chemical pharmaceuticals, and the maximum period of data exclusivity is typically eight years or less.

Since nations increasingly seek to harmonize their intellectual property and exclusivity regimes, one may question whether the data and market exclusivity periods established by other nations are truly intended to foster research and development, or rather to set the stage for shorter exclusivity periods in the United States so as to stimulate the follow-on industry at the expense of the branded. However, in light of the fact that in most of these nations the periods of data and market exclusivity for biosimilars are identical to the analogous long-established periods for traditional chemical pharmaceuticals, it seems evident that the aim of each nation when implementing a biosimilar exclusivity period was to achieve a balance that would stimulate both the branded and follow-on pharmaceutical industries.

C. United States Obligations under International Law Conflict with a 12-year Data Exclusivity Period

Another essential consideration in establishing an exclusivity period for biologics in the United States is the extent of US obligations under international and regional treaties. Pursuant to the World Trade Organization (WTO)'s Trade-Related Aspects of Intellectual Property Rights (TRIPS) Agreement, WTO member states are obliged to ensure effective protection against unfair competition by protecting confidential information. As noted by one expert, Article 39.3 of TRIPS imposes two obligations on WTO member states to protect information that they require to be submitted as a condition of securing marketing approval of a new chemical pharmaceutical product. First, member states must protect against unfair commercial disclosure of information that requires considerable effort to obtain and which is submitted to governmental agencies as undisclosed test or other data. Second, member states must protect such data against disclosure, whether to the public or even within the government, except where necessary to protect the public, or unless the government can ensure that the data, if disclosed, would be protected against unfair commercial use (Kogan, 2011).

While Article 39.3 of TRIPS does not establish a particular fixed time period during which data relating to pharmaceutical marketing approval are to be protected against unfair commercial use and disclosure, both the United States and the EU advocate for a reasonable fixed period. While a draft version of TRIPS Article 39.3 did specify a time period of "generally no less than five years," members of the generic pharmaceutical industry opposed this approach. For example, the European Generic Medicines Association asserted that "TRIPS Article 39.3 does not require the implementation of the type of data exclusivity that the United States, EU and other countries provide for pharmaceutical products" (Kogan, 2011, p. 530).

Thus, while TRIPS does not specify a required data exclusivity period, the five-year period contained within Article 18.9.1(a) of the KORUS Free Trade Agreement that was signed by both the US and South Korean governments in 2007, prior to the enactment of the BPCIA, is considered TRIPS-compliant (Kogan, 2011). There is concern among some stakeholders, however, that the branded biopharmaceutical industry, in negotiating further free trade agreements subsequent to the BPCIA's enactment, will seek to impose a 12-year data exclusivity period. A period of this length will face opposition from the US's trading partners. For example, nine nations—Australia, Brunei, Chile, Malaysia, New Zealand, Peru, Singapore, the United States and Vietnam—are currently negotiating the Trans-Pacific Partnership Agreement (TPPA).

The US pharmaceutical industry advocates at least 12 years of data exclusivity for biologics under the TPPA, stating that the KORUS FTA did not include this only because it was enacted before the BPCIA. In July 2011, 40 members of the US House of Representatives wrote to President Obama advocating that the TPPA include 12 years of data exclusivity in order to ensure that foreign countries would provide the US biopharmaceutical industry with adequate protection. In response, 10 Democratic House members wrote to the US Trade Representative in August 2011 urging that any data exclusivity provisions included in the TPPA be "voluntary" and akin to "comparative periods of protection in the U.S.," presumably, in their view, fewer than 12 years (Kogan, 2011, pp. 536–7).

Two days later, on 4 August 2011, another group of seven House Democrats led by Representative Henry Waxman (D-CA), the leading champion of the legislation creating an abbreviated approval pathway for generic chemical pharmaceuticals, wrote to President Obama recommending that, with respect to negotiating the TPPA, since the BPCIA had been enacted only recently, "the consequences of mandated 12 years of biologics exclusivity are not yet known" (Kogan, 2011, p. 537). He warned that the inclusion within the TPPA of a 12-year data exclusivity provision for biologics would violate the US's international trade obligations (Kogan, 2011).

Members of Congress on both sides of the issue sought through these letters to communicate to the Obama administration before the start of the eighth TPPA rounds that occurred in Chicago in September 2011. While US government negotiators had hoped to make progress on outstanding issues including data exclusivity at this negotiating session, US- and European-based healthcare activists attempted to defeat the US position by reporting how the "USTR's proposed IP chapter [would] . . . require[e] all developing countries to give up the additional flexibilities [previously secured from] the . . . May 10th [A]greement" (Kogan, 2011, p. 538). In addition, US government negotiators also met some opposition from their Australian and New Zealand counterparts, who had been lobbied by their own regional health activist groups concerned that a TPPA with longer patent and data exclusivity periods would impede access to affordable drugs (Kogan, 2011). One report prepared on behalf of Public Citizen in Australia noted that the US "may seek as many as twelve years' exclusivity for biologics (biotech medicines)" which would "represent a major change to Australian law with potentially dramatic financial consequences" (Kiliç & Maybarduk, 2012).

Political leaders in the BRICS nations (Brazil, Russia, India, China and South Africa) as well critique US requests for a 12-year data exclusivity period for biologics. Indeed, they have characterized even the current five-year data exclusivity period offered to innovators of chemical pharmaceuticals as exceeding the parameters of TRIPS (referred to as TRIPS-plus). Some developing nations permit compulsory licensing of pharmaceuticals, and data exclusivity provisions could possibly impede the approval of medicines produced under a compulsory license, thereby rendering such licenses ineffective. In addition, in certain WTO nations that do not have to grant patents for pharmaceuticals until 2016, such as India, data exclusivity could prevent the registration of generic versions of medicines.

IV.   THE FUTURE OF THE BPCIA

The US Supreme Court's ruling in favor of the Patient Protection and Affordable Care Act (*National Federation of Independent Business v. Sebelius*, 2012), of which the BPCIA forms a part, ensures the continued vitality of the BPCIA. Several paths for future clarification of the market and data exclusivity periods are possible. Congress may choose to amend the Act to render the data and market exclusivity periods clearer. Alternatively, Congress may leave interpretation of the BPCIA to the FDA, which has been charged by Congress with fleshing out the parameters for approving follow-on biologics.

Any further consideration of the BPCIA should take into careful account differences in data and market exclusivity periods in the US and EU. In the past, lack of harmonization in this regard was not of significance to manufacturers crafting their generic development strategy because most firms were regionally focused. This has changed due to the emergence of global generic firms, and there is a concomitant need for generic manufacturers to pursue multi-national product development strategies that take into account differences in exclusivity terms among various regional markets. The data exclusivity periods of five to eight years in other nations that have established abbreviated approval pathways for follow-on biologics offer some evidence as the data exclusivity period that is likely to comport well with EU law as well as US treaty obligations.

NOTES

*   I would like to thank Professors Daniel Cahoy and Lynda Oswald for inviting me to present this work at the May 2012 Patent Law Colloquium sponsored by the Stephen M. Ross School of Business at the University of Michigan and the Smeal College of Business at Penn State University. The participants at that colloquium offered helpful comments for which I am grateful. Thanks are also due to my colleagues in the Law Department at Baruch College, City University of New York, who offered helpful suggestions and insights at our Faculty Scholarship Workshop. Copyright 2013, Donna M. Gitter.
1.   A biopharmaceutical, or biologic, is a pharmaceutical product that is derived from a living organism and used in the prevention, treatment, or cure of human disease.
2.   The FDA defines an abbreviated application as "one that relies, to at least some extent, on the Agency's conclusions regarding the safety and effectiveness (or safety, purity, and potency) of an approved product."

REFERENCES

Beaver, N., Maebius, S. & Rosen, D. (2010). Update—United States Enacts Approval Pathway for Biosimilars. *Mondaq Business Briefing*. Retrieved from http://www.mondaq.com/unitedstates/article.asp?articleid=98250

Biologics Price Competition and Innovation Act of 2009 (BPCIA), 42 U.S.C. § 262 (2010).

Biotechnology Industry Organization (2007). *A Follow-On Biologics Regime Without Strong Data Exclusivity Will Stifle the Development of New Medicines*. Retrieved from http://www.bio.org/sites/default/files/FOBSData_exclusivity_ 20070926_0.pdf

Brill, A. (2008). *Proper Duration of Data Exclusivity for Generic Biologics: A Critique*. Retrieved from http://www.tevadc.com/Brill_Exclusivity_in_ Biogenerics.pdf

Drug Price Competition and Patent Term Restoration Act of 1984, Pub. L. No. 98-417, 98 Stat. 1585 (as amended).

Duane Morris (2011). *Alerts and Updates: FDA Proposes Pre-marketing User Fees for Biosimilar Product Manufacturers Comparable to Fees for Branded Manufacturers*. Retrieved from http://www.duanemorris.com/alerts/FDA_ biologics_price_competition_innovation_act_user_fee_biosimilar_biological_ 4073.html

Engelberg, A.B., Kesselheim, A.S. & Avorn, J. (2009). Balancing Innovation, Access, and Profits—Market Exclusivity for Biologics. *The New England Journal of Medicine*, **61**, 1917–18.

Evans, I. (2010). Follow-on Biologics: A New Play for Big Pharma. *Yale Journal of Biology and Medicine*, **83**(2), 97–100.

Federal Trade Commission Report (2009). *Emerging Health Care Issues: Follow-on*

Biologic Drug Competition. Retrieved from http://www.ftc.gov/os/2009/06/
P083901biologicsreport.pdf
Fidler, B. (2012). FDA Issues Key Generic-Drug Guidelines. *The Deal Pipeline.*
Retrieved from http://www.thedeal.com/content/healthcare/fda-issues-key-
generic-drug-guidelines.php
Follow-On Biologics: Hearing Before the Senate Committee on Health, Education,
Labor and Pensions, 110th Cong. 3 (2007) (statement of Nicolas Rossignol,
Administrator, European Commission, Pharmaceuticals Unit). Retrieved from
http://help.senate.goc/imo/media/doc/Rossignol.pdf
Golec, J. & Vernon, J.A. (2009). Financial Risk of the Biotech Industry Versus the
Pharmaceutical Industry. *Applied Economics and Health Policy*, 7(3), 155–65.
Grabowski, H. (2008). Follow-on Biologics: Data Exclusivity and the Balance
Between Innovation and Competition. *Nature Reviews Drug Discovery*, 7,
479–88.
Grabowski, H., Long, G. & Mortimer, R. (2011). Data Exclusivity for Biologics.
Nature Reviews Drug Discovery, 10, 15–16.
International Federation of Pharmaceutical Manufacturers and Associations
(2011). *Data Exclusivity: Encouraging Development of New Medicines.* Retrieved
from http://www.ifpma.org/fileadmin/content/Publication/IFPMA_2011_Data
_Exclusivity__En_Web.pdf
International Standards Group (2007). *The IP Academy: Overview and Comparison
of Data Exclusivity in Israel and in Selected OECD Countries.* Retrieved from
http://www.stockholm-network.org/downloads/publications/ip/d41d8cd9-IP-
Academy%20International%20Standards%20Group%20-%20DE-%20April%
2007.pdf
Kiliç, B. & Maybarduk, P. (2012). Dangers for Access to Medicines in the Trans-
Pacific Partnership Agreement: Comparative Analysis of the U.S. Intellectual
Property Proposal and Australian Law. *Public Citizen.* Retrieved from http://
www.citizen.org/documents/Australia-TPPA-chart.pdf.
Kogan, L.A. (2011). The U.S. Biologics Price Competition and Innovation Act
of 2009 Triggers Public Debates, Regulatory Policy/Risks, and International
Trade Concerns. *Global Trade and Customs Journal*, 6(11/12), 513–38.
Letter from AARP, Aetna, CVS Caremark et al., to Dr. Margaret Hamburg,
Commissioner, Food and Drug Administration (2011). Retrieved from http://
patentdocs.typepad.com/files/genericsletter-exclusivity.pdf
Letter from Representatives Anna G. Eshoo (D-CA), Jan Inslee (D-WA) and Joe
Barton (R-TX), to the U.S. Food and Drug Administration (2010). Retrieved
from http://patentdocs.typepad.com/files/letter-to-fda.pdf
Letter from Senators Kay Hagan (D-NC), Orrin Hatch (R-UT), Michael Enzi
(R-WY) and John Kerry (D-MA) to Dr. Margaret Hamburg, Commissioner,
Food and Drug Administration (2011). Retrieved from http://www.hpm.com/
pdf/1-7-11%20Senate%20Biologics%20letter%20to%20FDA.pdf
Letter from Senators Sherrod Brown (D-OH), John McCain (R-AZ), Charles
Schumer (D-NY) and Tom Harkin (D-OH), to Dr. Margaret Hamburg,
Commissioner, Food and Drug Administration (2011). Retrieved from http://
patentdocs.typepad.com/files/senator-letters-exclusivity.pdf
*National Federation of Independent Business et al. v. Sebelius, Secretary of Health
and Human Services et al.*, 567 U. S. ____, 132 S.Ct. 2566 (2012).
Noonan, K.E. (2011). Data or Market Exclusivity? (Perhaps) Only Congress
Knows for Sure. *Patent Docs, Biotech and Pharma Patent Law and News Blog.*

Retrieved from http://www.patentdocs.org/2011/01/data-or-market-exclusivity-perhaps-only-congress-knows-for-sure.html

Patent Act of 1952, 35 U.S.C. §§ 1-376 (1952).

Patient Protection and Affordable Care Act, Pub. L. No. 111-148, §§ 7001–03, 124 Stat. 119, 804–21 (2010).

Rimmington, S. (2009). 12 Years of Data Exclusivity for Biologics? *Essential Action*. Retrieved from http://www.wcl.american.edu/pijip/go/blog-post/12-years-of-data-exclusivity-for-biologics

Schacht, W.H. & Thomas, J.R. (2009). Follow-on Biologics: Intellectual Property and Innovations Issues. *Congressional Research Service*. Retrieved from http://www.ipmall.info/hosted_resources/crs/RL33901_090320.pdf

Trapp, D. (2010). Health Report Law Gives Biologic Drugs 12-Year Exclusivity. *American Medical News*. Retrieved from http://www.ama-assn.org/amednews/2010/04/12/gvsa0412.htm

Vogenberg, F.R., Larson, C., Rehayem, M., & Boress, L. (2012). Beyond the Cost of Biologics: Employer Survey Reveals Gap in Understanding Role of Specialty Pharmacy and Benefit Design. *American Health and Drug Benefits*, **5**(1), 23–30. Retrieved from http://www.ahdbonline.com/feature/beyond-cost-biologics-employer-survey-reveals-gap-understanding-role-specialty-pharmacy-and-?page=0,1

Index